DRINK*

✱ A User's Guide

DRINK*

*A User's Guide

Tom Hickman

EBURY PRESS

1 3 5 7 9 10 8 6 4 2

Copyright © 2003 Tom Hickman

Tom Hickman has asserted his moral right to be
identified as the author of this work in accordance with
the Copyright, Designs and Patents Act 1988.

All rights reserved. No part of this publication may be
reproduced, stored in a retrieval system, or transmitted in any form
or by any means, electronic, mechanical, photocopying or otherwise
without the prior permission of the copyright owner.

First published 2003 by Ebury Press,
An imprint of Random House,
20 Vauxhall Bridge Road, London SW1V 2SA
www.randomhouse.co.uk

Random House Australia (Pty) Limited
20 Alfred Street, Milsons Point, Sydney,
New South Wales 2061, Australia

Random House New Zealand Limited
18 Poland Road, Glenfield, Auckland 10, New Zealand

Random House South Africa (Pty) Limited
Endulini, 5a Jubilee Road, Parktown 2193, South Africa

The Random House Group Limited Reg. No. 954009

Printed and bound in Denmark by Nørhaven Paperback A/S, Viborg

A CIP catalogue record for this book
is available from the British Library.

Cover designed by Keenan
Interior by seagulls

ISBN 0091889197

✳ A User's Guide

CONTENTS

Introduction: A LESSON FROM HISTORY	ix
1. THE BODY AND BOOZE	**1**
Let's have a drink	1
Some physiology	5
Ethanol and ethnicity	8
A measured approach	9
Hair of the dog	11
2. THE GREATEST INVENTION: THE WHEEL... OR ALCOHOL?	**18**
Which came first, bread or beer?	18
Grain, grape and apple: a guide	19
Liquid food and medicine	23
Food and drink in one	24
What *is* alcohol?	29
The boozy brilliance of humankind	32
Putting the 'con' in connoisseur	33
3. BEER'S HIT AND MISS HISTORY	**39**
Them and us	39
A matter of style	43
Back to beer basics	46

CONTENTS

Beer *boring*?	51
PS: there's no such thing as a beer belly!	55

4. CIDER: NEITHER WINE NOR BEER — 58

5. WINE: VIVE LA RÉVOLUTION! — 62

The British: non-growing ... but grateful	72
The night they invented champagne ... in England	77
Put a cork in it!	82

6. SPIRITS: THE BAD BOYS OF BOOZE — 85

A word about wood	87
Brandy	88
Brandy-fortified wines	91
Whisk...y	94
Rum	98
Vodka	102
Gin	105
Absinthe and tequila: spirit(s) of the age	108

7. MONKS AND THE LIQUEUR HABIT — 114

8. SHAKEN AMERICA ... STIRRED BY THE COCKTAIL — 118

High art of drinking – or low farce?	121

9. DESIGNATED DRINKING PLACES AND THEIR NAMES — 125

Early English communal drinking	125
Public drinking – the US model	128
The common drinking experience	129
Signs of the times	136
Famous watering holes	140

CONTENTS

10. SOME THINGS DRINK MAKES PEOPLE DO (AND NOT) — 144
- The real you? — 144
- Aggro...holics? — 147
- Alco...heroics — 150
- Emotional baggage not stowed: air rage — 152
- Sex and drink: double trouble — 155
- A good idea at the time... — 161

11. THE ROAD TO DRINK-DRIVE — 165
- Breathe into this, sir — 169

12. DRINK, WOMEN AND THE YOUNG — 174
- Women and drink — 174
- The young and drink — 181

13. ALCOHOL, CHURCH AND STATE — 185
- Booze and belief — 185
- Authority's ambivalence — 192

14. OH, NO YOU DON'T! — 197
- Temperance and prohibition — 197
- The hangovers from prohibition — 204
- Islam, Koran, interpretation — 205

15. OH, YES WE DO! — 209
- Prohibition? What prohibition? — 209
- It was ever thus ... — 211
- Eastern (broken) promise — 214

16. ALCOHOL ADULTERATED, BOOZE BLACK MARKET — 219

CONTENTS

17. PRODIGIOUS DRINKING — 223
- National characteristics — 223
- The intemperate 18th century — 226
- Toasts and other excuses — 232
- World drinking league — 237

18. DISASTROUS DRINKING — 240
- I can handle it! — 240
- I can't handle it! — 242
- 'An illness of unknown cause' — 247
- Help! — 251
- To drink or not to drink: that is the question — 255
- Who's doing the abusing – you or it? — 259
- Sex, drink – and more physiology — 263

19. FAMOUS DRINKERS — 267
- Inebriated rulers and leaders — 269
- Writers: the drinking prize — 273
- Alcoholic career openings — 278
- I don't mind if I do… — 278

20. IT'S GOOD FOR YOU, HONEST! — 280

AFTERWORD — 286

INDEX — 291

✱ A User's Guide

INTRODUCTION

A lesson from history

It can't be claimed that anyone discovered alcohol – it's part of nature's bounty, formed when airborne yeasts come into contact with any carbohydrate vegetable matter. Neolithic men and women would have first tasted it in rotting fruits some 6,000 to 10,000 years ago, possibly having watched one or other animal species giving themselves an alcoholic buzz. Just like people, animals in the wild are partial to getting off their face – chimpanzees have been observed enjoying something more than a tea party and elephants have been seen staggering along after an intake of fermented fruit, flapping their ears to clear their

'THERE are two reasons for drinking: one is, when you are thirsty, to cure it; the other, when you are not thirsty, to prevent it. Prevention is always better than cure.'

– Thomas Love Peacock

DRINK | A USER'S GUIDE

heads – in which, possibly, pink men in hobnail boots are rolling barrels.

Early humankind had practical as well as recreational reasons for developing alcohol production: fermentation stopped bacterial growth, which meant that juices didn't spoil, and foods prepared with alcohol kept longer. By the Middle Ages, when many springs and wells had become contaminated, it was wise to avoid water, which frequently caused sickness and sometimes death. Nothing much had changed by the Restoration. Water was now piped under the streets of many cities, but it was tainted by the deteriorating elm pipes that carried it and was ill-tasting enough before cesspits overflowed into the cellar tanks – which frequently happened. A hundred or more years later, things were possibly worse, as the 18th-century novelist Tobias Smollett indicated in *Humphrey Clinker*:

> *If I would drink water, I must quaff the mawkish contents of an open aqueduct, exposed to all manner of defilement; or swallow that which comes from the river Thames, impregnated with all the filth of London and Westminster – human excrement is the least offensive part of the concrete, which is composed of all the drugs, minerals and poisons used in mechanics and manufacture, enriched with the putrefying carcasses of beasts and men, and mixed with the scourings of all the washtubs, kennels and common sewers within the bills of mortality …*

INTRODUCTION

Boiling water was, of course, possible, if infinitely more cumbersome without the aid of the gas and electricity that we take for granted. Anyway, the wisdom of historical experience was plain: stick to alcohol, and from the 17th to the 19th century, Europe and the colonies did so with extravagant conscientiousness, going on what can best be described as a bender that makes the much-criticised drinking habits of the 20th and early 21st centuries look positively abstemious.

The introduction of tea, chocolate and coffee in the mid-18th century helped take the edge off excessive alcohol consumption by giving people something else to drink to excess. Warnings against the infusions were as dire as those (unheeded) warnings about alcohol. They supposedly rendered enthusiasts 'incapable of performing the offices of Digestion' (the essayist William Hazlitt was said to have died from tea addiction). In Prussia, Frederick the Great tried to ban coffee, ordering the populace to drink alcohol instead.

In England in the second half of the 19th century, another royal did his bit for coffee and for temperance – albeit unintentionally. The Prince of Wales and future Edward VII loved his booze – more than his mistresses if less than his food, hence the sobriquet of Tum-Tum – and certainly never stinted himself. But he took to joining the ladies for coffee after dinner rather than staying with the chaps, who traditionally proceeded, with the ladies' withdrawal, to drink themselves under the table – literally. Thus the chaps had no choice but to join Tum-Tum. Suddenly, rendering yourself insensible was no longer de rigueur; in fact, it soon ostracised you from society.

xi

DRINK | A USER'S GUIDE

Across the centuries, alcohol has been prescribed as a medicine, traded as a commodity, collected by connoisseurs, used in religious ritual and regarded as a symbol of national identity. It can't be denied that it's had a hand in shaping history. It contributed, for example, to the English losing the Battle of Hastings. Having defeated the Vikings at Stamford Bridge and been force-marched 170 kilometres (275 miles) to the south coast to take on William's Normans, you might have expected Harold's army to have wanted nothing more than a good night's kip. Instead, while the Normans spent the eve of battle in rest and prayer, the English got tanked up and were seriously hung-over in the morning, 1066 thus becoming the first date that anyone remembers, for all the wrong reasons from an English point of view. If it weren't for alcohol, the Pilgrim Fathers might have landed somewhere other than Plymouth Rock. The log of the *Mayflower* shows that when beer was running low (and for the voyage to the New World more beer was loaded aboard the vessel than any other commodity), the passengers 'were hasted ashore and made to drink water so that the seamen might have the more beer'. The storming of the Bastille wasn't the beginning of the French Revolution as is usually claimed. In fact the Revolution started days earlier with riots in those areas outside Paris that were about to be enclosed by an extension of the city walls – which would have made the wine sold in the bars there liable to municipal tax for the first time.

All societies, without exception, have made use of intoxicating substances, but alcohol has always been the most

INTRODUCTION

popular. Today, 90 per cent of British adults imbibe, and so – illegally – do a third of 13-to-16-year-olds. In the UK alone, we spend over £1 million *an hour* on alcohol, according to the Salvation Army, who disapprove of drinking and may be exaggerating to make their point, but probably aren't.

Why do people drink? To flaunt that they're rich, to forget that they're poor, to forget their troubles, to be companionable, to celebrate, to hide fear, lose inhibitions, reward themselves, pick themselves up. They drink for every reason you can think of and for no reason at all. No doubt a systematic cross-cultural examination of the use of alcohol in different societies could establish deeper insights. In the end, however, it all comes down to one thing: people drink because they like it. 'I drink, therefore I am,' Descartes didn't write. Perhaps he should have.

✳ A User's Guide — 1

THE BODY AND BOOZE

 ## Let's have a drink

Most people know that alcohol is a drug, but have collective amnesia on the matter. They prefer to regard alcohol as a stimulant. It perks you up, gives you a glow, makes the world go round. Stimulating is the word.

The first drink or two certainly make you feel good, relaxed, cheerful. If you've got problems, they don't seem so bad. After three, four, five – what problems? And you've begun to realise how fascinating other people's conversation

> 'REALITY is an illusion created by a lack of alcohol.'
> – N.F. Simpson

DRINK | A USER'S GUIDE

WHAT THEY SAY ABOUT DRINKING ...

'I drink to make other people interesting.' – George Jean Nathan

'Drunkenness is temporary suicide: the happiness that it brings is merely negative, a momentary cessation of unhappiness.' – Bertrand Russell

'Wine sets even a thoughtful man to singing, or sets him into softly laughing, or sets him to dancing. Sometimes it tosses out a word that was better unspoken.' – Homer

'Booze may not be the answer, but it helps you forget the question.' – Source unknown

'Always do sober what you said you'd do drunk. That will teach you to keep your mouth shut.' – Ernest Hemingway

'Wine makes a man better pleased with himself; I do not say that it makes him more pleasing to others.' – Samuel Johnson

'The hard part about being a bartender is figuring out who is drunk and who is just stupid.' – Richard Braunstein

is, if not as fascinating as yours. Yes, you're being a bit loose-mouthed, but hey!, you're on top form. Is that Aristophanes down the end of the bar? 'Quickly, bring me a beaker of wine, so that I may wet my mind and say something clever.' I'm quoting Aristophanes. Give good ol' Aristophanes a drink on me. 'S not Aristophanopanophanes? Give 'im a drink anyway.

If you get up and go home now, you'll get there safely, and if you have a thumping head in the morning you'll still make it to work on time. If you stay and carry on, after eight or ten

THE BODY AND BOOZE

drinks your speech will be slurred, your vision blurred, your sense of balance gone and your co-ordination shot, and you'll be emotional. From here on time is out of joint (although you're still in the place) and, as Henry Peacham wrote over 350 years ago in *The Art of Living in London*: 'Drunken men are apt to lose their hats, cloaks, or rapiers, nor to know what they have spent', except in your case it's coat, briefcase or mobile (*did* you leave the laptop in the office?).

Eight to 12 hours hence you'll have the onset of a hangover to look forward to, which will be partly due to poisoning, partly due to your body's reaction to withdrawal from alcohol, and partly due to the pleasure of reviewing your behaviour (or what you can remember of it), which quite possibly ran the gambit from jocose to lachrymose to bellicose to comatose. When you wake up, wherever it may be, your mouth will feel, as Kingsley Amis put it, 'as if it had been used as a latrine by some small animal'. You'll be nauseous and have the shakes (the only exercise he ever got, the modern world's most celebrated drinker, W.C.

HO! Ho! Yes! It's all very well,
You may drunk I am think, but I tell you I'm not,
I'm as sound as a fiddle, and fit as a bell,
And stable quite ill to see what's what.
I under do stand you surprise a got
When I headed my smear with gooseberry jam;
And I've swallowed, I grant, a beer of a lot
But I'm not so think as you drunk I am.

– J.C. Squires

DRINK | A USER'S GUIDE

EUPHEMISMS for drunkenness: tight, sozzled, merry, well oiled, legless, canned, crocked, wrecked, smashed, ripped, ploughed, paralytic, pie-eyed, stinko, blotto, trolleyed, mullered, bombed, slaughtered, blitzed, bladdered, wrecked, trashed, twatted, spannered, seeing two moons, smelling of the cork, swinging from the chandeliers, well gone, rat-arsed, shit-faced, arse-holed, out of it, off your tits, pissed as a pudding/fart/newt, drunk as a drum/wheelbarrow/boiled owl/brewer's horse/tinker/fiddler or fiddler's bitch (the fiddler at wakes, fairs and dances was paid in liquor).

Quite a few euphemisms are nautical: half-seas over, three sheets to the wind, main brace well spliced, back teeth afloat, lapping the gutter, can't see a hole in a ladder.

'Tired and emotional' was a euphemism coined in the 1960s by *Private Eye* for the Labour Deputy Prime Minister George Brown, who when under the influence habitually made a fool of himself in public.

Fields, said). It'll be then that you'll want to die and you'll promise never, ever to drink again.

A few drinks are fine – they'll even improve your health (see Chapter 20). Beyond that, however, alcohol doesn't bring serendipity, just the illusion of it. Alcohol isn't actually a stimulant, it's a depressant, just like tranquillisers and barbiturates. Its initial stimulating effect isn't due to its direct action on the brain but because it makes the adrenal glands discharge feel-good hormones. What it does after that, in proportion to its concentration in the bloodstream, is shut down activity in what Woody Allen called his second-best organ.

THE BODY AND BOOZE

 ## Some physiology

Your body goes on red alert as soon as it detects that you're drinking. Given time, it manages to get rid of up to 10 per cent of your alcoholic intake by channelling it via the kidneys into the bladder, by exhaling it through the lungs, and by sweating. But, essentially, to neutralise the toxic consequences of what you're getting down your neck, the body relies on two enzymes: alcohol dehydrogenase (ADH), over three-quarters of which is in the liver – your in-built detox clinic – and its co-worker, the circulating aldehyde dehydrogenase (ALDH).

PARADOX ONE
A belt of very strong alcohol may be absorbed more slowly than an average one. Why? The shock to the pylorus, the opening from the stomach into the small intestine, is so great that it closes off, preventing the alcohol's passage onwards; and it's through the wall of the intestine that the alcohol gets into the bloodstream.

PARADOX TWO
You might think that drinking alcohol with a carbonated mixer would lessen its impact, but the dilution is offset by the mixer's fizziness, which speeds up absorption. Researchers at the University of Surrey compared a group drinking bubbly champagne with a group drinking champagne that had been allowed to go flat. After five minutes those drinking the bubbly – which comes with a concentrated carbonation of an estimated 47 million bubbles to the bottle – had 0.54 milligrams of alcohol in their system; those drinking the flat champagne had 0.39 milligrams.

DRINK | A USER'S GUIDE

The problem is, the mechanics work more slowly than you can drink. In an hour, one standard drink (half a pint of beer, a glass of wine, a single measure of spirits) raises the blood alcohol concentration (BAC) of a healthy man of average build to about 0.02 per cent, or 20 milligrams, of alcohol per 100 millilitres of blood. By this time, however, his body will have cleared only 15 milligrams of alcohol, so it's already slipping behind. If he drinks five pints across three hours he isn't likely to think he's overdone it, but five pints will leave him with a toxic load of 155 milligrams of alcohol in his blood, nearly twice the legal UK drink-drive limit of 80 milligrams.

This example is simplistic in that it doesn't take into account such factors as whether the drinker has food in his stomach, or eats as he drinks (high-protein foods like cheese and nuts, and anything fatty – the typical late-night takeaway – slow absorption), and his psychological state (stress prises apart what are known as tight junctions in the intestine wall, giving the alcohol a helter-skelter ride into the bloodstream). Whatever factors are operating, the body is put under maximum pressure when drinking is sustained, so to speak, BAC to BAC.

Water isn't most people's first choice of beverage on a night out, except for the young at raves, but it's a vital part of

IT may come as a shock to teetotallers, but our bodies produce alcohol naturally. Small but measurable quantities are present in the liver, brain and blood, in the muscles and in the large intestine.

THE BODY AND BOOZE

> 'I never drink water. That's the stuff that rusts pipes.'
> – W.C. Fields

the defence system where alcohol is concerned. Because it occurs naturally in the body's cells and organs, it's the ultimate 'mixer', diluting your alcoholic intake, though at a cost – for every pint of alcohol, you lose $1\frac{1}{4}$ pints of water. It's dehydration that causes that raging morning-after thirst.

Because a big man has more water content than a small man, he's likely to be able to drink more (though, of course, a small man may have a larger than normal liver and vice versa). But a small man is likely to be able to drink more than a big woman. Firstly, a woman's body has more fatty tissue and in consequence less water than a man's – 52 per cent against 61 per cent – and, of course, on average her body weight, and thus her storage capacity, is several stones less than a man's. Consequently, women absorb alcohol more quickly. Secondly, while having proportionately as much ADH in their liver as men, women lack the enzyme in their stomach where men have it, and which gives them what's called 'first-pass metabolism' – in other words, in men some alcohol is prevented from reaching the bloodstream at all. Research also suggests that in women who drink heavily the pituitary gland in the brain stops producing ADH altogether – so that drinking has the same toxic effect on them as if they took their alcohol intravenously. Thirdly, premenstrual hormonal changes every month reduce a woman's drinking capacity –

DRINK | A USER'S GUIDE

and fourthly so does the Pill, if you're on it, because of the oestrogen it contains.

But some people just can't drink, or drink much, irrespective of build or gender: their bodies simply tolerate alcohol less well than normal, like Cassio in Shakespeare's *Othello*, who tells Iago: 'I have very poor and unhappy brains for drinking.'

Ethanol and ethnicity

If women in the main can't drink as much as men, then a great many Japanese and Chinese have an even greater

FOR 300 years the Firewater Theory has maintained that Native Americans lack the ability to drink distilled alcohol. Recent laboratory research has shown that this is actually true of only a very small number, who have the same defect in the ALDH gene as the Japanese and Chinese. The high incidence of alcohol dependence and abuse among many tribes is a result of the severe controls that have prevented Native Americans from establishing acceptable drinking norms.

Before the Europeans came to America, the Native Americans drank weak corn beer – they were undone by whisky. In sub-Saharan Africa during the 19th century, other beer-brewing peoples were similarly undone by rum and gin, with which traders purchased ivory, rubber and slaves. A clergyman described the boats plying up and down the West African coast as 'simply wholesale liquor houses – rum in hogsheads, in casks, barrels, kegs, demijohns and stone jugs'. And, as he wrote in his diary, all along the coast the cry was 'Gin, gin!'

THE BODY AND BOOZE

problem with alcohol – or, more accurately, ethyl alcohol or ethanol.

As many as 40 per cent of Japanese and Chinese people – and as many as one in five Jews, the latest research suggests – have a mutation in the gene that encodes ALDH, the secondary enzyme that completes the job of metabolising alcohol. In consequence, the alcohol remains in their blood and tissues in a partially degraded state – and even minimal drinking rapidly causes symptoms that a Westerner experiences only after enough drinks have shut down sentience to the point where he or she doesn't notice. These symptoms are deeply unpleasant and help to explain why Israel has one of the lowest levels of alcoholism in the developed world. The Japanese, however, appear to be prepared to push through the alcohol intolerance barrier.

A measured approach

'Too much is enough' isn't a practical philosophy for a long or healthy life. But where do you draw the line? In the last decade or two, medical opinion has suggested that an upper limit for men is 21 standard drinks a week and for women 14 standard

'I am not a heavy drinker. I can sometimes go for hours without touching a drop.'

– Noel Coward

DRINK | A USER'S GUIDE

drinks – with a standard drink being half a pint of beer, five fluid ounces of wine or 1^1/$_2$ fluid ounces of spirits. Men downing 50 or more a week and women 35 or more are probably going to end up with a liver like the late Oliver Reed's.

But even these levels of intake have been qualified by a study done in 2002 at the London School of Hygiene and Medicine. The first major research to take a drinker's age and statistical longevity into account, this concluded that men should have no more than two units of alcohol a day and women no more than one unit a day before the age of 44 – only then can they allow themselves the generally accepted upper limits of consumption.

But assessing your alcoholic intake is a confusing business. Take beer. The guidelines are based on a 3.5 per cent strength (alcohol by volume, or ABV), but many beers are now typically 5 per cent, and some strong beers and lagers are 2^1/$_2$ times that – so what you may think of as a single unit could actually be 2^1/$_2$ units. Also, cans often contain not half but about three-quarters of a pint, so if you've put away three and think you've kept more or less within recommended daily limits, you're wrong: you've had 4^1/$_2$ units. And that's without considering the ABV.

As to wine, the tables are based on a strength of 9–11 per cent, but today 12–13 per cent is nearer the mark. So a standard glass of wine isn't one unit but 1^1/$_3$ or more, converting the six standard 125-millilitre glasses in a 750-millilitre bottle into eight. That bottle shared between two is four units on each person's tally. To compound the situation, when you're drinking at home, the glasses are almost

THE BODY AND BOOZE

certainly larger than those little ones in the pub; and if you're drinking spirits you're not measuring what you pour with an optic.

Bottom(s up) line: tt's a pinch of salt to a slug of hooch that you're drinking more than you acknowledge. Most drinkers fool themselves that they're not drinking as much as they are, especially when they're having a good time. If they do acknowledge it and promise themselves to make up for it later, it's a promise quickly forgotten. If you're wise, you'll aim below the suggested weekly benchmarks – say, two units a day if you're a man, and one if you're a woman. Or drink nothing unless you're equipped with a calculator, a measuring beaker and a hydrometer.

Hair of the dog

I've a head like a concertina,
I've a tongue like a buttonstick,
I've a mouth like an old potato,
and I'm more than a little sick

– Rudyard Kipling

You've told yourself to be sensible. After the third you'd decided to say 'not for me, thanks', but you hadn't noticed the hostess pour the fourth and you're not sure whether there was a fifth, though you do remember thinking, what the hell, one more won't hurt me.

But it has. It is. It hurts. A lot. Thought is difficult, speech all but impossible. The room still swirls, you want to vomit

DRINK | A USER'S GUIDE

VOMITING: involuntary forcible expulsion of stomach contents through the mouth, usually preceded by nausea, pallor, sweating, excessive salivation, and slowing of the heart rate.

Vomiting occurs when the vomiting centre in the brainstem is activated … [by various bodily messages but also] by the chemoreceptor trigger zone, which is itself stimulated by the presence in the blood of poisons or certain other substances.

Once activated, the centre sends messages to the diaphragm, which presses sharply downwards on the stomach, and to the abdomen wall, which presses inwards. Simultaneously, the pyloric sphincter between the base of the stomach and the intestine closes and the region between the top of the stomach and the oesophagus relaxes. As a result, the stomach contents are expelled upwards through the oesophagus. As this happens, the larynx (voice-box) is tightly closed by the epiglottis to prevent vomit from entering the windpipe and causing choking.

*– The British Medical Association
Complete Family Health Encyclopedia*

again but you've done that twice already and you know there's nothing left, but still 'your stomach climbs up like spiders and rubs, purring, against the roof of your mouth…' in the words of Gerald Kersch.

Most of us have been there, done that, got the T-shirt.

'Hangover', the universal English term, is an American coinage, though in the 1890s it was usual to talk about being overhung. Other languages have their own, more graphic expressions – the French, in translation, means 'wood mouth', the German 'wailing of cats', the Norwegian 'carpenter in the

THE BODY AND BOOZE

brain', the Swedish 'pain in the hair roots', the Italian 'out of tune', the Cuban 'gnawing in the stomach', the Portuguese 'kill the beast'. The Burmese *gaungit* translates as 'clapper of the temple bell'. The Spanish have three common sayings, meaning 'pounding of waves on rocks', 'the ooze' and 'nail in the head'.

Different peoples have evolved different remedies for mitigating the pain, ranging from cow dung (the Ruthenes of the Carpathian Mountains) to sparrow droppings in brandy or tobacco (the Magyars of Hungary). The ancient Assyrians swore by swallow's beak in myrrh; the Egyptians and Greeks by eating cabbage; and the Romans by fried canary (Pliny the Elder recommended powdered pumice stone or lightly cooked screech owl eggs). In medieval England it was bitter almonds, sometimes with vinegar. Eighteenth-century London thought saloop – in its own right a popular beverage of sassafras, milk and sugar, which was sold for three halfpence a bowl from stalls on wheels – was the best possible remedy for what it called the 'womblety cropt'.

Traditionally, some Germans think that a breakfast of red meat and bananas does the trick; the Dutch go for salted herring; the Italians for olives by the handful; the Swedes for two tablespoons of butter or cream; the Chinese for fish soup

'FOR a bad hangover, take the juice of two quarts of whiskey.'

– Eddie Condon

DRINK | A USER'S GUIDE

or spinach tea; the French for black coffee with salt. Puerto Ricans rub a slice of lemon under their drinking arm; Haitians stick 13 black-headed needles into the cork of the bottle that caused the carnage; and Russians, as you'd bet, opt for the hair of the dog.

PREVENTION being better than cure… One 17th-century almanac advised the reader to 'take the lungs of a hog; roast it, and he who eateth thereof shall not be drunk that day however liberally he takes his wine'. This was on the right lines – having food inside you before you start drinking (or eating while you drink) is the best precautionary measure. It stops the alcohol getting into the bloodstream in a rush. Pasta and cheese are good absorbents, and a glass of milk puts a lining on the intestinal wall. So does salad oil, if you can face it – Alfred, Duke of Edinburgh (brother of Tum-Tum Edward VII) thought this method helped him to drink the Russians under the table.

Drinking metabolically 'clean' liquor like vodka (first choice), gin or white wine is a big damage-limitation measure – countless flavourings along with ageing add impurities to the likes of whisky, port and brandy, and red wine can be lethal. Beer falls between the 'clean' and the 'unclean' choices – the darker the more dangerous. Sticking to one type of drink is a wise move, as different drinks have different chemical make-ups and react together in different ways.

The rule of thumb is that your body can deal with one unit of alcohol an hour; drinking water between units of alcohol slows down your consumption and flushes your system. Drinking water before going to bed is good news: it continues the flushing process and helps you to avoid the dehydration that booze causes – worth a trip or two to the bathroom in the small hours.

THE BODY AND BOOZE

'THE best way to cure a hangover is to avoid alcohol the night before.'
– Cathy Hopkins

What works? The truth is – nothing. Once the alcohol is in your bloodstream you have to wait for nature to take its course, and on average, first to last, it takes 20 hours. You could cleanse your blood in a couple of hours if you had access to a dialysis machine, but that isn't really a starter. You can, however, take steps to have a soft rather than a crash landing.

Apart from the obvious toxic effects, alcohol makes the body lose significant amounts of vitamins (mainly B and C) as well as nutrients, causing varying degrees of metabolic shock. Replacing the losses makes sense. So take a multivit. And drink water to help remove the circulating poisons, preferably with salt, not just to help with dehydration but because the digestive system, research shows, is much better at taking up an isotonic solution. Throw in some sugar – it'll disguise the salt and will help replace the glycogen stores in the liver that the alcohol has raided. Fruit juice provides more sugar as well as vitamin C needed to mop up the surfeit of damaging free radicals that are a by-product of the liver's efforts to render alcohol harmless. Tomato juice is an alternative source of C and has its own armoury of antioxidants, as have eggs (best swallowed raw, if the nausea will let you). Eggs also put back vitamin B – little wonder that Prairie Oyster (egg yolk, olive oil, tablespoon tomato ketchup, salt and pepper, Tabasco, Worcestershire

DRINK | A USER'S GUIDE

sauce, vinegar or lemon juice) has as many fans as a Bloody Mary. A banana is not only an antacid and sugar-provider but also puts back lost potassium and magnesium.

Whatever you try, and whatever combination you try, the hair of the dog, much favoured by Gold Rush miners, isn't to be recommended.

Hair of the dog does bring some relief to start with, because the new alcoholic jolt stops the liver processing methanol – which releases acid into your system and makes you feel bad – and makes it go back to processing ethanol. But the methanol has to be dealt with eventually – hair of the

SEASONED drinkers nowadays think Berocca, a brand-name pick-me-up, is top of the tree as a hangover remedy – it has a balance of everything that booze depletes. In Australia, its country of origin, Berocca is often handed out to delegates at conferences where overnight stays are involved, and many Aussies wouldn't dream of going on a binge without a trusty tube in their pocket.

IN the 1850s in San Francisco, a Miss Piggott kept a waterfront saloon, where in the morning she served her hangover special to a customer who'd just woken up – equal parts of gin, brandy and whisky laced with opium. When he staggered to the door, he was met by one of her two male partners together with a blackjack, Miss Piggott pulled a lever and the unfortunate fell right into a waiting rowing boat – to awaken (again) as the member of a crew bound for Australia or the Far East. He had a bigger hangover, too.

THE BODY AND BOOZE

> 'ALCOHOL units 9 … cigarettes 30 … 9 a.m. Oh God, feel awful … horrible sick acidic hangover.'
>
> – Tuesday, 19 December, *Bridget Jones Diary*

dog just puts off the moment, and when it comes, it'll be that much worse.

In the meantime, you lie in a darkened room. You've rung in sick, food poisoning, something you had at a dinner party last night. And you suffer. You make resolutions about your future drinking, you blank your mind. The suffering goes on. You have no one to blame but yourself. True, true. The piper must be paid, you know that. But does the bastard have to play *so loud*?

✱ A User's Guide   2

THE GREATEST INVENTION

The Wheel ... or Alcohol?

 Which came first, bread or beer?

'Without question, the greatest invention in the history of mankind is beer. Oh, I grant you that the wheel was also a very fine invention, but the wheel does not go nearly as well with pizza.'

– Dave Barry

How long has humankind been boozing? Twenty thousand years? Ten? It's usually argued that the introduction of grain-growing made brewing possible, but there's a counter-argument – that what drove Neolithic peoples towards stable agriculture, the first giant step towards civilisation, wasn't the desire to make bread but the desire to produce booze.

Ever since the archaeologist James Death put forward the

THE GREATEST INVENTION

theory a century ago, his fellow archaeologists, and those other 'ologists' – anthropologists, biologists, evolutionary psychologists – who involve themselves in piecing together some approximation of pre-history, have been intrigued. The fact is that in the Neolithic period cultivated cereals seem to have constituted no more than 4 per cent of the diet, so they were never a staple, and as they provided precious little flour, is it more likely that they were mashed up to make beer?

A dismissive scholar once wrote: 'Are we to believe that the foundation of Western civilisation was laid by an ill-fed people living in a perpetual state of partial intoxication?' Well, could be. In which case the brewer's is an older profession than the baker's, and even, it's suggested, the potter's – though the potter would have come along pretty smartly to meet the brewer's demand for something reliable to put his beer in.

You can, at a pinch, imagine a world without the wheel. People can *walk*. But a world without *alcohol*?

Grain, grape and apple: a guide

The earliest *archaeological* evidence of wine production dates back 7,000 years, though there's some dispute as to whether a site in the mountainous regions of Iran is older than another

'TO alcohol! The cause of – and solution to – all of life's problems.'
– Homer Simpson

in the foothills of south Georgia in the Caucasus. The earliest *documentary* evidence of alcohol usage is of beer in Sumeria (in present-day Iraq) a couple of thousand years later – and the first known recipe, in the Sumerian tablets, is for beer, not bread. Beer drinkers everywhere would be proud of the Sumerians: they considered beer making to be the only profession under divine protection.

Beer established its primacy as the source of ancient-world booze because barley, from which it was ideally made, was less fussy about climate than the vine. Even where the vine did grow, it took a while for people to discover how to graft male and female stems and thus make the plant self-propagating – in the wild the vine has unisex flowers on separate plants and only the female produces fruit. The grape's poor sugar content also had to be improved.

The ancient Egyptians thought beer was too common to offer to the gods, though they were extremely enthusiastic about the brew – 'the mouth of a perfectly happy man is filled with beer', they were fond of saying. Travellers from wine-drinking nations thought Egyptian beer 'not much inferior to wine', though it's recorded that the brew was full of grain husks, which is why the Egyptians invented the drinking straw – to save the trouble of picking husks out of their teeth.

The earliest wines were mostly not made of the grape. The Egyptians made wine from pomegranates, figs and dates and, by all accounts, very fine wine too. It was possible 5,000 years ago for hosts to ask their dinner guests whether they'd prefer red or white, sweet or dry. In other cultures, the first 'wine' was mead – alcohol made from fermented honey. Even the Greeks were mead drinkers before they were grape-wine drinkers. The Francs, Saxons and Scandinavians drank mead even after they had started brewing beer, and mead is still the national drink of Poland – where they also make excellent plum wine.

Did the ancient Egyptians drink cider? They grew apple trees along the Nile delta after all. There's no direct evidence, but it would be injudicious to assume they didn't – they thought of pretty much everything else.

The cider drinkers were mostly in the Euro belt between the grape-growing south and the grain-growing north, on a diagonal from Bavaria to Somerset in the toe of England, with a detour into northern Spain. The Romans were the Johnny Appleseeds of the ancient world who, when they arrived in England in 55 BCE, found the villagers of Kent drinking cider and liked it so much, they introduced it across their Empire. Julius Caesar was such an enthusiast that he had cider-apple tree seeds and saplings taken to Rome, though not much came of it.

The Greeks and the Romans spurned beer. It was a barbarian brew which some Greek physicians believed caused leprosy. 'The people of the Mediterranean began to emerge from barbarism when they learnt to cultivate the olive and the vine,' the historian Thucydides said. Greek and Roman wine was usually sweet and at the upper end of potency – 15 or 16 per cent proof – and scented with flowers, perfume or an infusion of myrrh and rushes. It often absorbed the tang of pitch or resin used to seal amphoras and, on occasion, of the sheep and goats that wineskins were made of. The Romans favoured adding tree resins: pine, cedar, or terebinth, which

DRINK | A USER'S GUIDE

Pliny described as the 'best and most elegant' – just as many modern wines get their characteristic vanilla flavour from oak. The only modern carry-over of the ancient tradition of resinating wine is Greek Retsina.

HOW LIQUID IS YOUR COLLATERAL?

In Sumeria 4,500 years ago, beer was actually used as currency. Among the Lepcha people of Tibet today, alcohol is considered the only proper payment for teachers.

Across Europe for centuries under the feudal system, the nobility paid their debts in wine, and up to the 1800s farm labourers across Europe received a beer or cider allowance as part of their wages – the quantity increased during haymaking.

Many labourers in many industries were part-paid in alcohol, brewery workers, hardly surprisingly, among them. In Scotland's distilleries, men enjoyed a drop of what they produced, lining up for a dram at the start of the shift and at clocking off (and, in the more generous distilleries, at noon and mid-afternoon). The practice came to an end with changes to health and safety regulations in 1978.

In the latter half of the 18th century in American communities west of the Allegheny Mountains, bottles of bourbon were often placed in church coffers instead of cash.

During the time of the slave trade on the west coast of Africa, alcohol was frequently used as payment, while on the other side of the continent, along the caravan routes to the markets of the interior, people commonly swapped alcohol for other goods up to 150 years ago. That's what happened in cash-strapped communist countries, too.

THE GREATEST INVENTION

> A peculiar custom of the ancient Greeks, not shared by other ancient wine-drinking cultures, was to add water to their wine. Half and half or one to three was too strong, a quarter too weak. Five parts water to two of wine was the ideal.

When the Romans first came into contact with the beer-quaffing Gauls, their sensibilities were shocked: 'Their bodies, being large and delicate and fully of flabby flesh, grow by reason of excessive eating and drinking of beer, heavy and corpulent, and quite incapable of running or hardship.' Mind you, by the time the legions had got further east and met up with the Germanic tribes, many had taken to beer – just as they did to barbarian trousers. Back home people simply thought they'd gone native.

Liquid food and medicine

When that bulldog boozer Winston Churchill was asked if he'd consider cutting down on his drinking, he replied, 'But isn't alcohol food?' He believed that brandy in particular was necessary for a balanced diet, rather as people in the 18th century believed that alcohol was vital in balancing the humours (fluids) of the body.

Very probably from the time that our ancestors experienced the psychotropic buzz of booze, it was also seen as a food and a medicine. According to one 17th-century tract, 'It scowereth all scurf; it sloweth age; it cutteth flegme; it pounceth the stone; it expelleth gavel; it keepeth the head

DRINK | A USER'S GUIDE

> 'I HADN'T the heart to touch my breakfast. I told Jeeves to drink it himself.'
>
> – Bertie Wooster

from whirling, the mouth from maffling, the stomach from wambling, the heart from swelling, the belly from wirtching, the cuttes from rumbling...' This, in fact, is about whisky, but it hardly matters: you can read similar claims for beer, wine and other spirits. All distillations were at first medicines, even if they didn't stay that way for long.

Collectively they were known as *aqua vitae* or *eau de vie*, in Gaelic as *usige beatha* or *usequebaugh* – 'the water of life'. Liqueurs were concoctions that came from the alchemists' search for the elixir of youth, and if they never found it, a lot of people since have thought they didn't come up far short. A divine hand was seen in the bounty of spirits, as the name indicates. From the Middle Ages to just over a hundred years ago, the word 'spirituous' – containing much alcohol – was a synonym for 'spiritual'; and colonial Americans referred to all alcohol as 'the Good Creature of God'.

Food and drink in one

In the hospitals of Restoration London, the sick were entitled to three pints of hospital-brewed beer a day and an unspecified amount of ale. Across Europe in the 18th century, trust was placed in the curative powers of wine, and the sick were given half a pint a day 'of a strong kind'; convalescents got a

THE GREATEST INVENTION

quart. Caudle, originally a medieval home remedy – eggs, bread, sugar and spices in whatever alcohol was knocking about – remained popular.

Three thousand years ago, physicians in Athens were prescribing absinthe for anaemia, jaundice, gout and rheumatism, and during the Algerian War in the 1840s French soldiers were issued with absinthe as prevention against malaria. In the Middle Ages, bitters were dispensed for menstrual cramps and diarrhoea. Four hundred years ago the Swedes were treating headaches, kidney stones and toothache with vodka, at a time when the English were using gin as a remedy for kidney complaints. When Spanish flu struck Mexico after World War One, doctors prescribed tequila, just as monks and nuns dispensed liqueurs 600 years earlier as a remedy against the Black Death.

Whisky has always been considered a cure for the common cold, and brandy a cure for almost everything (100 years before Churchill, Lord Byron was treating his epilepsy and malarial fever with brandy, as well as vast quantities of cider) until largely replaced as the medicant par excellence by champagne, in the 19th century. Flu, pneumonia,

---

AS late as the 17th century, housewives would take a large cock, pulverise it until every bone was broken, and stick it in a cloth bag into a batch of ale with a few pounds of raisins – and a quart or two of sack (sherry) if they had it – which they then boiled up. Cock ale was the result. Smith's *Compleat Housewife* suggested adding some mace and a few cloves – and warned that the cock had to be 'flea-ed first'.

DRINK|A USER'S GUIDE

> 'I HAD a bad cold and a fellow told me that the thing to do for it was to drink a quart of whiskey and go home to bed. On the way home another fellow told me the same thing. That made half a gallon.'
> – Mark Twain

> IN 1920 a British advertising agency polled drinkers about why they drank Guinness. Among the most common responses was, 'Because it does me good' – which formed the basis of Guinness's long and successful advertising campaign. The slogan 'Guinness is good for you' is attributed to crime writer Dorothy L. Sayers, a copywriter in the agency at the time.

puerperal fever, malaria, typhoid, typhus, cholera, diabetes, consumption: champagne was the medical profession's answer. In 1873, seven London teaching hospitals between them ran up a champagne bill of £8,000, astonishing for the time. Some patients became alcohol dependent because of their lavish treatment – but so did many more during the period who were prescribed soothing syrups, cough medicines, sleep inducers and painkillers, which mostly had a heavy brandy base.

That alcohol has genuine medicinal benefits is recognised today. Doctors often recommend a whisky or brandy for those with circulatory problems, and those in need of building up are advised to try stout, as were many soldiers returning from fighting in the Far East after World War Two. In Victorian England oyster stout was widely regarded as *the* supplement drink, and nutritional milk stouts emerged in the

THE GREATEST INVENTION

early 1900s. They're still going strong in Britain and the US, though in Britain it is now illegal to use the word 'milk' in connection with them – but Mackeson, the best-known British stout containing lactic sugar, still displays a butter churn on its label. At one time Whitbread's Extra Stout was advertised as 'Recommended for Invalids' and an invalid stout was still popular on the Australian market in the 1990s.

Healthy Irishmen who want to take no chances with their health down copious quantities of Guinness for its preventative properties and feel their digestion blessed as if by the wing of an angel. They say it's an aphrodisiac, too – without mentioning that beyond a certain intake wirtching of the belly is almost guaranteed.

All alcohol provides some physical benefit. Neanderthal beer was apparently a thick brew of the consistency of gruel, or thin porridge – which, on reflection, made early humankind beer eaters rather than beer drinkers. Sumerian and Egyptian mums sent their sons off to school with two jars of beer in

---

THROUGHOUT history alcohol has been used as an antiseptic. It was also used to deaden surgical pain – it was just about all the medical profession had until, on the cusp of the 18th and 19th centuries, the first anaesthetic gas was produced.

A SNACK food company has developed lager-flavoured crisps. These are made with brewing yeast and hops but contain only trace amounts of alcohol. The company is now working on a real ale variety.

DRINK | A USER'S GUIDE

addition to three small loaves to ensure they grew up big and strong, just as for centuries boys at Eton had a daily allowance of beer – and were punished if they didn't get through it. In 18th-century England small children were fed a dram of rum several times a day, much in the same way that these days they might be given cod-liver oil.

Medieval ale and beer could be on the chewy side, but they were full of protein and carbohydrates, which made them a good source of sustenance for noble and peasant alike – 'a quart of ale is a dish for a king,' Shakespeare says in *A Winter's Tale*. Ale and beer certainly enlivened what the poor had to eat, which consisted of bread and pea or bean soup for breakfast, lunch and dinner. To this day East European breakfasts are often accompanied by a shot of spirits.

So unshakeable was their belief in the goodness of alcohol – irrespective of amount imbibed – that even as evidence of the deleterious effects of over-consumption piled up, people in 19th-century France refused to accept that the findings could apply to wine: 'meat makes flesh, and wine makes blood', they continued to say. And it wasn't that they were absolutely wrong.

HEAVY drinkers often eat little, satisfying their calorific requirements by the glass. As a result, chronic alcoholics are prone to nutritional deficiency, particularly of thiamine (vitamin B1). Some drinkers bloat (as did the recently deceased Rod Steiger during periods when he was having problems with alcohol); others waste – a lot of alcohol can irritate the stomach and reduce appetite.

THE GREATEST INVENTION

> 'WHAT contemptible scoundrel stole the cork from my lunch?'
> – W.C. Fields

The benefits of booze, according to modern understanding, have little to do with nutritive value (which in the case of Neanderthal and medieval brews came from ungerminated grains and unconverted natural sugars). From time to time proposals have been made to fortify alcoholic drinks with vitamins, especially the vitamin B complex, but these have been rejected as a possible encouragement to drink.

The body needs food to maintain its cells and to give it energy. Food consists of calories. So does alcohol: one gram of alcohol is worth seven calories (and one ounce is worth 200 calories) – almost twice the number of calories contained in one gram of carbohydrate. Regrettably, unlike the calories in food, those in alcohol are 'empty' – they provide some energy but almost no bodybuilding value, beyond in some cases traces of vitamins and minerals.

What *is* alcohol?

Alcohol is a colourless liquid, C_2H_5OH, which is undrinkable in its pure form. The alcohol in wines and ciders is produced by fermentation with yeasts of the sugar contained in whatever fruit is used. The alcohol in beers and stouts is produced by the conversion of the starch in grains to sugar

DRINK | A USER'S GUIDE

> KOSHER spirits and wine must be made by orthodox Jews. They remain kosher only if opened and poured by an orthodox Jew.

by malting, the sugar then being fermented by yeasts. Spirits are distilled from malted liquors or wines – the liquid is heated and the alcohol, which condenses first, is run off and captured. Roughly speaking, beers and ciders are about one part alcohol to 20 parts water, wine is between one part alcohol to five to ten parts water, and spirits are half and half.

Alcoholic strengths are easy to understand when expressed as a percentage by volume. Typical percentages are:

ciders	*1–8 per cent*
beers	*3^1/$_2$–10 per cent*
'natural' wines	*8–14 per cent*
vermouths and aperitif wines	*18 per cent*
dessert, sweet and post-prandial wines (sherry, port, muscatel)	*18–22 per cent*
cordials made of flavoured spirits (anisette, curaçao, maraschino)	*25–40 per cent*
spirits	*40–70 per cent*

In the US system of measuring alcoholic strength, each degree of proof represents 0.5 per cent of alcohol, so that a liquor having 50 per cent alcohol is 100 proof. The British way of doing things is downright confusing. Here, an alcoholic

THE GREATEST INVENTION

> SMIRNOFF vodka was advertised in the sixties by celebrities including Woody Allen, Zsa Zsa Gabor, Benny Goodman and Harpo Marx. Sean Connery advertised Jim Bream whiskey, David Niven Carling Red Cap Ale, and Liberace once made a commercial for Blatz beer from his hometown of Milwaukee.
>
> Strangely, Salvador Dali appeared in an Old Angus Scotch ad with the hilarious printed quote from the Spanish artist, 'It's really the tops'.

> WHEN exactly 1 gallon of pure alcohol is mixed with 1 gallon of pure water, the result is 3.5 per cent less than 2 gallons. This is because the molecules of alcohol fit into the spaces between the atoms of water.

drink is 100 per cent proof when its weight is $^{12}/_{13}$ the weight of an equal volume of distilled water at 51°F, and different drinks are expressed as degrees over or under proof. In practice, this means that whisky of 80 degrees proof in the US is 70 degrees proof in Britain. Coincidentally, the strongest that any alcohol can be is 190 per cent proof. Above this, the liquid draws moisture from the air and self-dilutes.

If the British way of measuring sounds baffling, you can also blame them for the odd designation of 'proof' in the first place – from the days when they used pure alcohol in water to moisten gunpowder. Just enough 'proved' to be what permitted the gunpowder to hold together and still burn.

DRINK | A USER'S GUIDE

The boozy brilliance of humankind

'One bourbon, one scotch, one beer.'
— *George Terigood and The Destroyers*

The grape may be the fruit of choice for making wine, barley for making beer, and any grain for distilled spirits, but people

---

SOME drinks are tied into religious beliefs or are specific to certain cultures ...

Among the Chagga mountain people of East Africa, men who become blood brothers drink beer in which their blood and saliva is mixed.

In Central and South America, chichi is a drink that begins with people chewing grain and spitting it into a vat – the enzyme in saliva changes the starch to sugar, which then ferments.

Among the Bagonda people of Uganda, the widows of a recently deceased king have the honour of drinking the beer in which his entrails have been cleaned.

The Uape Indians of the Upper Amazon in Brazil put the ashes of their cremated dead into casiri, the local alcoholic drink.

The Cocoma tribe of Peru drink the ground-up bones of deceased relatives in a fermented brew, believing that the dead are better off inside a warm friend than in the cold earth.

Vietnam has a popular liqueur made from lizard's blood.

China produces a Three Penis wine, made from one part seal, one part dog and four parts deer.

THE GREATEST INVENTION

> LET others laugh, let others snicker,
> We're all related in our love of our liquor.
>
> – Official poem www.alt.drunken.bastards.org

across the ages have used what they can get their hands on to produce alcohol: berries, fruits and flowers, sap from cacti or palm trees, even the leaves and bark of trees – the taverns of colonial New England were once renowned for their birch, spruce and sassafras beers. Poor Russian peasants manage something alcoholic by fermenting stale rye bread, and the Mongols, living in a land virtually bare of vegetation, knocked up kumis, from fermented mare's milk – a method of production still practised by some nomadic tribes today.

While you may not find any of the above on the off-licence shelves, you may find any one of over 3,500 branded drinks. Whatever of these is your tipple, it links you back across the centuries, even to the ancient world. Every drink you take is a sip of history.

Putting the 'con' in connoisseur

> *'It's a naïve domestic little Burgundy without any breeding, but I think you'll be amused by its presumption'*
>   – James Thurber, cartoon caption

Booze is a bluffer's paradise. Average drinkers just want to drink: they know what they like (and can afford), they drink it, and are content. In that they're like the bibulous barrister

DRINK | A USER'S GUIDE

Horace Rumpole, John Mortimer's fictional Drinking Everyman, whose tipple happens to be the rough claret in Pommeroy's winebar – or Château Thames Embankment as he calls it.

Occasionally, of course, the average drinker (you, quite probably) will run into someone who is not content simply to drink, someone who needs to anatomise what passes his lips, and to pontificate – someone like Rumpole's colleague Claude Erskine-Brown, for example, who, delicately sipping something more patrician than Rumpole's plebeian plonk, opines: 'The point of drinking wine, Rumpole, is to taste the trapped sunlight.'

Such *bon mots* directed at the average drinker (you, quite probably) can make the bluffer hidden within rise up …

Bluffers don't have to have a clue about the deeper mysteries of wine or whisky or beer or whatever tipple is involved. They must, however, be sound on basics of the kind scattered throughout this little book (and far more authoritatively in many other places!), they need a smattering of the towering brand names in their chosen category, and a stock of arcane facts that can be trotted out as occasion demands: 'Centuries of resistance to lager brewing in the German city of Cologne resulted in koelsch beer – a unique ale/lager hybrid, you know.' 'As it happens, the Huguenots grew vines when they first arrived in America, but they found it was more profitable to grow tobacco.' 'The most fully flavoured Scotches comes from the isle of Ilay – "You either love them," someone wrote, "or wonder what's the attraction of smelling hospitals." '

THE GREATEST INVENTION

But a handy vocabulary is the easiest way of flagging up alleged connoisseurship (with the proviso of not confusing, say, light lager with dark stout, red wine with white or blended whisky with malt). And it's pretty unchallengeable. You can't go wrong by discussing the 'body', 'complexity', 'nose' (with wine 'bouquet' is better), 'balance', 'finish', 'roundness', 'softness' or 'smoothness' of any tipple. Or lack thereof.

Beer can be talked about in terms of 'hoppiness', and beers and spirits in terms of 'graininess' and 'maltiness' – and beers, spirits and wines in any other terms you think you can get away with: 'toasty', 'roasty', 'tarry', 'nutty', 'chocolatey', 'buttery', 'earthy', 'perfumy'. Vanilla is a good word to throw out, as are toffee, coffee, marzipan and mint. 'Oaky' is a good all-purpose word, as virtually every brew that's aged is aged in barrels. Where wine is concerned, commenting on its tannin – which gives wine its keeping quality and the bite that makes it either zestful or wrinkles your socks – is de rigueur; or you can employ even more esoteric terms such as 'svelte', 'bog-boned' and even 'gossamer-like'.

Word combinations are limitless and can be put together on a mix 'n' match basis: a gossamer-like palate – why not? A multi-layered finish. A lingering complexity. As Humpty Dumpty said, words mean what you choose them to mean.

It helps if what you say bears some relation to what you're drinking, but conviction is all. It does, admittedly, take chutzpah to deliver the likes of 'I'm getting barnyard funky with a touch of gun smoke – and do I detect old leather?'

A question in the voice is always advisable: 'Nice round taste, quite a lot of pepper – it's not a Shiraz?' Told it's no

DRINK | A USER'S GUIDE

A BLUFFER'S GUIDE TO THE BREWS TO BOAST ABOUT:

BEERS: Budweiser Budvar (Czech pilsner)

What to say: 'All over the world there are brewers who presume to style their beers "pils", "pilsener" or "pislner" and they're not fit to take a bottle opener to Budweiser. Budvar — which bears no relation to America's favourite beer. Czech Bud — which, incidentally, is sold in the US as Czechvar — is the beer that aficionados might crawl over broken glass to drink. The grassy Saaz hops impart a very delicate aroma, noticeable beneath the more obvious vanilla notes. The softness on the palate … the lingering subtlety…

'On the other hand, the Belgians are the world's greatest brewers, there just isn't a bad Belgian beer. Have you tried any of the Trappist brews…?'

BRANDIES: Ragnaud-Sabourin (cognac); Château de Laubade (Armagnac)

What to say: 'Everyone knows that Martell, Hennessey, Courvoisier and Rémy Martin — who between them account for four-fifths of cognac sales outside France — are excellent cognacs, but for my money Ragnaud-Sabourin sounds the grace notes. Frankly it's the yardstick by which to judge all cognacs. But it is rather spirity — never drink it under 20 years old.'

'You have to taste Laubade to appreciate its finesse, its depth of flavour and colour. Not for nothing is it the favourite of several European royal families.'

WHISKIES: The Macallan (Scottish malt), Chivas Regal (Scottish blend), Connemara (Irish malt), Makers Mark (US bourbon)

THE GREATEST INVENTION

What to say: 'The Macallan is the only Scottish malt aged exclusively in sherry barrels – hence it's sherry-like qualities, of course. But it's roundness, richness, mellowness is unmatched this side of heaven – and the palate is positively lascivious!'

'Chivas Regal? What's to say about the whisky that's regarded worldwide as the final word in Scotch? Enough said!'

'I'd rather go for individuality, so while the world drinks Jameson, Bushmill and Tullemore Dew, my Irish whiskey is Connemara. It's Ireland's only peat-dried single malt and perhaps too smoky for some. But the balance is superb. Honey overtones … A hint of heather …'

'Yes, yes, everyone's heard of Jack Daniels, Jim Bream, Wild Turkey, Old Crow. But what about Makers Mark bourbon? Deep, complex in flavour and aroma – and as smooth as silk.'

RUMS: Pirassununga 51 (Brazil)

What to say: 'There's a perennial argument whether rum or vodka is the most popular spirit in the world but there's usually no argument that Barcadi is the biggest spirit brand – except I believe that title belongs to Pirassununga 51. You really should search it out!'

VODKAS: Chopin (Poland)

What to say: 'The five big world hitters are Smirnoff (America), Finlandia (Finland), Wyborowa (Poland), Stolichnaya (Russia) and Absolut – and frankly there's absolutely no consensus on which is the best. Of the bunch I rather favour Absolut, probably only because I think of it as the vodka for those who can't spel – and you have to admire the adverts. But I've found a new label, no advertising behind it, and it's rather good…'

DRINK | A USER'S GUIDE

> **GINS:** Bombay Sapphire (Britain)
>
> *What to say:* 'Truth to tell all gins are pretty similar, like vodka. If I wanted to impress I'd go for Tanqueray – the favourite of John Kennedy, Bob Hope and Frank Sinatra, you may know. But I rather like Bombay Sapphire – I just like the pale-blue tinted bottle ...'
>
> **TEQUILA:** Dos Reales Anejo (Mexico)
>
> *What to say:* 'There's only one name in tequila in world terms and that's Cuervo – and Cuervo 1800 deserves to be the number one seller, I admit. But I'm rather taken with Dos Reales Anejo. Unusual deep amber, rich bouquet, hint of sweetness – not unfairly compared to the best brandies.'

such thing you can reply, smiling, 'Thought not ...' That's a good way of not losing ground more often than not, but there's always the chance that you'll run into a better bluffer – or someone who really knows what they're talking about. In which case, you can still step out of the ring gracefully.

Finally, a word of warning. The more you know about a drink the more you're likely to want to know. You'll start reading books. You'll have an urge to go to an evening class and cancel the beach holiday for a tour of château vineyards, Scottish distilleries or Bavarian breweries. *Before you know it, you'll have trained yourself to be dissatisfied with drinking 'Château Thames Embankment', or its equivalent, which before was perfectly acceptable ...*

A User's Guide

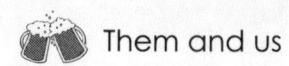

BEER'S HIT AND MISS HISTORY

Them and us

'You can't be a real country unless you have a beer and an airline. It helps if you have some kind of a football team, or some nuclear weapons, but at the very least you need a beer.'

– Frank Zappa

Strictly speaking, early beer was ale. The words are now interchangeable, although these days 'ale' isn't used much unless it's humorously – or by chaps who still wear cravats with their blazers and insist on calling the publican 'mine host'.

Historically, however, ale was beer made without hops, and had to be drunk within days or thrown away because it soured. Beer was ale with the addition of hops, which not only gave it its distinctive bitterness but also preserved it. Gauls and other Celts, Saxons, Nordics and Germanic tribes

DRINK | A USER'S GUIDE

> LITTLE Estonia has been in *The Guinness Book of World Records* twice: once for having the word with the highest number of consecutive vowels (jäääärne, meaning 'beside the ice') and once for having the strongest bottled alcohol (99 per cent ABV).

> BOHEMIAN hops were so prized that in the 10th century King Wenceslas (*that* Wenceslas) ordered the death penalty for anyone caught exporting cuttings from which new plants could be grown.

drank ale, until someone had the bright idea of putting what was then a medicinal plant into the brew and 'made medicine that tasted good'.

Hopping the beer was well established in Germany by the 11th century. The English had to wait a few hundred years for the Dutch to introduce them to the practice, continuing to drink ale, which, contemporary sources suggest, was sometimes good and sometimes closer to medicine. In any event it wasn't until the 15th century that the English were knocking up a brew that a modern palate might recognise.

Making beer was a hit-or-miss business up to the Middle Ages, until it was noticed that where others often did the missing, those who did their brewing next to bakeries always did the hitting – due to the quantity of yeasts in the air. Brewing continued to depend on airborne yeasts until the 19th century, when a Danish botanist found a method of growing yeast in culture. Europe and the Americas quickly adopted this pure-culture technology. True to the perversity

BEER'S HIT AND MISS HISTORY

of their character, the British and Irish didn't do so until the 20th century.

Once, every castle, monastery and great estate did its own brewing, and so did the big taverns. From the 14th

> AFTER filming in the desert for *Ice Cold in Alex*, John Mills's favourite beer was Carlsberg. In David Lynch's *Blue Velvet*, the psycho local gangster (Dennis Hopper) drank Pabst Blue Ribbon.

> BREWING is essentially a simple process: add barley to water, chuck in hops and yeast – beer. But the skill is in the execution.
>
> Barley can't be mashed directly to make the wort (the liquid that's beer before it's beer) because the starch in the kernel is insoluble, so the grain is first soaked and then spread on racks until it germinates. Enzymes produced in this process break down the starch. The malt, as the barley is now called, is kiln-dried, becoming darker the higher the temperature. The darker the resulting brew, the richer the taste; the lighter the malt, the lighter the beer.
>
> From ancient times barley has been known as the best grain for brewing, but many others have been used, often in combination. Such haphazardness didn't allow for much consistency and often induced wirtching of the belly. In 1516 Bavaria passed the *Reinheistgebot* – the pure beer law (still upheld) – which stipulated that all beer was to be brewed only from barley. One brewery, however, retained the right to continue brewing wheat beer, and later Count Maximilian I earned a fortune from the monopoly – which wasn't lifted until the 18th century.

century on, individuals with an eye for the main chance set themselves up to supply others, but it wasn't until the 18th and 19th centuries that brewing reached its peak, with the foundation of the great family dynasties – the likes of Samuels Whitbread and Smith, William Younger, and Arthur Guinness in Britain; the German immigrants Anheuser-Busch, Miller, Coors, Stroh, Schlitz and Pabst in America – who saw their work not so much as a trade but as something closer to a mission from God.

Even when they started using yeast cultures, the British and the Irish went their own perverse way. Everyone else used bottom-fermenting yeast, which, once the initial tumultuous

---

THE Kulmbach brewery in Bavaria produces a doppelbock of 13.2 per cent – the world's strongest beer. This no mean feat. An alcohol concentration of over 11 per cent kills even the toughest yeast and therefore arrests fermentation. The brewery's answer is to refrigerate its Kulminator brand until ice starts to form in it. Water freezes before alcohol, so the removal of the ice concentrates the beer.

UNTIL 1842, when brewers in Pilsen in the Austrian province of Bohemia devised a process to make clear golden lager, all beers were cloudy. Introduced at a time when the old drinking vessels of wood or leather and the ceramic stein were being replaced by glasses through which the clarity of a drink could be appreciated, Pilsen's product took Europe and America by storm. Britain resisted – but turned from murky porters to clear, pale amber ales.

BEER'S HIT AND MISS HISTORY

> GEORGE Washington, Benjamin Franklin and Thomas Jefferson, signatories of the Declaration of Independence, all enjoyed a spot of home brewing.

fermentation in the wort is done, falls to the bottom of the vat; British and Irish top-fermenting yeast remained as a frothy layer on the surface of the beer.

A matter of style

All beer is brewed in one of two styles: lager (German for 'storage' – in Germany beer is 'lagered' in cold caves for several months) or ale, the official description for top-fermented brews, even though the historical definition of 'ale' erroneously indicates that hops aren't used. Perhaps the brewers of the British Isles insisted on keeping the word because they were miffed that it took so long for someone to tell them about hops. On the matter of style, the British and the Irish are not as one when it comes to stout. The Irish prefer to think of stout as a third type of brew and object to it being called beer (which it is, but respect the viewpoint).

Top-fermentation, bottom-fermentation: it may seem trivial, but it isn't. The type of yeast is the essential determining factor in the end result. Subtleties stem from yeast preference: bottom-fermenting is carried out at a lower temperature, which restricts the yeast's ability to impart its fruity

DRINK | A USER'S GUIDE

> IN the 18th century 'brown' ale was an English sweet beer – the century had an outrageously sweet tooth. The introduction of a further duty on malt made brewers cut back on the amount they used and introduce more hops, thus creating a beer 'so bitter that I could not drink it' the visiting Casanova said. Some people liked this 'bitter' mixed with regular beer – half and half.
>
> In the early 1720s a mellow brew, four or five months in the making, was introduced and was favoured as a breakfast drink by the working classes – among them the market porters, who gave the drink its name. Stronger porters such as Guinness became known as 'stout' (heavy) porters. When the general popularity of porters declined, these brews became simply 'stout'.

> 'WHY is American beer served cold? So you can tell it from urine.'
> – David Moulton

flavour, aromatics and 'yeastiness'; so does the fact that the yeast is working bottom up, not top down.

All of this leads to what is seen as the major difference between indigenous British beers and most of those from the rest of the world – the temperature at which they're served. Continental-type lagers are typically served at 3°C, and American lagers are often served at an even lower temperature, whereas in Britain non-lager beer is supposed to be served above 12.2°C. British traditionalists, who care mightily about this, lob taunts about anaesthetised taste buds and

BEER'S HIT AND MISS HISTORY

get back a volley about the unpalatablity of warm, liquidised vegetable patches, but no one else really cares – chilled lager has been the most popular beer in the UK for over three decades. Lager, which accounts for over 90 per cent of US consumption, now accounts for nearly two-thirds of the entire UK beer trade and three-quarters of the take-home sector – with the number one seller Belgian Stella Artois.

NAMES FOR BEERS

By the nature of things, the names of beers are often those of the founding brewers; others have a historical or locational reference, or are just fun, and some manage both. Not all but most of the names that show a cheerful irreverence belong to microbreweries. A sample ...

America Bastard Ale, Old Leghumper (from a brewery called Thirsty Dog), Hog Heaven, Chicken Killer, Moose Drool, Butt Head, Bluebeery, Pipe Organ (from a brewery called Church Brew Works), Back Hand of God, Old Horizontal, and I'll Have What the Gentleman on the Floor is Having.

Britain Dog's Bollocks, Skullsplitter, Lifeboat (from a brewery called Titanic), Old Growler, Tar, Blunderbuss, Coal Porter and Janet Street Porter.

Belgium Delirium Tremens and Sudden Death.

Czech Republic Thirsty Monk.

China Reeb (yes, beer backwards).

The beer served in Mo's in *The Simpsons* is Duff – it just made creator Matt Groening laugh.

DRINK | A USER'S GUIDE

> ALTHOUGH Germany pasteurises its beer for export, it doesn't for consumption at home, where turnover is so fast the product is never in danger of deteriorating. The fact that much German beer doesn't 'travel' has thus helped Germany avoid the centralisation occurring elsewhere.

By the 1970s in Britain, real ales – beers that are 'alive' with the yeast and with hop leaves still in the cask in the pub cellar – stouts and porters appeared to be disappearing in the lager tide, and the 10 per cent of American beer that wasn't lager looked to be drowning, not waving. In Britain it didn't help that the breweries, in a search for what might be popular, chose to dumb down, moving to keg beers that were filtered, pasteurised and carbonated – and bore very little resemblance to beer, as far as many beer lovers were concerned. Older British traditionalists may still have a nightmare from which they awake shouting 'Watney's Red Barrel!' as Americans with long memories might similarly cry out, 'Billy Beer!'

And then, something happened ...

Back to beer basics

You must have seen the film *Network*, in which Peter Finch as the crazed newsman turned evangelist announces to America on TV, 'Tell them you're not going to take it any more' – and heads appear out of windows across the nation yelling into the night sky, 'We're not going to take it any

BEER'S HIT AND MISS HISTORY

more!' Well, what happened in the beer world wasn't so instantaneous but, in its way, it was just as dramatic.

In the US, microbreweries began to spring up, going back to handcrafting beers in the old ways. In Britain, a few beer lovers sitting in a pub one night decided they weren't going to take it any more and formed the pressure group CAMRA – the Campaign for Real Ale.

Today, there are up to 300 microbreweries in Britain and over 1,300 in America, all lovingly producing from original recipes and experimenting with new, and flavouring their ales with a wide variety of ingredients such as carrot, lemongrass, cabbage, spices, and even port and whisky. Honey is a

---

IN 1880 Budweiser was America's first national brand, but it was Pabst, a decade later, that was the first to sell over a million barrels in a year.

BEER wasn't sold in bottles until the mid-1800s. During the communist era all beer bottles in the Eastern bloc were the same – empties returned for the deposit went to the nearest bottling plant to be washed and used again with a different label.

Beer in cans appeared in 1935, and the world's first snap-top can in 1962. In 1989 came the widget, a plastic bubble that releases pressurised gas when a can is opened, giving beer a creamy head. In 2002 a South Korean entrepreneur announced the can that chills itself: a gas, released when the ringpull is tugged, spirals up a coil, reducing the temperature of the contents from 28°C to 4°C in 15 seconds.

DRINK | A USER'S GUIDE

favourite addition, often in wheat beers (when more than half the sugar in a beer is honey it becomes mead). There are dozens of different fruit beers, peat or hardwood smoked malts and even beers during the brewing of which large heated stones are added directly to the boiling brew.

But despite these efforts, the major companies' hold over the international market is growing stronger. In 1989 the 30 largest brewing outfits worldwide produced less than half the globe's beer. Now the top 10 sell one beer in three. Micros in Britain and the US have barely made a pinprick in the big boys' sales, most producing only 50 or so barrels a week, and only a few producing more than 100 barrels.

CAMRA's biggest achievement, after 15 years of lobbying, was to get the major breweries to allow a guest real ale in their pubs – something now under threat from the European Union, which is trying to force Britain to widen the law to include any draught beer on the grounds that it discriminates against imports. No other EU country has been asked to introduce legislation to widen consumer choice.

SUCCESSIVE generations of Theakstons ran the family brewery in Marsham, in Yorkshire, England, until 1983, when it was sold to a regional brewer, who in turn sold it on to a conglomerate.

When a site next to the old family business went up for sale in 1992, Paul Theakston bought it and started brewing again – under the name of the Black Sheep Brewery. Enjoy the irony – and let's hear it for the little guy.

BEER'S HIT AND MISS HISTORY

> 'BREWED under licence' are three words that are enough to chill the heart of all drinkers of imported beers, for they mean they haven't been imported at all and the dreaded curse of globalisation has struck.
>
> When a beer is first sold in any country, it's shipped from the country of origin. But once the local brewing giant has done the marketing and established the brand, it's brewed in the same vats as the indigenous beer – and its authenticity and original characteristics are lost, or at least diminished.
>
> Even Guinness in its 19 worldwide versions isn't a patch on what's brewed on the Liffey, and that includes London. If you're drinking Guinness abroad, look out for exported Foreign Extra, which has more oomph than regular. If you're in Belgium, look even harder – Dublin brews an exclusive, even more powerful 'Extra' for the Belgians.
>
> Always check: imported or brewed under licence …

Nevertheless, they've done wonders for choice and the heritage of beer history. And they've made the large companies add specialist beers to their output at a time when giant international conglomerates have been swallowing national and regional breweries across the world and – given the intricacies of cross-licensing and contract brewing – it's difficult to keep up with who 'makes' what, never mind the name on the label.

Some microbrewers have even brought bottle-conditioned beers back on to the shelves, brews that could almost have been counted on one hand in the seventies and which appeared to have become all but extinct by the early nineties. These beers, which undergo a secondary

DRINK | A USER'S GUIDE

IT was Russian Czarina Catherine the Great who inspired the brewers to create Russian Imperial Stout. Until then, exporting stouts was a problem: by the time the barrels reached the Baltic ports, most of the beer had turned stale. To combat this, the brewers produced a highly hopped, high-alcohol brew that could survive the journey and which, they claimed, 'would keep seven years'. It's not too likely that was put to the test – Catherine and her court had a voracious appetite for the stuff.

The problem of time and distance was even greater for the 18th- and 19th-century brewers trying to meet the call for beer from the large numbers of troops and civilians in the outposts of Empire. The three- to five-month passage to India, through considerable temperature fluctuations, was too much for the porter of the time. There was also the fact that drinking preferences in a hot climate suggested a need for something less dark and sweet.

Pale ale, copper or reddish-bronze in colour, had been around for some years, but India Pale Ale (or IPA) got a heftier hopping and extra grain and sugar during fermentation – which kept the yeast alive and the brew sparkling during the long voyage. One head malter at an English brewery about to enter the market tasted a rival's IPA and spat it out, it was so bitter to his taste. But the troops in India loved it. The shipment in 1800 surpassed the entire amount of beer that had gone to the subcontinent in the previous 100 years.

The ale was export-only until 1827, when an outward-bound ship carrying it was wrecked in the Irish Sea; the cargo was auctioned off in England and the locals found out what they'd been missing.

IPA is the granddaddy of the world's pale ales and was quickly taken up in the US, where some brewers replaced their older ales with it, trying to stem the lager revolution.

fermentation in the bottle, have a shorter sell-by date than pasteurised beers, and the big boys could no longer be bothered, although in England small batches of Russian Imperial Stout, the bottled beer with the longest continuous history, still appear.

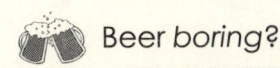

Beer *boring*?

'Twenty-four beers in a case. Twenty-four hours in a day. Coincidence? I think not.'
— *Fox Mulder*

It might make Norm fall off his stool in *Cheers* or Barney fall off his in Mo's, but in the third millennium many people, according to research, find beer boring. People in most northern European countries, North America and Australasia are drinking less beer than they did, and it's forecast that by 2010 they may be drinking as much as 20 per cent less than today.

For many years the Germans were the world's biggest beer drinkers, averaging 160 litres (280 pints) per person per year. For the last three years, however, they've been back in third place, behind the Czechs and the Irish, their consumption down to 125 litres (220 pints). But that's 25 litres (44 pints) ahead of the British, whose consumption has fallen by 13 per cent since 1990. The Americans are behind the British; over 20 years, average American intake has dropped from 92 litres (161 pints) to 82 litres (143 pints). Even the Australians, usually imagined as even going to the dunny

DRINK|A USER'S GUIDE

> ACCORDING to research conducted in the USA's major supermarkets:
>
> Those who engage in extreme sports drink more than the average person.
>
> Golfers and hunters prefer domestic light beer.
>
> Sixty-three per cent of those who drink inexpensive beer are men.
>
> Skiers are 89 per cent more likely than average to drink red wine and premium beer.
>
> Comedy club-goers drink wine that costs more than $10 a bottle.
>
> Those who attend R&B/rap/hip-hop concerts are nearly twice as likely as average to drink sparkling wine and champagne.

> ALCOHOL advertising is banned in Estonia, but there is no law defining what alcohol is. The Saku brewery advertises on television and sponsors a TV programme from its pub in the capital, Tallinn.

with a tinny in their hand, have slipped from seventh to ninth place among beer-drinking nations.

It's little wonder that the conglomerates' eyes are on new markets in Eastern Europe: by 2010 beer drinking in Russia – where beer is officially classified as non-alcoholic – is calculated to jump by 140 per cent. The other big growth area, China, is a closed market to Westerners, but its beer production has been growing at an annual rate of 25 per cent in the past decade and the Chinese predict that they'll pass the

BEER'S HIT AND MISS HISTORY

Americans as the world's biggest producer in the next two or three years.

However much beer sales are down compared with the past, Britain, Germany and America remain beer-drinking countries, although there's a strong cultural difference in that in Britain and Germany beer is classless, while in America it epitomises the working man – a legacy from pre-Prohibition, when only immigrants (mostly German and Irish) remained indifferent to anti-drink feeling and carried on supping regardless.

An earlier incident that clearly marked out beer as the drink of the working man involved that other great American passion, baseball. In 1882 a National League was established to attract a better class of patron. It doubled ticket prices, banned Sunday games – and prohibited beer. St Louis, Philadelphia, Cincinnati and other brewing centres refused to go along with

---

AMERICANS down 80 million cans of beer daily, most of it Budweiser and Miller Lite, the two leaders outside Texas, where Shiner Bock and Ziegen Bock are as widely appreciated. An obsession with dieting has been responsible for Miller's success, although many think the product has little to do with beer. 'People who drink lite "beer" don't like the taste of beer; they just like to pee a lot,' says the solidly authentic Capital Brewery in Middleton, Wisconsin.

'LIGHT beer is an invention of the Prince of Darkness.'
– Inspector Morse

this policy and formed their own American Association, keeping entrance tickets at 25 cents, retaining fixtures on Sundays (the workers' only day off) and serving beer.

The National League was short-lived.

The big boys of brewing pour megabucks into advertising and from time to time get rapped over the knuckles, especially in the US, where they worry excessively about the young being seduced into alcoholic ways. Anheuser-Busch were criticised for the Budweiser frogs just because kids liked them as much as Bugs Bunny.

Once upon a time, brewers bought 30- and 60-second TV advertisement slots. Then they sponsored whole TV shows. Now, with the continuing fragmentation of broadcast media across cable, satellite and the Internet, and the new wave of recording technologies able to screen out ads altogether, advertisers need a cunning plan to corral all the distracted

---

IN Denmark, where alcohol advertising is banned in print and at the cinema, and where a ban on all broadcast alcohol advertising is threatened, Carlsberg has created its own advertising medium – a chain of stores that sells only comic books, sports trading cards and CDs. The shops are decorated with Carlsberg's logos.

'SON, when you participate in sporting events, it's not whether you win or lose … it's how drunk you get.'

– Homer Simpson

BEER'S HIT AND MISS HISTORY

WESTERN-STYLE beer wasn't introduced into Japan until the beginning of the 20th century, but it now accounts for over three-quarters of alcohol consumption. Most beer is lager – with *happoshu* (low-malt beer – lite again) accounting for over a fifth of the market – and all of it comes from just four brewers: Asahi, Kirin, Sapporo and Suntory – the 'newcomer' in 1964. Japanese law once forbade the setting up of a brewery unless it could produce two million litres (3.5 million pints) a year, but this has now been reduced to 60,000 litres (105,600 pints) – which may pave the way for microbrewers.

Beer in Japan is expensive: Joe Sixpack-san has to stump up the equivalent of about £21 ($14) for his sixpack.

Incidentally, Japanese sake, made from rice, is almost always called wine, but in fact it's beer. The confusion arises because its 14–17 per cent alcohol content takes it out of the usual beer class and because it's not carbonated as the modern beer drinker expects. Uniquely, sake isn't fermented with a yeast but with a fungi.

eyeballs. With the *World Beer Games* perhaps they've found one. Launched in June 2002 in the US and Canada, the Games involved 17 nations (including the UK and Ireland) and featured such events as the pint curl, the empty can toss and the pint chug. Turning the commercial into the show could be the way of the future.

PS: there's no such thing as a beer belly!

For centuries in northern Europe, the beer belly – or what Charles Dickens termed 'an aldermanic corporation' – was

DRINK | A USER'S GUIDE

> RESEARCHERS in Beth Israel Deconess Medical Center in Boston, USA, have identified the enzyme responsible for the accumulation of midriff fat. When mice were fed large amounts of it, they developed what looked like beer bellies. Several drug companies are now looking at the possibility of switching off the enzyme, which would, they hope, help men reduce their overhang.

regarded as lending a dignified appearance; a belly not only gave a man physical substance but proclaimed his material wealth. The likes of Gustavus Adolphus of Sweden, Martin Luther, Handel and J.S. Bach were proud of their potbellies – bellies born of the dedicated raising and lowering of their pots, or tankards. In modern parlance, we're talking beer gut, and male pride in this protuberance remains prevalent in Germany, as well as in the US, the UK, Canada and, perhaps more than anywhere else, Australia. There, possessors enjoy beer-gut festivals, beer-gut beauty parades and beer-gut barging contests, in which they bang their bellies into each other, sumo-like, while balancing on a suspended beam with their hands tied behind their back.

A pint of beer is the equivalent of as many as six slices of bread. It contains between 180 and 300 calories, compared with a glass of white wine's 85 or a gin and tonic's 140. Twenty-one pints of beer a week increase an individual's weight by about 2 kilograms (1 pound). A year's accumulation – disregarding such factors as levels of activity – is 24 kilograms (52 pounds). And the bulk of that on most sedentary, committed beer drinkers arrives around the midriff.

BEER'S HIT AND MISS HISTORY

Medical practitioners in many Western countries are trying to scare the paunchy by telling those with a waist measurement of 97 centimetres (38 inches) or more that the kind of fat that sticks around the middle is associated with diabetes, high blood pressure, heart disease and some forms of cancer. They're even dropping 'beer gut' in favour of the message-delivering (they hope) 'fatty food gut'.

The paunchy seem not to care – according to the Dietary and Nutritional Survey of British Adults, one-third of men in the UK live on a fast food and beer diet. And, it seems, regard their beer/fatty food belly with macho attachment. 'A woman can never be the equal of a man until she has a beer belly and can still walk down the street feeling sexy,' runs the joke, which will be a good deal less funny if the beer belly makes its owner go belly up before his time.

'BEER drinker Matt Royale is suffering from repetitive strain injury caused by lifting too many pint glasses. Matt, a 26-year-old psychology student from Manchester is in pain after drinking 24 pints of bitter a week.'

– British newspaper report, 2002

'NOT all chemicals are bad. Without chemicals such as hydrogen and oxygen, for example, there would be no way to make water, a vital ingredient in beer.'

– Dave Barry

✱ A User's Guide 4

CIDER: NEITHER WINE NOR BEER

> *'Cider was, next to water, the most abundant and the cheapest fluid to be had in New Hampshire, while I lived there, often selling for a dollar per barrel. In many a family of six or eight persons, a barrel tapped on Saturday barely lasted a full week.'*
>
> – Horace Greeley (19th century)

The Boston Tea Party could just as easily have been called the Boston Cider Party…

During George III's reign in the 18th century, England's restrictive laws forced the American colonies to trade only with

> WHEREAS in Britain the word 'cider' refers to an alcoholic drink, in the US 'cider' is unfermented apple juice; the alcoholic variety is called 'hard cider'.

CIDER: NEITHER WINE NOR BEER

the mother country and to use her ships for commerce. England heavily taxed all imports, including cider – and monopolistically forbade the setting up of commercial cider mills.

In 1773, in an act of protest, the merchants of Boston disguised themselves as Indians, boarded an English ship in the harbour and threw overboard its cargo of tea. History records that the import tax on tea had become a symbol of English oppression. What seems to have got lost with the passage of time is that a second ship was also at anchor in the harbour, carrying cider, and that the tax on cider was equally a symbol of English oppression. The Bostonians weren't daft enough to consign that cargo to the sea – they took it home to drink, an action, perhaps, too prosaic for history.

Recent history has tended to be dismissive of cider yet it's unique, neither wine (though made like wine) nor beer (though drunk like beer) – and produced in as wide a variety of styles as either.

Introduced to cider making by the Romans – who'd learnt its rudiments from the English Saxons – the Norman French raised production to a sophisticated level and brought their methods to England after the Conquest. Cider making was already an industry in France and quickly became a priority in

> COLONIAL Americans sometimes made a near spirit-strength brew by boiling four barrels of cider into one barrel. This 'cider-royal' was usually called gumption.

DRINK | A USER'S GUIDE

> THE apples used in cider making are more closely related to crab apples than eating apples and have a high tannin content. Pomologists divide them into two broad categories: bittersweet and bittersharp. The best ciders are the result of careful blending.
>
> The first step in the cider-making process is to crush the harvest to a pulp known as the pomace. Traditionally, this was strained through straw but these days it's more usually wrapped in cloth. The 'must' is transferred to vats or casks, and the drink's dryness or sweetness is dependent on how long the fermentation is allowed to continue.
>
> To obtain a clear cider, the must is filtered to remove sediment; for cloudy ciders the must is retained. Most commercially produced ciders are carbonated (though less so in America than in Europe), mainly to avoid sparkling wine taxes.

England, where wine wasn't plentiful and the French lords wanted something on the table that they could drink. Throughout the Middle Ages strongly spiced cider was at least as popular as ale among the populace. It was also prescribed by doctors for baldness and was bathed in by ladies who believed it stopped ageing.

Cider's popularity in Britain peaked in the mid-17th century, after which it was overtaken by beer, but it remained the American beverage of choice for nearly 200 years more. In colonial times, a town's importance was judged by its volume of cider production, but cider gradually began to lose ground, its popularity finally plummeting with the arrival of millions of immigrants from beer-drinking cultures.

Today, France is the world's largest cider producer,

CIDER: NEITHER WINE NOR BEER

followed by Spain and Britain. Cider drinking is big in Asturias and the Basque region of Spain (where the cities have plentiful *cideria* bars) and in Normandy and Brittany in northern France. Here cider is accorded the reverence of being sold in champagne-like bottles. Indeed, as a promotional come-on, some restaurants give a bottle of cider to a table instead of the usual bottle of wine.

In the last decade cider has made a modest comeback in both Britain and the US, largely because there has been a move away from the mass-produced offerings to more traditional varieties – as with beer. But many in Britain can't quite take cider seriously; it's never quite shaken free of early 20th-century gags about country yokels in smocks, with string tied around their knees.

'YOU know, most people don't know the difference between apple cider and apple juice, but I do. Now here's a little trick to help you remember. If it's clear and yella', you've got juice there, fella! If it's tangy and brown, you're in cider town.'

– Ned Flanders

CIDER is produced in most temperate countries of the world and, unlikely as it may sound, also in Central and South America.

✱ A User's Guide

WINE: VIVE LA RÉVOLUTION

*'Who loves not wine, woman and song
Remains a fool his whole life long.'*
— Martin Luther

France has cultivated the vine for millennia, America for 200 years. France has always produced the finest wines in the world, and assumed it would always be that way. But in the last decade or so with, admittedly, more than a little help from its friends in what in wine terms is known as the New World, the US has shaken France to its cellars. And in a rush, or so it has seemed, French wine sales have been jostled everywhere.

Strictly speaking, wine production in California — where over 90 per cent of US wine comes from — did begin with a rush: the Gold Rush of 1849. Gold fever brought half a million get-rich-quick hopefuls into a state that had a population of 14,000; when the gold fever subsided, the realisation that

WINE: VIVE LA RÉVOLUTION

Californian conditions were ideal for the vine led to 'wine fever'. Plants went into the ground at a terrific rate. By 1856 there were one and a half million vines; six years later there were eight million.

Like the rest of the New World – whose other principal members are Australia, South Africa, New Zealand, Chile and Argentina – the sunshine state was on a steep learning curve, packing into decades experience that the Old World had had centuries to cultivate. The wines got better; the Old World, and France in particular, looked down from on high and paid little attention.

CALIFORNIA isn't the only place in the US that produces wine. Oregon in the Pacific Northwest is a wine region, as are Washington and Idaho. Indiana is no longer a winegrower, although it had the USA's first successful commercial vineyard, planted in 1802, and was the centre of the nation's wine industry until the 1830s.

A BOTTLE of Château Lafite was sold to the late Malcolm Forbes for a world-record price of £105,000. It had been found behind a wall in Paris, embossed 'Th.J' – the property of Thomas Jefferson when he was American ambassador to France. The bottle was put in the Jefferson Museum. Heat from a nearby spotlight shrivelled the cork ... and the museum possessed the world's most expensive bottle of vinegar.

The oldest bottle of wine ever drunk was a Steinwein, a German white, vintage 1540. It turned into a visit to the little boys' room for several lucky chaps in 1961.

DRINK | A USER'S GUIDE

DESPITE the wide variety of grape species, six are responsible for the lion's share of all wines currently on the market, either used exclusively or blended with minor percentages of others. These are (with some help on pronunciation for the phonetically challenged):

REDS

Cabernet Sauvignon (*ca-ber-nay so-veen-yawn*): dry, dark, powerful.
Worth saying: 'This wine was made to be aged.'
Descriptors: currants, chocolate, mint, toast.

Merlot (*mer-lo*): softer, fruitier (and friendlier at a younger age).
Worth saying: 'Always distinctly Merlot.'
Descriptors: rose petals (flowers OK), blackberry, strawberry jam.

Pinot Noir (*pee-no ne-wah*): light purple, true core of fruit.
Worth saying: 'Typically complex.'
Descriptors: cherry, cranberry, earth, truffle.

WHITES

Chardonnay (*shar-doh-nay*): rich, intense, typically aged for a short time and/or fermented in oak.
Worth saying: 'Ah, the great white grape of Burgundy.'
Descriptors: butter, vanilla, tropical fruit.

Sauvignon Blanc (*so-veeyawn bl-on*): fresh, lively, may or may not be oak aged, but if it is has a strong smoky character.
Worth saying: 'Sometimes, you know, the wine is known as fumé blanc.'
Descriptors: mown hay, melon, fig, spice.

Riesling (*rees-ling*): typically very fruity and sweet when from Germany.

WINE: VIVE LA RÉVOLUTION

But unencumbered by Old World custom and methods that in some ways creaked, the New World embraced new technology. More to the point, it mostly didn't muck about with (often incomprehensible) regional names in the Old World tradition: it just stuck the grape variety on the bottle. And, from around 1990, the world woke up to the idea that, while it was true that the superlative wines of France were still the best, the best of the New World could be every bit as good – and, at the lower levels of merely very good and good, were damn sight better value.

In the face of the New World onslaught on their markets, the French got up on their high cheval and, while conceding that New World 'varietal' production (which they made sound like a dirty word) was not without merit, it was the output of *scientists*, where theirs was the output of *artists*. The president of the Institut National des Appellations d'Origine called a press conference to state that French wine was a unique interaction of soil, climate and topography (*terroir*) that was impossible to imitate. 'There are thousands of chardonnays, but there is only one wine from Bonnezeaux,' he loftily intoned.

According to the French, New World wines sacrificed subtlety for strength, and complexity for fruit, fruit, fruit; they

---

Worth saying: 'A cold climate makes for a late harvest, which is why this is often overripe.' (But Riesling from less cold places, such as Alsace in France, can be dry, so take care.)
Descriptors: floral, apricot, honey.

DRINK | A USER'S GUIDE

CHAMBERTIN is a red wine and Montrachet a white, both from Burgundy. The first is made from the pinot noir grape, the second from the chardonnay grape. If these were New World wines they would simply be labelled Pinot Noir and Chardonnay. A few other examples ...

OLD WORLD	NEW WORLD
REDS	
Medoc, Pauillac, St Emilion, Pomerol (Bordeaux or Clarets)	Cabernet Sauvignon, Merlot
Sauternes	Semillon, Sauvignon Blanc
Pommard, Nuit St Georges, Vosne Romanée (red Burgundy)	Pinot Noir
WHITES	
Chablis, Macon (white Burgundy)	Chardonnay
Beaujolais	Gamay
Crozes Hermitage, Cornas (North Rhône Valley)	Shiraz
Condrieu, Château-Grillet (Northern Rhône Valley, white)	Viognier
Gigondas, Vacqueyras, Château Neuf du Pape (Southern Rhône Valley)	Grenache
Sancerre, Pouilly Fumé (Loire Valley et environs)	Sauvignon Blanc
Reingau Trocken	Riesling
Mosel-Saar-Ruwer	Riesling and Muller Thurgau
None	Zinfandel
Chinon, Bourgueil	Cabernet Franc
Barolo, Barbaresco	Nebbiolo
Brunello de Montalcino	Sangiovese
Vouvray, Savennières blanc	Chenin/Chenin blanc

WINE: VIVE LA RÉVOLUTION

> WINE falls into two general groups, dry and sweet, depending on the taste and the percentage of sugar remaining or added after fermentation. They're measured on two scales: 1–9 for sweetness (dry, 0.6 per cent sugar, sweet, 6 per cent sugar) and A–E for 'body' (light to heavy). Reds are made from the skins, seeds and juice of red grapes; whites from the juice alone of white grapes. Rosé can be made from mixing red and white wine, but the better quality rosés are made from reds that have the grapeskins removed after 12 to 36 hours of fermentation. Sparkling wines contain the natural carbon dioxide that forms during fermentation and which is allowed to escape from still wines before bottling.
>
> Ordinary reds are usually aged in oak casks for two to three years (whites less, 'gluggers' not at all), and in some cases for up to 20 years.

boomed heartily rather than beckoned seductively. The semantics obviously didn't convince the wine-buying public. In 1990 the French export market accounted for 40 per cent of world sales, California for 5 per cent, and Australia for 1 per cent. During the following decade, France's sales halved – and are still being shaved a percentage point or two year on year. Over the same period, California's sales tripled and Australia's drew even with France's. Even California has reason to worry about Australia, which has penetrated the huge American home market.

Elitism cost the French dear. They found themselves having to destroy 600 million bottles of wine that they couldn't sell, and angry producers took to the streets, burning cars and trashing the headquarters of a wine merchant selling *Italian* table wine. Riot police with tear gas were called in. The

DRINK | A USER'S GUIDE

> OLD World, New World ... Italy, by some counts, has over a million wine producers; Bordeaux has over 12,000. In Australia just four companies dominate 80 per cent of the market, in the US the biggest five producers have 62 per cent of the market, and in Chile the biggest five command 50 per cent. The world's largest wine company in terms of volume is California's E&J Gallo – yet its output is only just over 1 per cent of world production.

> A TEXAS man has set the world record for the greatest number of grapes caught by mouth. Steve Spaulding, 40, caught 55 in one minute at a wine festival in Dallas.

government was forced to pay some vine growers to rip their vines out of the ground, and the French began to feel that if the *terroir* hadn't quite become the terror, it was, as a member of the Institut put it, 'an elegant, and uniquely French, instrument of surrender'.

During World War One, the Languedoc-Roussillon region – near the Spanish–Marseilles border – provided French troops with an annual 1,500 million bottles of its rough reds and the growers with a nice little earner. As starting another war to increase sales wasn't an option, France set about raising the quality of its vins de pays. Many producers turned to the New World to learn about technical efficiency; some have bitten the bullet and now label their wines by grape variety, even (*mon Dieu!*) in English. And a few are employing humour.

WINE: VIVE LA RÉVOLUTION

When it comes to self-deprecation, the French as a nation have appeared in the past to have experienced a humour bypass. Treating with levity something as serious as wine would, not so long ago, have been tantamount to farting in church. But since the late 1990s the French have been bottling some wines, aimed at Anglo-Saxon markets, with names like Fat Bastard, Old Git and Old Tart – terms of (often) affectionate abuse in Britain and Australia.

Fat Bastard, a chardonnay, is also a play on Batard-Montrachet, a grand cru from Burgundy's Cote d'Or. There's an Utter Bastard, too, a red made with Syrah grapes, and boxed sets are sold – you're ahead of me – as The Complete Bastard ... for some lucky bastard, *naturellement*. Old Git,

---

WHEN a wine's fermentation is finished, the must (wine's equivalent of beer's wort) is filtered off the dead yeast cells – referred to as the lees. A haze may still be left in the liquid, which down the centuries has been cleared by the introduction of a wide variety of fining agents, including pitch, chalk, clay, seawater, egg white and animals' blood. Bordeaux is still known for the use of egg whites, although nowadays it isn't always fined, and when it is, isinglass – a gelatin obtained from fish – is mostly used.

The name of Hungary's red wine, Bull's Blood, has nothing to do with the old method of clarification but refers to the way the town of Eger fought back against a 16th-century Turkish army. The Hungarians – their beards and tunics stained with the local plonk – were so ferocious that the invaders thought they must have been drinking bulls' blood. At least that's way that the Hungarians tell it.

another red, gets its name from the hand-picked, 45-year-old Grenache and Syrah grapes that go into its making. Old Tart, a white made from Terret and Sauvignon, is just unashamedly politically incorrect.

The labels of this triumvirate are cheerful cartoon drawings, in Old Tart's case depicting an archetypical busty blonde in a scarlet dress, glass in hand. The surrounding – English – sell-lines are zingy (sample: 'There really is no substitute for a bit of class in a glass, just ask any Old Tart'). Old Tart is apparently cleared from the shelves at Christmas in America by men buying something for their girlfriends.

SOME OTHER WINES WITH A SENSE OF HUMOUR

Out of the US comes Big House, from a vineyard behind the state prison in Santa Cruz, California. The label shows a prisoner escaping on his bed sheets. Love My Goat is a downright enigmatic one from a man who sold the New York state winery that bore his name, which he couldn't use when he started up in business again (at one point his labels read 'produced by He-Who-Cannot-Be-Named').

From South Africa we have Spatzendrek, which translates as 'sparrow shit'. The wine is made by Spatz Sperling, a one-time German immigrant whose name means sparrow. His first wine, according to a friend, 'tastes like shit'. The label shows a sparrow doing a whoopsy into the cask.

From Sicily, Le Fiat Door and Le Seat Door pun on both Piat d'Or and two car manufacturers.

WINE: VIVE LA RÉVOLUTION

> WINE labels were introduced around 1860, when the sale of bottled wines became widespread. Producers are obliged to stick to the following categories: designation (a wine's alleged quality, only obligatory with European produce), geographical reference, volume alcoholic strength, year of vintage (if European producers state this, then the wine must be 85 per cent of that year), name and address of the producer/bottler (often just a postcode these days), and varietal information – an optional category.
>
> Some countries require warnings to be printed on wine labels and are most common in the US, where there are often warnings for pregnant women, asthmatics, and those operating machinery.
>
> The labels of Château Mouton-Rothschild have a cachet no other wine can beat: every year its label is the work of a famous artist, such as Picasso.

France remains the world's biggest producer, exporting the equivalent of 100 Airbuses of wine a year, but enlightened Frenchmen think it'll take five years to halt the decline in sales, assuming it can be done. In the meantime, the New World isn't just sitting and waiting for the French to play catch-up.

France also has to contend with a big improvement in quality in the Old World, where euro grants have helped the likes of Spain and Portugal to re-equip massively. Greece and Italy are coming up on the rail, post-communist countries are regaining their wine-making self-respect, and Germany, long the 'weak giant' of wine-making Europe, is beginning to see the sense in adopting easier labelling,

DRINK | A USER'S GUIDE

> 'SPANISH wine is foul. Cat piss is champagne compared to this sulphurous urination of some aged horse.'
>
> – D.H. Lawrence

> TROCKENBEERENAUSLESE is a German wine made from vine-dried grapes so rare that it can take a skilled picker a day to gather enough for just one bottle.

though it still makes too many wines under the same names (Kabinett, Späatlese, Auslese) that may be sweet, dry or something in the middle, and English-speaking countries remain confused.

The British: non-growing ... but grateful

One thing the British can't claim to be is a wine-growing nation. They've tried – they were at it in the 8th century. The Normans were pretty unimpressed when they arrived 300 years later, and in the next couple of centuries sorted out the business as best they could, importing French vines. During this period nearly all the wine drunk in England was home produced.

But a great deal of what wound up on the table was plonk less than ordinaire, even when the table was royal. In the reign of Henry II, a fastidious Frenchman at Henry's court wrote home to say that 'The wine is turned sour or

WINE: VIVE LA RÉVOLUTION

mouldy – thick, greasy, stale, flat and smacking of pitch. I have sometimes even seen great lords served with wine so muddy that a man must needs close his eyes and clench his teeth, wry-mouth and shuddering, and filtering the stuff rather than drinking…'

Of course, wines were also shipped from France – at the time the English owned Acquitaine, the important wine-growing region centred on Bordeaux, which Henry's wife Eleanor brought as her dowry – but the practice was sporadic and sometimes dicey. Caskets flung about on a rough crossing often ceased to be airtight, and vinegary contents were common. Pepper was often added to try to disguise the deterioration.

The great monasteries of the 15th and 16th centuries raised English viniculture to respectability and did a brisk trade (as they did with their beers and ciders). It irritated the hell out of Henry VIII: the monastery lands belonged to the church, so he couldn't even tax the profits. Henry broke from the papacy to sort out his love life, but one of the reasons for the dissolution of the monasteries was to get his hands on their vineyards. Decline, however, was rapid, as vast quantities of imports crossed the Channel. By the 18th century, growing vines in England was only a hobby for the rich.

> THERE are 300 small vineyards in Britain today, which mostly started up in the 1980s. Between them, they produce more than two million bottles of wine a year, which, in view of the British weather, is a triumph – although no one seems to know who buys them.

DRINK | A USER'S GUIDE

If they can't produce the stuff, the British can drink it, although until the last decade or two only the rich had developed a discerning wine palate. Whether some of the wine that many in Britain were drinking in the 1970s and 80s could be described as wine is questionable – Henry II would only have drunk Yugoslavian Riesling, Don Cortez Spanish Chablis, and Hirondelle something or other in a really bad patch.

But since 1990, when the supermarkets got behind the New World revolution (and snaffled three-quarters of the entire wine trade), the British have had the opportunity to learn to discriminate, and they've taken it. Today, they've got more right to call themselves a wine-drinking nation than the French: three-quarters of the British population indulge, compared with two-thirds of their wine-growing neighbours. The number of wine drinkers in France continues to decline, and the average age of 'regular consumers' (those who drink at least a glass a day) has risen to over 55, compared with 35 a generation ago.

Forty years ago the French drank 120 litres (211 pints) of wine per capita per annum; today it's 58 litres (102 pints). Twenty years ago the British drank 7.7 litres (14 pints); today

> BLACK Tower ('the white wine in the black bottle') and Blue Nun were regarded as the height of sophistication in the 70s, and were a distinctive presence at dinner parties alongside the prawn cocktail, coq au vin and black forest gateau. Mateus rosé, in its squat, flat bottle, was the giveaway wrapped present of the decade, and once emptied could be converted into a tasteful [sic] sub-Habitat table lamp.

WINE: VIVE LA RÉVOLUTION

> **MULLED WINE**
>
> Mulled red wine – sugar, lemon and a pinch of nutmeg or cinnamon – isn't as popular as it used to be in Britain – the winters just aren't that cold any more. But in the 17th century mulled wine was in vogue, and nutmegs – gilded and beribboned – were given as gifts. Toffs carried nutmegs in their pockets, and fashionable women carried a silver or enamel nutmeg holder, just large enough to hold a single nutmeg; the inside of the cover had a little grater.

it's 22 litres (39 pints), and increasing at the rate of 5–10 per cent a year. In comparison, Italy's consumption is 43 litres (76 pints) – steady, Spain's 35 litres (62 pints) – rising, and Germany's 23 litres (40 pints) – steady.

American wine drinking is back at the British level of 20 years ago and is marginally on the rise after taking a heavy knock from the 'Just say no' anti-drugs and alcohol campaigns of the eighties (the peak Californian output of 1986, 587 million US gallons, fell to 449 million in 1993) but news of the 'French paradox' – the fact that despite their fatty food and Gauloise-smoking lifestyle the French have less heart disease, because it's suggested they drink wine – brought sales back up. The link between red wine in particular and good health has led to sales of red outrunning white for the first time in the US for two decades. In Britain red has overtaken white for the first time ever.

Up to a decade ago, wine was basically in the hands of old-style wine merchants, who made the ordinary punter feel as if on entering their emporia he or she should whisper and

DRINK | A USER'S GUIDE

> **Songs with wine in their titles:** 'Bottle of Red Wine' (Eric Clapton), 'Days of Wine and Roses' (Henry Mancini), 'Kisses Sweeter than Wine' (various), 'Strawberry Wine' (Deana Carter), 'Wine Coloured Roses' (George Jones), 'Wine into Water' (T. Graham Brown), 'Yesterday's Wine' (Merle Haggard), 'Red, Red Wine' (UB40), 'Lilac Wine' (Jeff Buckley).
>
> **Songs with wine in their lyrics:** 'Bottle of red, bottle of white' from 'Scenes from an Italian Restaurant' (Billy Joel), 'Eyes that look like heaven, lips like sherry wine' from 'Elvira' (The Oak Ridge Boys), 'History's lessons drowned in red wine' from 'Children's Crusade' (Sting), 'Please bring me my wine, he said. "We haven't had that spirit here since 1969"' from 'Hotel California' (The Eagles).

> WHEN the British wine writer Malcolm Gluck, began a newspaper column devoted to what was on the supermarket shelves, one conventional wine merchant in the Home Counties threatened him with castration. Established wine scribes poured scorn on this man who rated wines on a value-for-money basis and gave them points out of 20. But Gluck's *Superplonk* annual wine guide became a regular bestseller, even outstripping the sainted Delia Smith's cookbooks at Christmas.

perhaps genuflect. Now, wine is mostly sold in popular outlets, divested of spurious mystique. That, to a considerable extent, has been thanks to a new breed of wine commentators who have come to dominate wine taste and fashion in the English-speaking world.

Commentators of previous generations had tended to further the mystique, using terms like 'breeding' and 'character' to describe wine. They talked a lot about 'bouquet', too, and if

WINE: VIVE LA RÉVOLUTION

trying to be more defining chose to say things like Sauvignon Blanc 'smelled like cat's pee on a gooseberry bush' – which might be accurate but isn't appealing. In the new vocabulary wines now smelled like herbaceous borders, rain on tarmacadam, baked apples, Provence clay, even – famously – old wellingtons. Audiences were probably as often bemused as they were amused; but they were also enthused, and went out to buy the recommendations to taste and smell) for themselves.

The night they invented champagne ... in England

'I wish I'd drunk more champagne.'
— *Last words of John Maynard Keynes*

If the English want to get up the superior olfactory organ of the French (and they do, they do) they can always point out that they created champagne. Well, there's a bubble of two of truth in it.

For hundreds of years the French took the bubbles out of champagne – they wanted it to be like every other wine. 'These mad wines' they called the produce of Champagne.

'CHAMPAGNE tastes much better after midnight, don't you agree?'
— The film *Letter From an Unknown Woman*

DRINK | A USER'S GUIDE

Champagne is the northernmost of France's wine-growing regions; no sooner are its grapes picked and the fermentation from them begun than the long cold winter descends and the fermentation stops – until the warmth of spring brings a secondary action. For themselves, the French waited until this had cleared. But they shipped the still lively casks to England, where, it just so happened, the English had developed sturdy bottles that withstood the force of the trapped carbon dioxide. *Voilà!* Champagne. Haphazard and probably very little like what the French with subsequent due diligence developed, but, at the very least, proto-champagne.

CHAMPAGNE FACTS

Champagne is bottled in 10 different sizes: the half, the bottle, the magnum (two bottles), the jeroboam (four bottles), the rehoboam (six bottles), the methuselah (eight bottles), the salmanazar (12 bottles), the balthazar (16 bottles) and the nebuchadnezzar (20 bottles). Only the half, the bottle and the magnum are sold in the bottle in which they undergo secondary fermentation. The three largest sizes are rarely produced nowadays.

Champagne is labelled by sugar content, from Extra Brut (less than 0.6 per cent sugar – bone dry) to Doux (a minimum of 5 per cent sugar).

There are two methods of opening champagne: the more spectacular (but potentially wasteful) is thumbing out the cork. The more conservative hold the cork still and twist the bottle. Those who have a sabre handy can decapitate the bottle. It's called *sabrage*.

WINE: VIVE LA RÉVOLUTION

THE Romans devised the technique for blowing glass bottles, but these were thin-sided and unable to stand up to being knocked about. Not much had changed by the 17th century, when the English developed something considerably more robust … accidentally. Because timber was in short supply, they turned to firing their furnaces with coal, which produced higher temperatures – and consequently stronger glass.

Seventeenth-century bottles were onion-shaped, only becoming long-necked later and cylindrical later still, when people wanted to store them on their sides – which helped ageing and kept the cork from drying out. The concave indentation in the bottom of a bottle, dating from this time, was to strengthen the structure, not to give short measure.

In the 18th century the wine industry developed the ability to make standard-sized bottles, but different regions favoured different sizes – for instance, Burgundy and Champagne used 800-millilitre bottles and Beaujolais 500-millilitre bottles. The European Union brought about the standardised 750-millilitre bottle in Europe.

Once the French decided that champagne should sparkle, for a century and a half it was a dodgy business bottling it – the bottles exploded. A breakage rate of 15 or 20 per cent was normal, and 40 per cent not unusual. The producers couldn't gauge how much sugar needed to go into a bottle to ensure the second fermentation. Too much and it was look out for flying glass. The men in the cellars wore iron masks. It wasn't until 1836 that a chemist devised a method for measuring sugar levels.

An earlier problem was how to remove the sediment of dead yeast that the second fermentation leaves in a bottle.

DRINK | A USER'S GUIDE

> THE first recorded champagne house was Ruinart, founded in 1729. Möet (now Möet et Chandon, the largest of them all) began in 1743. By the end of the 18th century there were others, including Clicquot, Mumm, Perrier and Heidsieck (now Piper-Heidsieck, the champagne of the Hollywood Oscars) and, of course, Bollinger, awarded the Royal Warrant by seven British monarchs, and the tipple of James Bond and Edna and Patsy in *Absolutely Fabulous*.

> THE classic champagne glass derives from a mould of Marie Antoinette's breasts.

Nichole-Barbe Clicquot – widowed at 27 and finding herself in charge of the champagne house started by husband Phillipe – is credited with the solution. Initially, Veuve (widow) Clicquot cut holes in her kitchen table and stood her bottles in them upside down to bring the sediment into the neck. Not entirely satisfied with this method, she hired Antoine Muller, who hit on the idea of sloping the bottles at 45 degrees to start with, slowing turning them and increasing the slope to the perpendicular.

The process, when it was introduced, took eight weeks, even with a skilled *rumueur*, whose fast hands could rotate over 10,000 bottles a day. Nowadays mechanical methods are used, and have reduced the process from eight weeks to eight days (and, apparently, ended compensation claims for repetitive strain syndrome).

WINE: VIVE LA RÉVOLUTION

If you'd like to irritate the French further, you could point that that Dom Pérignon certainly didn't invent champagne – which many of the French believe to be the case (like many of the British, but there's no need to say that). The Benedictine monk, master blender though he was, belonged to the time that considered 'bubbly' to be bad wine making. So it's unlikely that he actually said, 'I am drinking stars', a statement often attributed to him. (Actually he might just have, because the French interest in bottling bubbly began just before he died, but given his lifelong quest to produce still wines, it isn't likely. Nine years later, Pérignon's pupil, Frère Pierre, wrote a detailed treatise on the master's work and nowhere mentioned sparkling wine.)

EVEN French champagne has lost market share to New World sparklers that have begun to rival it in quality – such as those from the Californian wineries Iron Horse, Jordan Vineyard, Winery S. Anderson, and Schramsberg. France still has the name, but it also has cases of champagne it can't sell. For one thing, it overestimated the new millennium demand and created a global glut. For another, 2000 saw the beginning of a worldwide economic slowdown triggered by the bursting of the internet bubble and suddenly there were no more multi-million dollar company launches and fewer bonuses to spend on bubbly – and there are only so many Formula One winners to waste the stuff. Exports to the UK, champagne's largest market after France itself, plummeted from 32 million bottles to 20 million.

At least two of France's most prestigious champagne house – Moët et Chandon and Louis Roederer – have started producing sparkling wine in California.

DRINK | A USER'S GUIDE

> THE only drink to be seen with these days among Manhattan's in-crowd of conspicuous consumers is the ostentatious Cristal champagne, which comes in at around $625 a bottle. More a fashion statement than a drink.

One would like to think that the quote attributed to Lily Bollinger of the champagne house of Bollinger is true in every syllable – it's the most delicious of all drinking quotes: 'I drink champagne when I am happy and when I'm sad. Sometimes I drink it when I'm alone. When I have company I consider it obligatory. I trifle with it if I'm not hungry and drink it when I am. Otherwise I never touch it – unless I'm thirsty.'

Put a cork in it!

In the early 17th century the English were happily stoppering their bottled ales with cork bungs; it was a small step to do the same to French champagne wine. Even if at that time the French had thought sparkling wine was worth bottling, which they didn't, they couldn't have done it: they were still using hemp-wrapped wood stoppers that barely

> IN early and later history, corks were tapered to fit into bottles. Only with the introduction of hand-held and then mechanical corking appliances did corks come to have straight sides. Champagne corks actually start out straight, becoming mushroom-shaped only after insertion – the change in shape is caused by pressure.

WINE: VIVE LA RÉVOLUTION

THE corkscrew was inspired by the gun worm or bullet screw, which extracted an unspent charge from a musket barrel. The first patent was granted to a Samuel Henshall of Middlesex in 1795.

Of many other patents, the most noteworthy are for the single-lever type, known as the 'butler's friend' or 'waiter's friend' and invented by the German Carl Wienke in 1882; the double-winged level, probably the most common household model, created by Englishman H.S. Heeley and patented in 1888; and the Walker Bell, a self-pulling corkscrew that draws the cork up into a bell shape that rests on the bottle, patented by American Edwin Walker in 1893.

If a cork is too crumbly to remove, gripping the neck of the bottle in red-hot tongs and then wrapping it at once in a cold damp cloth is supposed to make it snap clean off – or did in the days when red-hot tongs were handily in the fireplace.

One of the drawbacks of the plastic cork is that it's almost impossible to get the corkscrew out of the cork as soon as it's been withdrawn. Leave it for an hour or two, however, and the plastic contracts and the task is simple. Should you need to use the corkscrew immediately after the first use – buy another.

provided a seal for still wine never mind effervescent champagne.

Cork was used as wine-bottle bungs by the Romans in the first century CE but gradually fell out of favour. The English are credited with its reintroduction – first for ale, then for wine – importing it from Spain and Portugal, though one suspects that the Spanish and Portuguese had been plugging their bottles with cork all along and the story is an English spin on history.

DRINK | A USER'S GUIDE

> 'REMINDS me of my safari in Africa. Somebody forgot the corkscrew and for several days we had nothing to live on but food and water.'
>
> – W.C. Fields

Cork itself is now under pressure – from outside the bottle. The stripped bark of the *Quercus suber* oak tree is no longer the automatic stopper of choice. Many producers have turned to plastic and screwcaps. Traditionalists are horrified, regarding the dumping of cork as a harbinger of the end of civilisation. The Portuguese, unsurprisingly, maintain that cork is the only way to seal wine – and to abandon it threatens the existence of the wildlife that inhabits the forests where the cork oak thrives.

Ignoring tradition and emotive issues, cork isn't ideal for the job of stoppering wine. Sometimes it develops a mould that taints the wine (making it 'corked', as Basil Fawlty memorably didn't know); more generally it causes variation in quality from one bottle of the same batch to the next. Some producers are now using twist caps and even 'crown corks' – those crinkled metal caps on beer bottles – but most are turning to plastic, not just in the New World but also in the Old – the highly respected house of Michel Laroche is just one such producer, and it prints an invitation on its stoppers to visit the company's website to find out why.

A User's Guide

SPIRITS: THE BAD BOYS OF BOOZE

Until the 17th century, wine, ale and beer satisfied most of the civilised desire for alcohol, but then a variety of distilled spirits began to be widely available that were three, six, ten times more potent. Europe and the colonies – while still somehow finding time for exploration, scientific discovery, invention, artistic and literary achievement, and other trifles – went on the toot for 200 or more years.

It's a small step from alcohol to distilled alcohol: all that's additionally needed is a source of heat and a closed receptacle with a tube running from it. And there you have it: hard liquor. The reason alcohol can be separated out from water – and therefore concentrated – is because it boils at a lower temperature. The fumes rise in the still and are run off – originally into a leather hood but for the last 700 years into a copper vessel (copper is a virtually neutral metal). Essentially, distilling is controlled evaporation.

DRINK | A USER'S GUIDE

You can't say anyone in particular discovered the knack of distillation: it happened all over the world. The Chinese were distilling something fierce from rice beer in 800 BCE, and the same thing was happening around the same time in that part of India which is now Pakistan. The ancient Greeks toyed with distillation but didn't pursue it outside the laboratory, other than a little for medicinal purposes. When the Romans invaded Ireland they found the natives at it, as by then were the Scots, though how much relevance these brews had to their later whiskies is anyone's guess. Eight hundred years ago, the Irish were distilling something that a modern palate would take to be whiskey (we'll come to the 'e' in due course): the Book of Leinster records a feast at Dundadheann in the north which the guests left staggering after a skinful, setting out for Louth on the east coast and not recovering their senses until they got to Limerick on the west (look at the map).

The English might have found out about distillation from their doorstep Gaels if they hadn't considered them a bunch

---

THE early bulbous pot still has largely been replaced by the continuous still, which is more efficient and cheaper. But brandy, Calvados and malt whisky continue to be produced in pot stills – slower, but worth it, it's said, because every last subtle flavour is locked in.

The invention of the continuous still is attributed to a French-born Irishman, Aeneas Coffey, around 1830 – but in fact he pinched the idea. In his job as a customs official, Coffey came across a patented apparatus for distilling a continuous stream of *beer* – and knew a good thing when he saw it.

SPIRITS: THE BAD BOYS OF BOOZE

> MANY of the minor components of distilled spirits, which are present only in parts per million, are detectable by the senses of taste and smell but undetectable by analytical methods.

of backward ruffians. As it was, they learned from Western Europe, which, as with so much in medicine and science, learned from the Greeks via the Arab world and specifically from the Moorish conquerors of Spain.

Spirits were everywhere by the 17th century. Using the same techniques and custom-built stills, each country fashioned its own preferences. Many national distillations crossed borders, but the big five – brandy, whisky, rum, vodka and gin – quickly became dominant.

A word about wood

Distillation is only the first stage in the production of brandy, whisky, rum and tequila; the more interesting chemical reactions occur when the clear new spirit is matured in wood – classically in oak barrels but sometimes with the addition of oak chips, which speeds up the process for lesser drinks. The tannins in oak impart the spirit's colour and up to 70 per cent of its flavour, and the wood also removes some of the harsher elements.

Brandy is left in new casks for about a year – otherwise it would be over-oaked – before being transferred to older casks for the rest of its maturation process (a minimum of

DRINK | A USER'S GUIDE

two years for the youngest French Armagnacs, three for cognacs and up to 10 times as long for the finest brandies).

American bourbon whiskey is aged in oak barrels that have been charred on the inside, the degree of charring – on a scale of one to four, one being lightly burnt toast, and four being cracked like alligator hide and almost pure carbon – affecting the taste. The charring caramelises the wood sugar to varying degrees, releasing compound flavourings such as vanilla.

Regulations allow bourbon barrels to be used only once, which is fine and dandy as far as Canada, Scotland and Ireland are concerned: they use old bourbon barrels for maturing their whiskies. Scotland buys in 800,000 bourbon barrels a year, and also about 15,000 old sherry barrels, which produce lighter-coloured styles. Every time a barrel is used, its influence diminishes; distilleries keep barrels in service for three or four 'fills' – which can mean 50 years' service.

Rum and tequila are also aged in bourbon barrels.

Brandy

'Claret is the liquor for boys; port, for men; but he who aspires to be a hero must drink brandy.'
– Samuel Johnson

The word brandy comes from the Dutch *branntewijn* – 'burnt wine' – in the 14th century, perhaps 100 years after a Franciscan monk in Majorca had recommended the use of

SPIRITS: THE BAD BOYS OF BOOZE

'BRANDY, a noun. A cordial composed of one part thunder-and-lightning, one part remover, two parts bloody murder, one part death-hell-and-the-grave, and four parts clarified Satan. Dose, a headful all the time. Brandy is said by Dr Johnson to be the drink of heroes. Only a hero will venture to drink it.'

– Ambrose Bierce

ONCE the custom was to bring out the full aroma of brandy by heating it over a candle. Nowadays just caressing the glass – balloon shaped to allow the fumes to rise – with a warming hand is considered sufficient.

'Nosing' should be done in two stages, the first without swirling the glass and bringing the nose slowly to the brandy, so as to capture the variety of arising aromas; the second, after catching the breath, by sticking the nose into the swirled glass, to capture the subtler components of the bouquet.

red and white wine as distillates, and three popes and the Holy Roman Emperor Frederick II had subsequently taken to the stuff.

The Spanish have been making brandy longer than the French and, illegally at least, so have the Italians (who are convinced the word comes from the Piedmontese *branda*), but it's the French who have put their stamp unmistakably on it. The great brandies, cognac and Armagnac, some aged for as long as 50 years, are French – L'Esprit de Courvoisier, a cognac made from brandies distilled between 1802 (at the time of Napoleon) and 1931, sells for around £230 … a glass.

DRINK | A USER'S GUIDE

The French amuse themselves by arguing whether cognac or Armagnac is the greater; it was a well-known source of academic humour for many years at the prestigious Collège de France that structuralists and epistemologists drank Armagnac, and deconstructionists and radical Marxists drank cognac. Having a talent for arguing, the French amuse themselves further by saying that there are three great brandies by including calvados from Normandy – which, from a purist perspective, can be ignored as it's made from apples. (Brandy is made from other fruit other than grapes in many countries, notably Germany, where kirsch is made from cherries, and Serbo-Croatia and Romania, where slivovitz is made from plums.)

What's interesting about the French and brandy is that, when all the talking's done, they mostly prefer to drink the cheap, raw stuff sold in supermarkets, which is merely

---

'POMACE' brandies – distilled from the skins and pips that remain after the juice has been extracted from grapes during wine making – are known as *marc* in France, *grappa* in Italy and the US, and *bageceira* in Portugal.

UNTIL a few years ago, cognac producers refused to promote their brandy as a long drink, although the bulk of their production is taken either with ice or Coca-Cola. And the Chinese of south-east Asia (who are the biggest single market for cognac), like the Japanese, drink cognac with water throughout meals.

SPIRITS: THE BAD BOYS OF BOOZE

flavoured neutral alcohol. And the shot of Calvados that four or five million Frenchman start their day by downing at their local – which is so young it's virtually had to do its growing up on the way to the café – is rawer still: it could be used to put a sheen on the zinc-covered café bar.

Brandy-fortified wines

Brandy is the basis of fortified wines – sherry, port, Madeira – an idea developed in the 17th century by the Portuguese specifically for the English market; port, indeed, was once known as 'the English wine'. The brandy is added during the wine's fermentation, which arrests the conversion of sugar to alcohol, the extent depending on the point at which the brandy is introduced. Madeira, from the Portuguese island, is additionally baked over a period of months, something that was once achieved by passing it through the tropics twice – out and back – in barrels used as ship's ballast.

The big advantage of fortification in its early days, besides the increased alcoholic kick, was that wines produced by the process didn't spoil. An opened bottle of fortified wine will keep pretty much indefinitely, the exception being vintage port, which, unlike the others in the fortified family, is aged in the bottle.

Other ports are made by the solera method, the barrels being stacked high on top of each other in pyramid fashion, and the wine gradually siphoned down to the bottom over several years, with new stock being added to the top.

DRINK | A USER'S GUIDE

> GEORGE Washington had three sets of false teeth (wood, cow's teeth, hippopotamus tusk), which he soaked in port overnight to make them taste better.

Once ready, the port is sailed down the Douro river to the port of Oporto (yes, a lot of ports here), where running water keeps the atmosphere 'pure' so no contaminating odours interfere with the port's smell.

Port is bottled under armed guard – it's marketed under licence by the Portuguese government.

Once, all grapes for all wines were trodden to extract the juice. In wine production this practice has long died out, but it has only recently been superseded in the production of port, which requires maximum extraction of colour and tannins from the skins of the (principally) Maurisco grapes. Until 2000 teams of four, working in four-hour shifts, did the stomping, to music. Now they've gone – their bare feet replaced by temperature-controlled paddles.

Like the Portuguese, the Spanish are jealous of their local product's name (which comes from *Scheris*, the closest the once conquering Moors could get to pronouncing Jerez, the centre of the sherry region). In 1996 the name sherry was legally recognised as belonging to Spain alone, so imitators had to do a bit of repackaging. Remember Cyprus sherry?

Which brings us back to the 16th-century Dutch, who not only weren't bothered that the French claimed brandy, but

SPIRITS: THE BAD BOYS OF BOOZE

also weren't too bothered about the quality of the fortified wines they were knocking out themselves – they were too busy making money. They visited all the European ports, bought up every wine consignment they could get – quality irrelevant – and took it home to 'taint', to use the contemporary terminology, into fortified wine.

The stuff was so rough that 'taint' was probably the appropriate word, but the Dutch didn't make it for drinking

---

PASSING THE PORT

'Passing the port' is one of the oldest British drinking traditions, observed with almost religious intensity when naval officers are dining. The decanter is placed in front of the host, who serves the guest to the right, then passes it to the guest on his left, who passes it to the guest on his left, and so on back to the host – the port travels clockwise. In the event of the decanter not coming full circle, it's bad 'port-iquette' for the host to draw attention to this directly. Instead he will ask the person who last had it if he knows the bishop of Norwich. The question isn't meant to get an answer – just the return of the decanter. If, however, the answer 'No' is given, the host will say, 'The bishop is an awfully good fellow, but he never passes the port.'

THE Elizabethans indiscriminately used the word sack for all strong, dry sweet wines of the sherry family, wherever they came from. Some experts claim that sack was a different drink entirely, though Shakespeare at times refers to it as 'sherries sack'. You care? Falstaff didn't.

DRINK | A USER'S GUIDE

themselves (nor did they try to foist it on the English, who'd quickly become connoisseurs). The Del Boys of the age, they flogged it to the Frisians, Germans and Scandinavians, who didn't know any better and were in all likelihood anything but fortified by it.

Whisk...y

> 'Whisky to a Scotsman is as innocent as milk to the rest of the human race.'
>
> – Mark Twain

Scotch became the short of choice among the rich worldwide thanks to the dumpy little queen of England, a vineyard louse and American Prohibition. The queen was Victoria, the champion of all things Scottish in the 19th century, towards the end of which the phylloxera louse attacked France's vineyards, reducing the supply of brandy to a trickle. By the time the French recovered their production it was to find that the canny Scots had nipped in and pinched their market. The Scots had already taken the English market from the Irish, who until Victoria took the throne had dominated sales, and

---

NEVER drink whisky with water and never drink water without whisky.
– Scottish proverb

SPIRITS: THE BAD BOYS OF BOOZE

> ARRIVING in Scotland on the royal train, Edward VII offered the official welcoming party a dram of whisky, as was his wont. One of the party was a strict teetotaller but not wishing to insult the king took the glass and tossed it off in a gulp. 'What a man,' Edward said. 'Give him another.'

> MALT whisky, the original whisky, is made from barley. A single malt is just that: a malt whisky from one distillery. A blended whisky contains whisky from more than one distillery but, in addition, some of that whisky must be grain whisky – which may be made with one or more grains. Until the early 20th century, barley, wheat, oats and rye went into Irish whiskey. Today 15–50 individual whiskies of varying ages and from different distilleries often go into one blend. Despite the enormous growth in the popularity of malts, blends account for 95 per cent of Scotch sales.

they'd do it to the Americans in the following century, when a 13-year government ban on alcohol was imposed. By the time it was lifted, the Americans no longer had a manufacturing base.

It's of intense satisfaction to the Irish that in the last year or two their single malts have become more popular in the US than Scotch.

Why the Irish spell whisky with an 'e' and the Scots spell it without is one of those everlasting conundrums. The common Gaelic root is *woosk'akei*. The Irish like to say their whiskey has more in every respect, including letters in the word. The Scots riposte that the Irish can't spell and nor can

DRINK | A USER'S GUIDE

> IRISH coffee was made famous at San Francisco's Buena Vista Café after World War Two.

the Americans, who choose to follow the Irish. The vocabulary of international aviation makes no distinction.

The three great whisk...y-producing nations – America being the third – go about the business in different fashions. The Irish and Scots both use spring water and barley, but the Irish dry the barley in the sun (which isn't easy to find in Ireland) and the Scots use peat fires (same sun problem, practical solution) – hence the smoky flavours, which the Irish disdain (sun's better). And while the Scots distil their whiskies twice, the Irish distil theirs three times for (they say) greater depth, richness of colour and additional overlays of flavours.

When they began distilling whiskies in the 18th century, the Americans favoured rye as the grain. When the rye crop failed, a large estate in Bourbon County, Kentucky, turned to corn, which immediately became more popular than rye. It wasn't difficult to think of a name.

By law, bourbon must contain at least 51 per cent corn, which is mashed with rye in limestone water. If made by the sweet-mash method, the mixture is blended with barley and malt and – like beer – fermented with yeast. In the more popular sour-mash method, the mixture is blended with boiling leftovers from an earlier distillation – Jack Daniels is

SPIRITS: THE BAD BOYS OF BOOZE

uniquely filtered through sugar maple charcoal, which removes much of the 'corny' taste.

Today, the US and Japan are the world's largest consumers of whiskies. Whisky (without the 'e') is Japan's favourite import, but it's been making its own since 1923. The French now drink more whisky than brandy – brandy has been usurped even in its own backyard.

IN the US, maturation has to be for a minimum of two years; in Scotland and Ireland it's five years. But many whiskies are aged for 8, 12, 16, 25 years and beyond. In 1940, the Glenfiddich distillery in Banffshire, Scotland, set aside nine casks and let them stand for half a century. In 1990 they made 500 bottles available, each numbered bottle bearing a certificate signed by the great-grandson of William Grant, the distillery's founder, and sold out at £3,500 a throw. Today, the value of these bottles has doubled. When 12 bottles of Macallan 60-year-old single malt were auctioned recently in Milan, an unnamed Scot entered a sealed bid of £15,000 for each of bottles numbered 1–6, making this the world's most expensive Scotch.

THE whisky wheel is a flavour guide developed by research scientists. It helps to classify a product as clean, fruity, green/grassy, green/oily, meaty, metallic, musty, nutty, peaty, perfumed, sour, spicy, sulphury, sweet, vegetable, waxy.

DRINK | A USER'S GUIDE

Rum

> *'The chief fuddling they make in the island is Rumbullion, alias Kill-Divil, and this is made of sugar canes distilled, a hot, hellish and terrible liquor.'*
> – From a 17th-century description of Barbados

Rum fuelled the slave traffic of the American colonies. Slaves were bought in Africa and traded in the West Indies for molasses, which was converted into rum in New England, which was then traded in Africa for more slaves.

Until the War of Independence, rum was the foremost liquor distilled in the American colonies, dominating drinking habits to the extent that in places the word was used indiscriminately to mean any hard booze, though rum itself was invariably called Kill Devil, not just in slang but in bills of sale. Oddly, the Dutch in New Amsterdam – New York – called it brandy-wine. Only when the colonies were cut off after the war from the British Caribbean possessions did whiskey become rum's substitute.

Of the major spirits, rum is the one that retains the raw-material taste, which blending and maturing (a minimum of five to seven years for the full-bodied kind) round off but don't eliminate. It isn't drunk straight these days, except in rum-producing countries (where rum-flavoured tobacco is popular); most people prefer it in cocktails or in tall drinks like rum Collins.

SPIRITS: THE BAD BOYS OF BOOZE

BLACKSTRAP – rum with molasses (the thick dark-brown juice obtained from raw sugar during the refining process) and a little vinegar – was a huge favourite in America. Casks of it stood in every provision store and tavern, a salted codfish hanging alongside: a subliminal invitation to thirst. The Americans liked mixing rum with hard cider, too (applejack). 'If the ancients drank wine as our people drink rum and cider, it's no wonder we hear of so many possessed with devils,' said President John Adams – who to the end of his life started the day with a tankard of hard cider before breakfast.

Another big favourite in America – known in England but less regarded – was flip: two-thirds strong beer and a dash of rum, sweetened with molasses and heated with a red-hot poker. As the three- and four-quart flip glasses that are now collectors' items show, the drink was downed in vast quantities.

RUM is made from the leftovers of the sugar-making process. Once the juice from the crushed sugar cane is removed, a brownish-black liquid is left behind in the boiler. This is often used as a syrup for pancakes or waffles and, if boiled a second time, becomes treacle. But after a third boiling it becomes thick, black molasses – containing over 50 per cent sugar – and it's this that becomes rum.

The heavy dark rums of Barbados, Jamaica and Demerara in Guyana are made from molasses enriched with the skimmings that remain in the boilers. These attract yeast spores from the air, resulting in a natural fermentation. The light dry rums of Puerto Rico and the Virgin Islands, which date from the 19th century, employ yeast cultures.

DRINK | A USER'S GUIDE

Hardly surprisingly, considering that rum was the produce of islands in the middle of the buccaneering main, its association with pirates was strong. It was even stronger with the British Navy. For nearly 300 years, every man jack aboard a British naval vessel at sea was issued with a daily ration of rum. Before 1650, the issue was beer – often of such 'pernicious provision that it stands as abominably as the foul stagnant water which is pumped out of many cellars in London at the midnight hour'. Brandy briefly replaced beer and then, in 1687, was replaced by rum – half a pint, twice daily, half that quantity for boys.

In the 18th century, when drunkenness and lack of discipline were rife, Admiral Edward Vernon introduced a watering-down of the issue in the ratio of two to one (mixed on deck in the presence of the lieutenant of the watch 'so that no man is

---

THE biggest rum-drinking country today is the Philippines (83 million litres/146 pints per annum), just ahead of America (79.2 litres/139 pints per annum), followed by India (58.8 litres/104 pints per annum), Mexico (58.5 litres/104 pints per annum) and Germany (31.8 litres/56 pints per annum). Britain isn't a rum country (12.8 litres/23 pints per annum) and Spain (7.2 litres/12 pints per annum) is even less so.

IN the Caribbean, rum is sprinkled on a new baby's forehead for luck.

SPIRITS: THE BAD BOYS OF BOOZE

> 'FIFTEEN men on a dead man's chest
> Yo-ho-ho and a bottle of rum
> Drink and the devil had done for the rest
> Yo-ho-ho and a bottle of rum.'
> – Robert Louis Stevenson, *Treasure Island*

> WINSTON Churchill is usually attributed with saying that the traditions of the British Navy were 'rum, sodomy and the lash'. In fact he didn't say it – but said he wished he had.

> VERNON became disparagingly known as 'Old Grog', after the waterproof boat-coat he wore, which was made of a wool and silk material stiffened with gum and known as grogram. The term soon applied to the diluted rum but is now a synonym for anything alcoholic.

cheated of his share'). Twenty years later the evening issue was stopped; six years on, the remaining issue was reduced to a gill (an eighth of a pint); and in 1970, on what was called 'Black Tot Day', the last pipe of 'Up spirits' was heard – the rum issue was stopped altogether.

After he was killed in the Battle of Trafalgar, Admiral Nelson was brought home for burial in a barrel of booze. Generally the booze is believed to have been brandy, though some (mainly rum manufacturers) insist it was rum. In any event, by the time Nelson's body came ashore the barrel was drunk dry – and the navy has ever since referred to rum as 'Nelson's blood'.

DRINK | A USER'S GUIDE

Vodka

The Russians have a saying: 'Tea is not like vodka, which you can drink a lot of.' The belief is based on the tradition of *zakuska,* the serving of small plates of pickles, salami, sausages, salted herrings and mayonnaise-based salads – nibbling which sustains vodka drinking for hours. Many Russians sustain vodka drinking for hours without *zakuska*.

The word *vodka*, which literally means 'water', comes from *zhizenni voda* – 'water of life' – Russian for that universal belief in spirituous distillation as the water of life. Poland, Sweden, Finland and Norway also lay claim to its origination, somewhere around the 14th century. Recently, Russian historian Boris Uspensky and American ethnologist Allan Morris have suggested that the beverage made its first appearance 300 years earlier – on the island of Majorca.

IN Russia it was once believed that the corpse of a man who had died from drinking vodka could be dug up and dropped into a bog to make it rain.

THE Azerbaijanis, the non-drinking Muslims in a country at the toe of Russia, describe a difficult task by adding, 'I had to eat a whole sheep to do this.' The version favoured by their Russian neighbours is, 'I had to drink a lot of vodka to do this.'

SPIRITS: THE BAD BOYS OF BOOZE

> **CONGENERS**
>
> Congeners are minor chemical constituents of wine and spirits that nonetheless contribute significantly to the characteristics of their taste, aroma and colour. Some are in the primary ingredients and some are produced during fermentation – and many are reduced by purification (vodka has as little as 33 milligrams of congeners per litre). But other congeners are introduced from the wood of the barrels in which spirits are aged – the longer the ageing process the more concentrated the introduction. Most whiskies and brandies, for example, have 500 milligrams of congeners per litre, and others as many as 2,600 milligrams.

Whatever the claims, since the 17th century, when Peter the Great began flogging vodka to the rest of Europe ('Vodka is the aunt of wine,' he told the French), it's been synonymous with only one place. Two-thirds of Czarist Russia's income was generated by it.

Originally the drink was made from a mash of potatoes – the cheapest and most readily available resource. Ukrainian vodka (*gorilka*: 'up in flames') was made from wheat and the Russians scorned it – they only sold it in taverns. Nowadays, virtually all vodka is made from cereal grains.

It's tempting to say it hardly matters. Whatever goes in at the beginning of the distillation process comes out at the end of it, charcoal-filtered, without discernible aroma or taste and, because vodka isn't aged in barrels, without colour. In fact, like gin, vodka isn't aged at all. You could drink it straight out of the vat, diluted, of course – pure vodka is

DRINK | A USER'S GUIDE

> ACCORDING to his published diaries, the English theatre critic Kenneth Tynan heard that alcohol is best taken rectally. On 5 May 1974 he got his lover to inject 'a large wine-glass of vodka into my anus via an enema tube. Within ten minutes the agony is indescribable.'

> A NEW, but so far not widely spread fashion emerged in 1999: vodka sniffing. If inhaled for long enough, the fumes deliver a bigger thump to the cerebral cortex than when swallowed.

100 per cent alcohol: you could launch rockets with it. Once it was left like that to stop it freezing while being transported in Russian winters when otherwise the water content would have cracked the casks.

Vodka's attraction is its very neutrality. Only in Russia and Eastern Europe, where there's a long tradition of flavouring it with bison grass, lemon, honey and cranberry, is it drunk straight up; everyone else takes it in combination with other beverages, because it imparts no conflicting flavour.

For 25 years vodka has been the largest-selling spirit in the US and one in every four alcoholic drinks consumed in the world has vodka in it.

SPIRITS: THE BAD BOYS OF BOOZE

Gin

'Gin was mother's milk to her.'
– *Eliza Doolittle,* My Fair Lady

Dutch cheapo fortified wine may not have reached England, but Dutch gin did, and it knocked the English bandy, all but destabilising English society.

The Dutch weren't to blame for the English taking to gin in the way that they did. Then again, though, it was the Dutch-born king of England, William of Orange, who let it happen, because he wanted to damage the Catholic French and help his Protestant countrymen. To do that he placed prohibitive taxes on the import of French wines and brandy, encouraged the shipment of gin into England and then allowed anyone who applied for a licence to set up a gin distillery.

English soldiers fighting in the Low Countries in the early 17th century first came across gin – which the Dutch originators called *genever* from the juniper berries from which it was distilled, and which the English shortened to gin. When they came to make it themselves, the English at first used junipers, but then turned to a mixture of cereal grain and malt barley, only using juniper as a flavouring.

In late 17th-century England it was suddenly patriotic to be Protestant and gin drinking instead of Catholic and brandy drinking. Farmers of any or no religious persuasion were delighted – distilling gave them a market for their low-grade corn, which was unsuitable for brewing. Between 1688 and the turn of the century, consumption quadrupled to two million gallons, overtaking beer and ale. Within 30 years the country was awash in gin. It took the law another 20 years – by which time 19 million gallons of gin were being distilled annually in London alone – to exercise control.

The great distilleries have long since dropped juniper, flavouring the spirit with a combination of what's referred to as 'botanicals': orris, angelica, licorice, caraway, coriander, fennel and many more – each producer has their own guarded formula.

Today, the London dry style is favoured in the UK, North America, Spain and Australia, and the original *genever* style in Holland, Belgium and Germany (although, it's not *quite* the original, as it's now distilled from grains with the juniper going in as the main flavouring). In Holland more *genever* is drunk than any other spirit, socked back in small glasses like schnapps or aquivit, often with a beer chaser (or vice versa).

Genever is too pungent to be combined with other drinks. London dry style, however, is popular in cocktails and most popular as gin and tonic. The upper classes lost their taste for gin during the half-century that the working

> TANQUERAY gin, established in 1830, is still sold in a bottle shaped like a 19th-century London fire hydrant, which – like the Coca-Cola bottle and the Haig dimple – is protected by worldwide patent. The recipe is claimed to be contained in a black ledger with three locks, the keys of which are held by different individuals.

SPIRITS: THE BAD BOYS OF BOOZE

> 'DRY' was originally applied to London gin, indicating 'no sugar included'. Late 19th-century drinkers didn't understand the term – it had to be spelled out on the label. A rarely produced English gin, Old Tom, which has a noticeably sweeter taste because it does have added sugar, is said to have been the gin used in the original Tom Collins.

classes were on their gin spree. It was officers in India who made gin respectable again in the following century. To disguise the bitterness of the quinine they took against malaria, they invented 'Indian' tonic water – which, they discovered, went uncommonly well with gin. The combination became the de rigueur choice of expatriates sitting on the verandas of the British Empire, and of women in Edwardian society, because it looked like water and didn't smell on their breath. The idea of gin without tonic is still today like a carriage without a horse.

Gin, mixed with angostura bitters, another prophylactic in the tropics, has long been the drink of officers in the navy. Pink gin, as the combination is called, should ideally be made with Plymouth Gin, a drier brand than any other, made in the famous West Country naval town. It's also said that naval officers began drinking pink gin to ward off scurvy. One of these stories is certainly true.

DRINK | A USER'S GUIDE

Absinthe and tequila: spirit(s) of the age

> *'The first stage of absinthe is like ordinary drinking, the second when you began to see monstrous and cruel things, but if you can persevere you will enter in upon the stage where you see things that you want to see, wonderful, curious things.'*
>
> – Oscar Wilde

What links Roman charioteers with an Aztec goddess? Bohemian artists in Paris with Mexican peasants? The answer is two drinks, one with a recent history of being reviled and one with hardly any recent history at all.

No one would suggest that tequila is going to rival the spirituous big five, nor that absinthe will rival tequila, but in an age when most drinkers are young, capricious and regard themselves as a bit rebellious, both are on the radar.

In its modern guise, absinthe came from Switzerland at the beginning of the 19th century and at the fin de siècle was the most popular aperitif in Europe. It was favoured by wild painters and poets, and the ritual of preparing to drink it was like 'shooting up': a drizzle of water into the glass to turn it into a swirl of milky yellow-green (the 'green fairy'), then

> IN Tudor England 'purl' was composed of hot ale and wormwood; in his diaries Samuel Pepys mentions drinking it.

sipping through a perforated spoon containing a lump of sugar – without which absinthe would have been undrinkable for most people.

Absinthe would have been just another aniseed-flavoured liqueur if it hadn't been for the wormwood that made it so astringent – it was because of that bitterness that champions in Roman chariot races were given a cup of wine in which wormwood leaves were soaked, as a reminder than even victory has a bitter side. It was wormwood that led the French medical profession to proclaim that absinthe alone was the cause of alcoholism – which could never be caused by, say, French wine – and to substitute the term 'absinthism'.

Such pronouncements caused hysteria. Many countries finally came to regard absinthe as we sometimes regard crack cocaine and from 1910 began to ban it. America followed; as did France itself in 1915, on much the same grounds as Britain legislated against whisky: the French government thought it was weakening the troops, who had a monthly ration.

But absinthe, the only booze ever singled out for international extermination, never went away entirely. It continued to be made in several countries, notably Czechoslovakia, by far the biggest producer then and now. And in the last five years or so it's appeared behind bars almost everywhere, including America – where, technically, it's still illegal – and the UK, where, interestingly, it never was banned.

Enough time has passed for a sense of perspective to show that 'the absinthe binge', as it was called, never really existed. Yes, absinthe was a craze and at its height, Pernod, France's

DRINK | A USER'S GUIDE

> LIGHTNING struck the Pernod factory in 1900, causing an alcohol fire that raged for four days. Hundreds of thousands of gallons of absinthe were lost in the Doubs river, which was flavoured with anise for miles downstream.

biggest absinthe distillers, were making five million gallons. But most of that was for export, a drop in the worldwide alcoholic bucket – in France the consumption of absinthe was never above 3 per cent of total alcohol consumption per year.

Time also shows that many of the experiments carried out on animals to prove the dangers of the green fairy hardly followed scientific protocol. Injecting a cat with pure essence of wormwood to prove it caused epileptic fits was irrational: the active ingredient in wormwood, thujone, is a neurotoxin, but absinthe had 35 drops of wormwood to the quart, less than two drops to the glass – Chartreuse, vermouth and bitters all contain small amounts of thujone.

That absinthe contributed to insanity was less a conclusion drawn from the laboratory than from the antics of the likes of Verlaine and Van Gogh – who were both mentally unstable and alcoholics before they even discovered absinthe. Sterility, blindness, death? Absinthe was implicated, but, even allowing that at 70 per cent proof it delivers the highest jolt of any spirit, it's debatable whether it is more injurious than any other. Verlaine downed 20 absinthes a day. Down that much – or even half – of any straight spirit and you'll be seeing more stars than ever Dom Pérignon might have seen.

SPIRITS: THE BAD BOYS OF BOOZE

It wasn't until the margarita cocktail that tequila was seriously considered drinkable by anyone except men in big hats (Mexican natives and American cowboys on the cattle trail south of the border). And then in the 1990s Mexico suffered an economic crisis and the peso plunged out of sight, making imported spirits too expensive for everyday consumption. Fashionable Mexicans started drinking tequila neat, like whisky. Women took to tequila. Tequila spread to the States – where it's now the fastest-growing spirit – and then to everywhere else.

Ten years ago, the agave plant, from which tequila is

ABSINTHEURS include the painters Manet, Degas, Toulouse-Lautrec, Gauguin, Van Gogh and Picasso; the poets Baudelaire, Verlaine and Rimbaud; and the writers Poe, Wilde and Hemingway. Degas, Manet and Picasso all painted scenes that involved absinthe, with Degas's *L'Absinthe* causing Francophobia in England. Van Gogh depicted it many times – his obsession with ochres and pale greens are said to stem from his love of absinthe. Hemingway mentions absinthe in *Death in the Afternoon* and *For Whom the Bell Tolls*. Others who enjoyed a snort of the green fairy included playwright Alfred Jarry (who rode his bicycle with his hands and face painted green in homage to it), Sigmund Freud and Josef Stalin.

THE Russian word for absinthe is *chernobyl*.

DRINK | A USER'S GUIDE

made, was virtually worthless, rotting in the field. Today, when there are 600 different tequilas being exported all over the world, there's a shortage of agave – the plant takes eight to twelve years to mature. Growth was already unable to keep up with demand by 1997, but then El Niño brought fatal frosts and an infestation killed hundreds of plants. Bandits have been hijacking lorries and stealing the agave out of the field. No wonder tequila prices have jumped.

Tequila owes its existence to mescal, a drink that originated with the conquistadors, who were in search of something with more punch that pulque, the drink the Aztecs first tasted after lightning struck and cooked an agave plant – the Aztecs thought the aromatic sap that oozed out was the lightning transformed by the gods.

The difference between mescal and tequila is that for the one the giant heart of the agave (weighing between 35 kilos/80 pounds and 91 kilos/200 pounds) is roasted, and for the other, steamed.

'A computer lets you make more mistakes faster than any invention in human history – with the possible exceptions of handguns and tequila.'
– Mitch Ratcliffe

IN 1999, US beer giant Anheuser-Busch rolled out Tequiza, a lager made with agave nectar and lime. It's become one of the four best-selling specialist beers in the US – even if you can't pronounce it without stuttering.

SPIRITS: THE BAD BOYS OF BOOZE

THE agave isn't a cactus as is frequently thought – it's a member of the lily family, despite its man-sized, sword-like growth. While we're at it, there's no worm in tequila as is also popularly believed; it's in mescal – and it isn't a worm but a butterfly caterpillar. The caterpillars, which live in the agave, are hand-harvested during the rainy season, sorted, stored, and placed in the bottles near the end of the process. Originally the worm was a test of 'proof': if it disintegrated there wasn't enough alcohol present to keep it intact.

THERE are three qualities of tequila: silver, gold and anejo. Silver isn't aged – it goes straight into the bottle; gold is aged for about a year; and anejo is aged for up to four years. The Westerner is advised to stick to anejo – silver is quite definitely tongue-stinging, throat-burning hooch.

The tradition has emerged of downing tequila with a wedge of lemon or lime and a lick of salt. The order in which this should happen is disputed by aficionados, but lick, sip, suck is usual. In Malaya, José Cuervo, *the* name in tequila, have a national promotion in which a man licks the salt from a woman's breasts and, after downing his shot, sucks from the lime she holds in her mouth.

You wonder why it isn't running here.

A User's Guide — 7

MONKS AND THE LIQUEUR HABIT

Nearly 500 years ago, a Benedictine monk tasted a liqueur he'd perfected and exclaimed: 'Deo optimo maximo!' or, in a loose translation, 'Jesus H. Christ, what a winner!' Not quite 100 years later, a Carthusian monk tasted a liqueur he'd perfected – and said nothing. Probably not that he wasn't just as excited, but the Carthusians are a silent order.

Once the practice of distillation began to spread in the 12th and 13th centuries, it was only another step to flavouring concentrated spirits with herbs, roots, barks and spices. For a couple of hundred years these 'waters' (back to aqua vitae) were alchemical potions; later they were used to mask the unappealing aroma of spoiled meats and vegetables (and were popular, because of their sweetness, in custards and desserts); only gradually did they become pleasurable drinks.

The Italians were the first to appreciate liqueurs for their own sake, in the 14th century. As they were mad about nuts,

MONKS AND THE LIQUEUR HABIT

they made most of theirs with walnut, hazelnut and pecan bases; many Italian liqueurs are still nut based. The Italians were also mad about peppermint and bitters, a liqueur that they downed in one therapeutic dose as a digestive tonic. They still drink bitters as aperitifs, but these are too, well, bitter for almost everyone else. Outside Italy they are used primarily to add a hint of, well, bitterness, to cocktails. The major exception is Italian Campari, drunk as an aperitif around the world, and vermouth, the catalyst in the martini's alchemy. Other of the world's best-known bitters are Angostura, Amer Picon, Byrrh, Fernet Branca, Radis.

With the marriage of Catherine de Medici to French monarch Henry II, the fashion for bitters spread to France – Catherine was a dab hand in the distillery. Soon most noblemen in the Western world had a small still and their ladies took pride in their own recipes, which included ingredients from the East and the New World; oranges, chocolate, cinnamon and ginger were highly prized.

The monasteries were at the centre of liqueur concoction. The French anise liqueur Cusenier Mazarine, for instance, derived from a recipe of the Abbaye de Montbenoit's, the

> VERMOUTH is a principal ingredient in the cocktail barman's trade. An aromatised wine flavoured with as many as 50 different berries, herbs, roots, seeds and flowers, it takes about a year to make. On its own, vermouth is the world's favourite aperitif but, according to *Wine Spectator*, less than 10 per cent of people who drink it have any idea what it consists of.

DRINK | A USER'S GUIDE

herbal liqueurs of Aiguebelle and Carmeline are Cistercian, and La Senancole is Trappastine.

IT would be a mistake to think that only the monasteries claim liqueuring excellence. By the middle to end of the 16th century, a number of commercial distilleries had formed, including the Dutch Bols and the German Danzig Goldwasser.

The French company Marie Brizzard produces more than 40 different liqueurs.

Two of the world's most famous concoctions – Cointreau and Drambuie – sound as if they should have been created in medieval monasteries, but weren't: the brandy-based, orange-flavoured Cointreau has been made by the French Cointreau family only since 1849; and the whisky-based, heather-, honey- and herb-imbued Drambuie only since 1909.

If you want to believe it, the recipe for Drambuie is said to be the personal one of Prince Charles Edward Stuart – Bonnie Prince Charlie himself. He is said to have given it to the family Mackinnon, who sheltered him on the island of Skye after his defeat at Culloden in 1746.

Other favourites: Advocaat (egg yolks, grape brandy), Amaretto (almond and apricot flavoured), Cachaça (sugar-cane spirit), crème de cassis (blackcurrant flavoured), crème de menthe (white or green, made from mint leaves), crème de cacao (chocolate flavoured, distilled from cocoa beans), Curaçao (orange flavoured), Galliano (aniseed dominant), Grand Marnier (Curaçao, with cognac base), Kahula (coffee), Kummel (caraway and aniseed flavoured), Pernod (aniseed flavoured), Tia Maria (rum based, with coffee extract), Triple Sec (sweet white Curaçao).

MONKS AND THE LIQUEUR HABIT

But in popularity, nothing has touched the glory of golden Benedictine, distilled by Dom Bernardo Vincelli in the French abbey of Fécamp about the year 1510, or the green of Chartreuse, the masterpiece of an unnamed monk in the French monastery of Grenoble in 1605.

Chartreuse is still made by the Carthusians, who now operate out of a distillery site just down the road from the monastery. They don't actually taste their products during manufacture these days, content, apparently, to smear a little on the back of the hand to tell by smell whether the aromatic balance is right. Chartreuse also comes in yellow or white, according to the flavourings used. These include palm leaves, peppermint, orange peel and spices.

In contrast, Benedictine has been secularised. It vanished in the upheavals of the French Revolution, its secret lost for half a century. Then the old recipes were found and it's been back in production since 1836, its ingredients a closely guarded secret but known to include hyssop, melissa, cinnamon, tea, thyme, coriander and nutmeg. In Europe it's sipped; Americans primarily drink it bottled as B&B – a combination of Benedictine and brandy.

If you take a look at the Benedictine bottle, you'll see that it still bears the golden imprint 'DOM', in memory of Dom Bernardo's (apocryphal, if you're the cynical type) first exclamation of appreciation.

A User's Guide — 8

SHAKEN AMERICA

Stirred by the Cocktail

'The barman recommended a "lightning whizzer", an invention of his own. He said it was what rabbits trained on when they were matched against grizzly bears, and there was only one instance on record of the bear having lasted three rounds.'
– P.G. Wodehouse

If gin owes much of its popularity to tonic, the cocktail owes much of its popularity to Prohibition bathtub gin – the illicit hooch purchased from the neighbourhood racketeer, and mixed in a container in the bath (because the container was usually too big to fit under the tap in the kitchen sink) with glycerine to smooth out some of the roughness, and then dosed with sugar, fruit seeds, fruit juices – to

SHAKEN AMERICA

disguise the terrible taste. This was the cocktail, which has defined the sophisticated end of American drinking ever since.

The cocktail existed before the roaring twenties. Combinations of spirits with sugar, water and bitters – bittered slings, notably the gin sling – were around over 300 years ago. Punch was a cocktail in all but name, and ice came in the mid-1800s, with commercial ice harvesting. The first cocktail book arrived in the 1860s. Before the 20th century, the mint julep, the daiquiri and the gin fizz were already being drunk, as was the most celebrated of all cocktails – the martini.

But the cocktail in countless different guises was a shaken America's antidote to Prohibition. The American essayist H.L. Mencken said that 17,964,392,788 different cocktails were possible and, while he was speaking with his tongue in his cheek, or possibly an olive – or a white pearl

---

WHERE does the word 'cocktail' come from? Most sources say it's indisputably American, but most sources are American, indisputably. France also lays claim, citing the word *coquetel*, an 18th-century concoction of wines; Mexico puts forward the tale of Coctel, the daughter of one of their kings who stopped a potential punch-up between her dad's militia and the US militia. Stories abound about fighting cocks, the colours in a cock's tail, feathers in men's hats, and much more. The least likely source cited is cock-ale. The most likely (maybe) is the English use of cocktail in the 17th century to describe a non-thoroughbred horse that nonetheless had thoroughbreds in its line.

DRINK | A USER'S GUIDE

> PUNCH came back from India to England and then onwards to the American colonies. *Panch* is Hindustani for five. The name was given because there were five principal ingredients: spirit, water, spice, sugar and some acid fruit juice.

> 'I must get out of these wet clothes and into a dry martini.'
>
> – Attributed to Alexander Woollcott and almost everyone who ever sat in on the Round Table with the in-crowd at the Algonquin Hotel, New York.

onion if he had a Gibson in front of him at the time – there were more than anyone could count.

Any bartender worth his salt had to know the recipes of as many as 300 different drinks, with names that reflected the sexuality of the era of hoods and molls, flappers and speakeasies: Bosom Caresser, Screaming Orgasm, Zipper Ripper, the Angel's Tit (yes, a cherry).

In the twenties, alcohol was the cocktail's main ingredient. Drinkers were after a fast fix. Harry Craddock, the barman at the Savoy in London in the cocktail's heyday – when it was the choice of the beau monde in Paris, Berlin and Venice as well as New York – said the best way to drink a cocktail was 'Quickly, while it's laughing at you'. But nowadays most drinks are long and the alcohol is a minor ingredient. The blender is as likely to be used as the shaker, too.

'New' cocktails are still being created but, hardly surprisingly, are really variations on a theme. The biggest change for

SHAKEN AMERICA

the cocktail has been the substitution of vodka for gin, fashionable since Ian Fleming gave his own preference to his creation, James Bond.

High art of drinking – or low farce?

Whether the cocktail is a concoction of high art, a drink so sublime that, as the actress Clara Bow said, 'Martini is a

---

LIQUEURS most used in cocktails: Advocaat, Amaretto, Benedictine, Cachaça, calvados, cherry brandy, Cointreau, crème de cassis, crème de menthe, crème de cacao, Curaçao, Drambuie, Galliano, Grand Marnier, Kahlua, Kummel, Orgeat, Pernod, Tia Maria, Triple Sec.

ONETIME bartenders: Tom Arnold, Sandra Bullock, Chevvy Chase, Bill Cosby, Kris Kristofferson, Bruce Willis.

THE Royal Society of Chemistry has asked an international fragrance and flavour company to investigate the difference between the martini that has been shaken, not stirred (the 007 way) and the martini that has been stirred, not shaken (the traditional way). It's claimed that shaking, not stirring, leaves fragments of ice that make the drink colder, and because more of the alcoholic surface is in contact with ice, the sensation in the mouth is different. Most master barmen are appalled and refuse to be shaken from the traditional approach.

DRINK | A USER'S GUIDE

THE martini (3–4 parts gin or vodka, 1 part vermouth, optional olive or, in a Gibson martini, a white pearl onion), the daiquiri (1 part white rum, 28g/1fl oz fresh lime or grapefruit juice, 2–3 dashes gomme syrup) and the margarita (1 part tequila, 1 part fresh lime juice, 1 part triple sec or Cointreau) remain the three big cocktails.

SOME OTHER FAMOUS CONCOCTIONS

Gin Alexander: two parts gin, one part crème de cacao, one part sweet cream, shaken; **Orange Fizz**: two parts gin, one part orange juice, one part lemon juice, a few drops of Pernod, arak or ouzo – then mixed half and half with soda water; **Pink Lady**: 2 jiggers gin, 1 egg white, tablespoon lemon juice, a few drops of sweet cream; **Singapore Sling**: 2 jiggers gin, 2 jiggers soda water, tablespoon cherry brandy, tablespoon lemon juice, several drops Benedictine and brandy, garnished with orange slice and sprig of mint; **Americano**: one part bitters, 1 part red vermouth, poured over ice cubes, served with slice of lemon (cold soda water optional); **Negroni**: as the Americano, with some gin or vodka.

Best known of the more modern cocktails is the Harvey Wallbanger, from the sixties: 1 part vodka, 150ml (5$^1/_2$ fl oz) fresh orange juice, 18ml ($^2/_3$ fl oz) Galliano. One that is now making a name for itself is the Sex in the City cocktail: 30ml (1 fl oz) vodka, 150 ml (5 fl oz) Cointreau, tablespoon limejuice, a splash of cranberry juice, shaken gently with ice cubes.

The restorative cocktail of the twenties still with us is the Bloody Mary: 1 part vodka, $^1/_2$ fl oz tomato juice, slightly more lemon juice, 2 dashes Worcestershire sauce, 1–2 dashes of Tabasco sauce, pinch of celery salt, black pepper. Nowadays a tequila rather than vodka restorative has become popular – known as a Bloody Maria.

SHAKEN AMERICA

> The Bloody Mary/Maria's rival, the Corpse Reviver, in three varieties: 1) 28ml (1fl oz) brandy, 18ml (²/₃ oz) sweet vermouth, 18ml (²/₃ oz) calvados; 2) 14ml (½ fl oz) gin, 14ml (½ fl oz) Cointreau, 14ml (½ fl oz) Lillet (a French apéritif), 14ml (½ fl oz) lemon juice, dash absinthe; 3) 28ml (1 fl oz) brandy, 28ml (1 fl oz) crème de menthe, 28ml (1 fl oz) Fernet-Branca.

longer word for joy', or a concoction of low farce for 'vulgarians with no palate' has always been a matter of conflict. For a long time in Paris the cocktail was confined to tourist haunts and places frequented by 'those suffering from Anglomania'. In a gastronomic book of 1932, cocktails were described as enough 'to make a shark retch or a crocodile vomit'.

More recently, in his magisterial *Dictionary of Drink and Drinking*, Oscar Mendelssohn fulminated that 'The ultimate degradation is Black Velvet, a blend of stout and champagne ... Both are honest beverages in their own right, but to mix them – one might as well spread onions on ice cream.'

But some serious drinkers have revered the cocktail. Hemingway was addicted to daiquiris. When he was in Havana he got the La Floradita Bar to double the rum and drank them

> DURING World War Two, distillers in the UK, the US and Canada shifted all production to industrial alcohol for the war effort – cocktails for Hitler.

DRINK | A USER'S GUIDE

> THE story goes that the champagne represents the nobility (when Prince Albert died in 1861, the bartender at Brooks Club in London felt that champagne should be in mourning, too), and the stout represents 'the common classes'. Prince Otto Von Bismarck of Germany might have words with Oscar Mendelssohn – Black Velvet became his favourite tipple.

> IT would make a master barman wince, but alcopops aren't so very different from cocktails – just their younger cousins, perhaps. In the late eighties and early nineties, the age of the rave, soft drinks and bottled water were rocketing in popularity at the younger end of the market – until alcopops (spirits in fruit juices, with an ABV of 4–5.5 per cent) came along and became the fastest-growing drink of all time.
>
> Alcopops were launched in 1995 in Australia, arrived in Britain, spread to the rest of Europe and two years later hit the US – where they're sometimes termed 'starter brews' or 'hard lemonades'. First on the UK market was Hooper's Hooch, just beating Two Dogs. Demand in the summer of '95 was so great that bars were limited to ten cases an order. Nowadays there are some 120 brands, including Barcadi Breezer, Red Square, Smirnoff Ice, Mog and Claw, Doctor Thirsty's Beetlejuice and Tangerine Scream.

frozen, saying they made him feel 'like a downhill glacier skiing feels running through powdered snow'. He always ordered doubles: Papa Hemingway, nicknamed Papa Dobles.

A User's Guide   9

DESIGNATED DRINKING PLACES

And Their Names

Early English communal drinking

Where there's alcohol there must be designated places for the communal drinking of it. Once, these were probably clearings in the forest – and quite possibly the English Saxons were still sitting in them when the Romans came and organised *tavernae* like the ones they had at home to sell wine, meals and bar snacks. The *tavernae* were opened for the soldiery, who perhaps in time could sign in Saxon guests. Maybe local brews were even introduced, as kind of guest ales. Anyway, by the time the Romans quit British shores, the natives had come to realise that a designated building had rather more going for it than the forest clearing, and the first alehouses were established.

DRINK | A USER'S GUIDE

> THE Romans adopted the tavern from the Greeks, but never the symposium – an intellectual drinking session for elite males who lounged around on couches drinking copiously and discoursing at great length – great, great length in the case of Socrates, who, Aristophanes moaned, never got drunk enough to stop, however much he drank, which made Aristophanes drink all the more until he 'was drowned in drink'.
>
> No Greek or Roman of any social standing would be seen in a tavern, although what Romans of social standing did in Britain is another matter. Rome did have the *lupanar*, side street concerns into which men slipped quietly, their heads covered, to enjoy what was the equivalent of the lock-in.

> THE better class of alehouse upgraded itself to offer some competition to the inns. There was a parlour that could be used as a sitting room by women travellers, or hired for the exclusive use of the wealthy. A sleeping room often had two or three beds in it – and single males frequently found themselves sharing one with a stranger.

In the 10th century there were so many alehouses in England that King Edgar decreed there should be only one per village. That didn't last long. By the early 17th century there were over 13,000 establishments of one kind or another where a drink was to be had – this in a population of five million. (As some yardstick, the UK today has some 60,000 pubs in a population of nearly 60 million, discounting all other kinds of outlets for alcohol.) Inns had grown up from the early

DESIGNATED DRINKING PLACES

Middle Ages, largely because the murder of Thomas à Becket in Canterbury Cathedral started an enthusiasm, which lasted 400 years, for pilgrimages to sacred sites. The monasteries, traditional accommodators of the weary traveller, were overrun by what were, in effect, the first package holidaymakers. To deal with them, they set up separate establishments, the inns – the Travelodges of their day.

But continuing urban expansion gave rise to the upwardly mobile professional classes who wanted more than the alehouse had to offer. The tavern appeared (a mere 1,400 years after the Roman model) a place of such epicurean satisfaction to the 18th century that Samuel Johnson opined: 'There is nothing which has yet been contrived by man, by which so much happiness is produced as by a good tavern or inn.'

THE good doctor kept his distance from the gin shops that mushroomed across London in his lifetime, parents of the infamous gin palaces of the following century.

In the fight against the growing menace of gin, the 1830 Sale of Beer Act removed all taxes on beer and allowed anyone to open a beer shop. By the end of the year there were 24,000 beer shops – and 46,000 six years later. However, the big breweries competed with the newcomers by transforming pubs into gin palaces, so called by the poor, who were mesmerised by the mirrors, new-fangled plate glass and gas lighting. Some gin palaces were purpose-built – and some were still going just prior to World War Two.

DRINK | A USER'S GUIDE

Public drinking – the US model

The archetypal American watering hole grew out of traditions imported from Europe and the garish innovation of the Old West.

The early taverns were English in concept but with the difference that they were kept by 'men of conscience' rather than the ruffians more common back home: a landlord was often a magistrate, an army officer of middle seniority, someone who held public office, or a well-to-do farmer whose establishment was near his fields. The contrast with what travelling Englishmen were familiar with was so great that they were said to laugh in disbelief.

In the expansion west, the tents and shanties serving booze morphed into the Wild West saloon, with bevelled mirrors often 3.5 metres (12 feet) or more high and 9 metres (30 feet) long (not something, whatever hundreds of cowboy movies show, that even a tanked-up cowpoke very often smashed in a brawl), much ornate carved wood and arm and foot rails in decorated brass.

The saloons that mushroomed across America drew

EARLY tavern keepers were known for their inquisitiveness, which annoyed Benjamin Franklin, who on entering an establishment was known to say: 'My name is Benjamin Franklin. I was born in Boston. I am a printer by profession, am travelling to Philadelphia, shall have to return at such a time, and have no news. Now, what can you give me for dinner?'

DESIGNATED DRINKING PLACES

something from the tavern and the establishment of the frontier, though 'men of conscience' were thin on the ground in many places. In the big industrial centres of the second half of the 19th century – the anthracite coal regions of Pennsylvania or the coal and silver mines of Colorado, for example – there was often a saloon for every 50 adult males. By 1907 there were 7,300 saloons in Chicago, as well as 1,000 'illegals' (and the city was spending more on booze than on food).

The common drinking experience

Taverns and alehouses were known as 'tippling houses' to most people in 17th-century England. Then they became 'tap houses' and then 'public houses' ('pubs') to the Victorians. To colonial Americans drinking places were 'ordinaries', only later 'taverns' and only later still 'saloons'. Whatever they were called, for centuries they were as central to their communities as the parish church. Only where the drinking was done could news and rumour be had – and companionship. So important was the watering hole understood to be in early colonial America that every town had to provide one of some kind by law, and was fined if it didn't. In the major cities they were places where well-to-do men gathered to do business, to buy and sell stocks and ships' cargo, and to read the newspapers; and where the poor could drink and find a little entertainment.

In the poor and overcrowded cities of America and Britain during the 19th century, many a pub and saloon was a dive,

DRINK | A USER'S GUIDE

WHAT'S the oldest drinking establishment in Britain? Even that rock of statistical certainty *The Guinness Book of Records* – which can tell you the largest, smallest, highest and longest-named – won't commit itself. Some possible contenders are so old there isn't any documentation, and at least 15 claim the distinction. The six most likely are ...

The Skirrid Mountain Inn, Abergavenny, Monmouthshire: listed as a pub in legal documents in 1110, it was also a courthouse for many centuries and the pubbing was probably part-time, which may discount it. James Crowther was hanged here in 1110 for stealing sheep, the first of many souls to be executed here. This is the only pub in the UK where you can order a hangman's lunch.

Ye Olde Fighting Cocks, St Albans, Hertfordshire: an 11th-century structure on an 8th-century pub site. It's verified that Cromwell stayed here – and kept his horse in what's now the bar.

The Old Ferryboat Inn, Holywell, Cambridgeshire: makes its claim on archaeological evidence that its foundations date back to 460, but there's no evidence that a pub stood here until around 1400.

The Bingley Arms, Leeds, Yorkshire: has records dating the core of the building to 953, but that isn't evidence that it served ale – which it was doing in the 1500s when it was called the Priest Inn.

Ye Olde Trip to Jerusalem, Nottingham, Nottinghamshire: claims to have been an inn when the crusaders stopped off on the way to the Holy Lands in 1189, the year Richard I became king ('trip' then meant 'resting place'). Documents show that a castle brewhouse stood on the site before this date – but that's it.

The Eagle and Child, Stow-on-the-Wold, Gloucestershire: this bar is part of The Royalist Hotel and dates from 947 – splinters of wood

DESIGNATED DRINKING PLACES

from the beams have been carbon dated. But it might be discounted on two grounds: it was closed for 16 years before the present owners took over, which spoils the record of continuity; and it's annexed to a hotel, which dents its authenticity.

The oldest tavern in America – where the historical timeline is shorter and there's more certainty – is Longfellow's Wayside Inn, Sudbury, Mass., called The Red Horse Tavern back in 1716. Henry Ford bought the place in 1923 to preserve it for future generations. In 1955 a fire destroyed two rooms but not the old bar.

The Deer Park Inn, Newark, near the University of Delaware, was built in 1851 on the site of another establishment dating from the mid-1700s. It is supposed to have a border marker of the Mason-Dixon line – which divided free and slave states – in the basement. During the Revolution, soldiers used the bar – and maybe Washington was one. In 1843 Edgar Allan Poe stayed here and fell on his face in the mud as he alighted from a carriage, probably tanked.

McSorley's Old Ale House, New York, opened in 1854 by John McSorley, had earned the title of America's most famous bar by the 1940s. The original name was Old House at Home, in honour of a pub in Ireland; McSorley changed it in 1908 after his old sign blew down. When John's son Bill took over, he paid no attention to prohibition and went on serving beer. He didn't even have a peephole – but many of his regulars were politicians, which was an even better safeguard.

McGillin's Olde Ale House, Philadelphia, Pa., was the Bell in Hand when William McGillin opened up in 1860, he and his wife offering patrons free potatoes with butter. They brought up 12 children there. It was the haunt of theatrical types, including Will Rogers, John Barrymore and Ethel Merman – and Billy Daniels once sang *That Old Black Magic* in the bar.

DRINK | A USER'S GUIDE

> Heinhold's First & Last Chance Saloon, Oakland, Calif., was built from the timbers of old whaling ships in 1860. It was a port pub and the last place a ferry passenger could drink on leaving – or the first on arriving. Heinhold's was a second home to Jack London, who liked to listen to sailors' tales here. Robert Louis Stevenson, Ambrose Bierce and Erskine Caldwell also drank here. When the 1906 earthquake destroyed San Francisco, the building and floor became severely tilted, as they remain.
>
> John Barleycorn, Chicago, Ill., dates to 1890, but its interest lies in the twenties when part of it was a Chinese laundry that fronted for the speakeasy (a 'blind pig') in the basement, where John Dillinger drank and often bought the house a round.

where the landlord was the biggest man in the community – he needed to be. The floor in most drinking places was covered in sawdust: in an age when people worked in dark satanic factories, the air was thick with soot from coal fires, and heavy smoking was the norm, everyone spat copiously; better class joints had spittoons, just like the gentlemen's clubs. But many establishments were respectable. Here, the servants of the upper and middle classes (and the menfolk of those classes) could drink in safety – and working men formed their political organisations, social clubs, benevolent and friendly associations, and trade societies.

Many landlords extended a helping hand to their customers by becoming a 'house of call' – a kind of employment exchange for itinerant craftsmen. Some gave credit and even hired out tools. In Britain a house of call was usually

DESIGNATED DRINKING PLACES

connected to a specific trade – hence the multitude of Carpenter's and Bricklayer's Arms.

The American saloon suffered a decline before, during and after Prohibition. Before it, the temperance movement stopped respectable men and women from drinking in public. During it, many saloons went out of business (though just as many moved the entrance to the back door and operated as speakeasies). Even when Prohibition came to an end, things didn't pick up as much as they might have – drinkers

---

MANY people associate pubs of the past with nothing more than shove ha'penny, shovelboard and dominoes, but for hundreds of years the English tippling house staged bear-baiting, badger-baiting and even ape-baiting, as well as cock-fighting, dog-fighting and pigeon shooting, not to mention boxing and wrestling. Some had their own skittle alleys (some still have them), bowling greens and cricket pitches.

British entertainments were echoed in the American tavern and saloon – though in the 18th century Americans moved from bear-baiting to dog and racoon contests and then to rat-baiting, which became the popular betting sport. Around 1880, admittance to an illegal price fight between men cost 50 cents – a dog–rat contest cost $1.50 to $5, the upper figure for a bout where 100 rats would be dispatched. Just as music hall grew out of the pub, vaudeville grew out of the saloon.

And now drinking places have karaoke. Once it was only drunken Irishmen who felt the need to get up and sing ('Danny Boy', inevitably). Now, thanks to karaoke, it's everybody – everywhere. The Japanese, who gave karaoke ('empty orchestra') to the world in the 1980s, have a lot to answer for.

DRINK | A USER'S GUIDE

> '[THE saloon] is a drowsy place. The bartenders never make a needless move, the customers nurse their mugs of ale, and the three clocks on the wall have not been in agreement for many years. The clientele is motley ... In the summer they sit in the back room, which is as cool as a cellar. In the winter they grab chairs nearest the stove and sit in them, as motionless as barnacles, until around six, when they yawn, stretch, and start for home, insulated with ale... "God be wit' yez," Kelly says as they go out the door.'
>
> – Joseph Mitchell (1940)

had got out of the habit of going out for a drink and the new beer can, and the refrigerator, made drinking at home that much more agreeable.

World War Two brought a boost, when the big US breweries were asked to set aside 15 per cent of their production for servicemen (a very different experience from World War One, when anti-beer hostility broke out because beer was so strongly associated with German immigrants). But it didn't last. In the forties and early fifties there were scores of saloons on every block in every working-class neighbourhood, where men met up for a couple of shots and a beer before the 7.30 factory whistle. The factories have mostly gone and so have the saloons – only one in a hundred remains, competing with newer bars and the 'brewpubs' that have sprung up across America.

Times have changed, just like society's attitudes to mixing work with drink and drinking with driving. Times have changed in the UK for pubs, too. During the second half of the 20th century, they were in a downward spiral from similar

DESIGNATED DRINKING PLACES

social forces, and thousands closed. The future of the rest might have been on the urinal wall, but at the beginning of the nineties they made big efforts to change their image – and the theme pub-restaurant chains were born.

The theme pub-restaurant, serving decent food – which the old-style pub mostly failed to do – made its appearance in many guises, but overwhelming in a style that you could call bucolic. The critics scoffed at their bare brick and flagged areas of floor, at the mix of agricultural tools and containers adorning rustic dressers and hung from walls of rough-hewn wood – where had they been found, Pa Larkin's farmyard?

Those who treasured the pub as it had been lamented that the different bars – public, saloon, lounge and 'smoking'

THE first 'brewpub' opened 20 years ago, when a change in the law allowed a brewery and an eaterie to be together on the same premises for the first time since prohibition. There are a handful of such establishments in Britain, but in the US there are over 1,000 and the number is expected to double in the next few years.

IF the effort to go to the pub is too much, the pub can come to you. An Irish company makes pubs for the garden, which come complete with the interior theme of your choice – traditional Victorian to fifties America, from sports to cinema to nautical – bric-a-brac, external signs and, of course, your own pub name. Each pub is pre-wired for light and heat, cooler, phone and satellite TV.

Log on to www.keenmacpubs.com

DRINK | A USER'S GUIDE

– which had once been social demarcations were in so many cases knocked through and made into one. Such traditionalists saw the Irish pub going about its business as it always had and noted that there were no theme bars in Ireland or in the Irish enclaves of America – every Irish bar was the real McCoy. (In fact the Irish bar is widely emulated from the Costa del Sol to Tokyo and in Britain has spawned chains called Scruffy Murphy's and O'Neill's – though this, as the Irish might say, is a horse of a different colour altogether.)

But the gripe misses the point: that the take-home segment of the beer-drinking market – which accounts for two-thirds of beer drinking in England, Scotland and Wales – just hasn't happened in the Emerald Isle. Ninety per cent of Irish boozing is still down the pub.

Anyway, Middle England loves the theme pub, which has largely saved the institution from tottering onwards into decline. And so the British pub lives on. The parish church, which suffered a parallel decline in the same years, has fared less well. A lot of churches have been sold off for a variety of uses – including being turned into pubs. No pub has been turned into a church.

Signs of the times

In ancient Rome a place where a drink was to be had was identified by the display of vines leaves above the door. In Britain – vine leaves being on the scarce side – the Romans hung a small evergreen bush on a pole.

Early alehouses followed the Roman example and hung

DESIGNATED DRINKING PLACES

out ale stakes: the kind used to stir the brew. In later centuries an establishment selling both ale and wine hung a bush on the stake – lateral thinking or what. The tradition lasted for some hundreds of years, then, gradually, inns, taverns and alehouses began to get names to differentiate them ('I'll see you tonight, down the place with the pole' – image the confusion) and painted signs followed – nice and simple so an illiterate people could be in no doubt as to what was where. At the end of the 14th century King Richard II made signs compulsory – not for anyone's convenience but for the official Ale Taster, whose job was quality control.

The early signs were simple: lions, dolphins, black swans; many were in the form of religious symbols: Sun, Star, Cross, Crossed Keys (the emblem of St Peter). Things got more complicated when words were added: many a sign commissioner was as illiterate as the signwriter, so the spelling was often as close to English (or Middle English and Early Modern English, to be picky) as is modern text messaging.

With time, historical and ecclesiastical references became corrupted, as did phrases and titles, in something like a game of Chinese Whispers. The Bacchanals came out as the Bag o' Nails, St Catherine's Wheel as the Cat and Wheel, the Infanta de Castile as the Elephant and Castle, Pique and Carreau (the spade and diamond in playing cards) as the Pig and Carrot, the motto 'Great God Encompassing' as the Goat and Compass.

The English writer Joseph Addison was puzzled for a long while by the Bell Savage, a common sign, which portrayed an Indian standing beside a bell. It was only after reading an

DRINK | A USER'S GUIDE

old romance translated from the French that he found out the derivation. The tale, which concerned a beautiful woman found in a wilderness, was entitled La Belle Sauvage. Well, we say 'belle of the ball', don't we? What's the problem?

It was very confusing to be a drinker during the English Civil War, but a very good time to be a signwriter. Alehouses, taverns and inns were used by both sides to billet their troops. As the war swung back and forth, the owner of an establishment had to be on his toes. One day, the Cromwell Arms, the next the King's Head – and hope the paint dried before it rained, and pray God the fortunes of battle didn't sway too quickly.

After the American War of Independence all the signs had to be repainted. Good old English names like St George and the Dragon, the Rose and Thistle and the Duke of Cumberland were covered with American eagles and portraits of George Washington. The General Wolfe, named after a well-known English officer, was a favourite image on colonial American taverns and signboards. After the Revolution he was painted out everywhere except in Newburyport, Massachusetts, where the old sign continued to swing 'in the very centre of the place, to be an insult to this truly republican town'. It's still swinging.

> SIGNWRITERS were generally inferior painters, but some great artists have painted pub signs, to earn a needed sum, to pay off a slate or maybe when simply pissed. Among this number are the likes of William Hogarth, Richard Wilson and George Morland.

DESIGNATED DRINKING PLACES

The antecedents of many signs are lost in history. Could the Vine and the Bunch of Grapes hark back to Roman Britain? Fanciful. The Chequers certainly does – some *tavernae* had a checkers board painted on the doorpost to show that the game could be played inside. The most common pub sign across the UK is the Red Lion – there are over 600 of them – dating back to the time of James I (already James VI of Scotland when he succeeded Elizabeth to the English throne in 1603), who ordered the heraldic red lion of Scotland to be displayed on all taverns. Another common sign is the White Hart, the heraldic device of Richard II, who, over 200 years earlier, had compelled London tavern keepers to display it. But there are a host of other names with royal connections: the King's Arms, the King's (or Queen's) Head, the Crown (sometimes with additions like the Septre), the George or King George, the Victoria, the Prince Albert and – although you have to wonder whether Charles II wasn't miffed about it – the Royal Oak, which alludes to the monarch's unregal refuge in a tree after his Civil War defeat at Worcester. But you don't have to look far, either, to find a Plough, a Badger, a Coach and Horses, a Fox and Hounds, a Duke of Wellington, an Admiral (or Lord) Nelson or a Cricketers.

Perhaps pub signs don't really add up to an anecdotal history of 400 years or so, but the patchwork of the most popular point up the respect in which royalty was once held and the pride the country once had in its military and naval might, its pioneering of road travel and steam, and its attachment to the countryside, which once gave most people their living.

DRINK | A USER'S GUIDE

There's nothing sacrosanct about pub signs – but there never has been. In Stamford, Lincolnshire, for example, the 18th-century Slaters Arms became the Sawyers Arms in the following century – and is now the Drum and Monkey. In North Howden in Yorkshire, the Railway is now the Sir Barnes Wallis, in honour of the man of Dambusters bouncing bomb fame. And why not?

The modern taste in pub names is for the humorous, the vulgar and the incomprehensible: the Slap-Up, Filthy McNastys, My Fathers Moustache, the Slug and Lettuce, the Pissed Newt. No doubt some signs past displayed the same characteristics. One thing that signs old and new frequently share: they really don't like apostrophes.

Famous watering holes

What makes a watering hole famous is frequently that the famous have drunk there. It also helps if they're old – the watering holes, that is. Like the Dove, in the outer reaches of west London, for example, where Charles II supposedly canoodled with Nell Gwynne 300 years ago. The designer and poet William Morris drank here for certain, and Graham Greene, and Hemingway.

In Victorian times Thackeray and Dickens frequented Ye Olde Cheshire Cheese in Wine Office Court, an alley off Fleet Street, London (Dickens gave it a name-check in *A Tale of Two Cities*), and in the 20th century Chesterton, Belloc and Conan Doyle all parked their ample literary behinds on the same wooden settles. Many years before (80 years after the

DESIGNATED DRINKING PLACES

NOTHING lasts for ever including famous watering holes, but the demise of the Stork Club, New York's most celebrated nightspot, brings a nostalgic tear to many an eye. Opened at the end of Prohibition, it was the epitome of gaiety, of men in black ties and evening hats, of women in capes and seamed stockings, of gold and blue drapery, chandeliers, incessant cocktail shakers and popping champagne corks – and a wine list that was six feet square.

Here the headwaiter didn't blink at a $10,000 tip. Here the Kennedys, the Roosevelts and Harrimans, the Duke and Duchess of Windsor, Chaplin, Hitchcock, Sinatra, Monroe and countless other A-listers were at home. Here Marlene Dietrich took a shine to Hemingway because, she said, she liked a man who liked martinis.

place was rebuilt following the Fire of London), Samuel Johnson moved in practically next door, but although Boswell assiduously chronicled the doctor's pubby perambulations he made no mention of the Cheshire Cheese. Is it possible that Johnson didn't use what must have been his local? Or was it such a regular thing that Boswell didn't think it worth mentioning?

It's the whiff of history more than the pleasant fumes of alcohol ... or the ambience .... or the company ... that places an establishment on a must-visit list. Imagine Joyce downing Guinness in the Brian Boru (now Hedigan's) on Dublin's north side, on the road to Glasnevin cemetery (the route's in *Ulysses*), scribbling phrases he overheard in his little book. Or Behan in the Palace, in Dublin's Temple Bar, telling the story of the drunk who'd found the grave of a friend in the

DRINK | A USER'S GUIDE

SCORES of books have been written about famous drinking places – of a particular town or city, of an area of a country, of a country, of the world. Here are a few:

Singapore: Raffles – one of the few really great 19th-century hotels in all of Asia, called by Somerset Maugham 'the legendary symbol for all the fables of the exotic East', and in the Long Bar of which the Singapore Sling was created.

Paris: Les Deux Magots – café on the Left Bank and seat of French existentialist thought where Jean-Paul Sartre and Simone de Beauvoir held court.

Las Vegas: The Carousel at the Circus Hotel – Hunter S. Thompson, a rolling stone came to a temporary stop, gathered material here for *Fear and Loathing in Las Vegas*.

New Orleans: The Old Absinthe House – watering hole in the famous French Quarter, visited by Oscar Wilde, William Howard Taft, Walt Whitman, Thackeray, and O. Henry when just a newspaperman called William Porter.

San Francisco: Vesuvio – the regular hangout of Jack Kerouac and other Beat poets on Columbus Avenue, and still a monument to jazz, poetry, art and the good life of the Beat generation.

New York: McSorley's Old Ale House – located at 15 East 7th Street, this is the oldest bar in the city, drunk in by Abe himself, John Steinbeck and most of the Kennedy men and, as already noted, it was a speakeasy during Prohibition.

Chumley's – haunt of Scott Fitzgerald, e.e. cummings and that man Hemingway. Another one-time speakeasy, Chumley's doesn't have a

DESIGNATED DRINKING PLACES

very same cemetery, scrutinised the statue of Jesus that the widow had put up, then said to his equally drunk companion: 'That not Mulcahy. Not a bloody bit like the man.'

So great is the American attraction to the cocktail that watering holes have become famous largely because this one or that one was created there: the Bloody Mary, for instance, made its appearance in Harry Bar in Paris (in 1921), the Bellini (champagne and peach juice) in Harry's Bar in Venice (in 1943), the Tahiti-style Mai Tai (dark and golden rum, triple sec – or Cointreau – almond syrup, lime, dash of grenadine) at Don the Beachcomber in Hollywood in 1934 or at Trader Vic's in Oakland, California, in 1944, depending on who you believe.

During prohibition richer Americans yearning for a legitimate drink took off for Europe, and in London the cocktail made the reputation of the American Bar at the Savoy (where for nearly 20 year an American barman who'd found himself out of work stateside was the resident high priest). For 80 years anybody who's anybody has been seen in the American Bar, including Hemingway. But Hemingway was to bars what Elizabeth I was to beds – except he really did drink in them all.

---

sign (old habits die hard); potential customers who don't know the place have to walk up and down Bedford Street until they find No 86.

White Horse – located at 567 Hudson Street at 11th Avenue, this is a gathering place for Greenwich Village bohemians. Steve McQueen is said to have tended the bar here, and Bob Dylan was a regular in the sixties. And it was here that Welsh poet Dylan Thomas was drinking before he collapsed and died in hospital.

✶ A User's Guide — 10

SOME THINGS DRINK MAKES PEOPLE DO

(And Not)

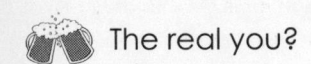

🍻 The real you?

'Some men are like musical glasses; to produce their finest tones you must keep them wet.'
– *Samuel Taylor Coleridge*

Philosophers down the ages have contended that drunkenness allows others to peer into a man's heart and soul: 'Bronze is the mirror of the outward form, wine the mirror of the mind,' Aeschylus is supposed to have said. That's highly literary – and nonsensical.

SOME THINGS DRINK MAKES PEOPLE DO

Two more commonly held views are that in your cups you reveal a heightened version of yourself, and that alcohol dissolves normal constraints (along with the brain cells) and turns drinkers into beasts. According to rabbinical teaching, Satan came to Noah when he was planting those vines and slew a lamb, a lion, a pig and an ape to teach him that man reveals the characteristics of all four in turn, according to the amount consumed. Reverse anthropomorphism has always held appeal. Four hundred years ago the Elizabethan writer Thomas Nashe drew on animal imagery to define types of drunk, among them the docile sheep staring blank-faced into his pot, the clowning ape talking gibberish, the roaring lion (roaring drunk) and the randy goat, 'when in his drunkenness he hath no mind but on lechery'.

Neither of these two positions is tenable, the first because it simplistically absolves the drinker from responsibility for his or her actions, the second because it claims that drunkenness shows itself only in limited and specific ways, and

'I trow that ye have drunken wine of ape.'
— Chaucer, Prologue to 'The Manciple's Tale'

'THE problem with some people is that when they aren't drunk, they're sober.'
— W.B. Yeats

DRINK | A USER'S GUIDE

> A study that involved giving alcohol to 1,000 green vervet monkeys revealed that they behave very much like human beings. The vast majority drink moderately and never before lunch, 15 per cent drink heavily, 15 per cent don't drink and 5 per cent are serious abusers who get drunk, pick fights and only stop drinking when they pass out.
>
> The research was conducted in St Kitts, where the monkeys have developed a taste for alcohol in the form of naturally fermenting sugar cane – and now hang about the island's bars to snaffle the leftovers.

because both they take no account of the drinker's personality and frame of mind. The Aztecs recognised that drink brings about a diversity of behaviour in different people at different times (maybe all on the same night and not necessarily in rabbinical progression). For whatever reason, they likened drunkens to rabbits, named their traditional brew *centzonttotochtli* (400 rabbits) and described types of drunkenness in terms of numbers of rabbits – 400 was a warrenful.

Historical and cross-cultural evidence overwhelmingly suggest that alcohol exaggerates the drinker's mood and expectations; all booze does is take the brake off. If the drinker is feeling happy, he (or she) becomes happier; if sad, sadder; if sexy, sexier. And if he left work feeling like thumping the boss, the person who just nudged his elbow at the bar is likely to make a handy substitute ... at least in some societies.

As someone once observed: 'If behaviour reflects expectations, then a society gets the drunks it deserves.'

SOME THINGS DRINK MAKES PEOPLE DO

Aggro...holics?

In certain countries, such as Britain, the US, Scandinavia, Australia and New Zealand, alcohol and aggression form an unholy AA.

The drinking cultures of these countries are referred to as 'ambivalent', which means that they allow drinking but feel guilty about it. They are also referred to as 'temperance' or 'dry', which sounds contradictory but actually indicates that, to greater or lesser extent, they try or have tried to forbid drinking. Other countries such as France, Spain, Portugal, Italy, Switzerland, Germany, Austria, Belgium and the Low Countries are referred to as 'integrated', 'Mediterranean', 'non-temperance' or 'wet', terms which raise no contradictions whatsoever. These countries have never given rise to serious prohibition or temperance movements and don't feel

---

AT a recent conference on drug policy, one chief constable was asked which drug did most harm. 'Alcohol,' he replied. 'My officers are not called out at 11.30pm on Saturday to deal with out-of-control dope smokers.'

THE expression 'mind your Ps and Qs' stems from the day that tavern keepers chalked up the pints and quarts a drinker drank for later payment; it was a good idea to keep an eye on the tally to make sure nothing was added. It was usual, when a fight was starting, for someone to warn other drinkers: 'Mind your Ps and Qs!'

DRINK | A USER'S GUIDE

guilty about their alcohol consumption – in some, even McDonald's can serve alcohol without anyone turning a hair.

The two groups of countries are separated by polarised mindsets. Many of the Spanish and the Portuguese, for instance, call in for a snort on the way to work, which is something the British and the Americans wouldn't dream of doing. But the Spanish and Portuguese wouldn't dream of going out at the weekend and bingeing into insensibility, as is not unknown in Britain and America. The big difference is that in non-temperance countries, a little alcohol is just part of the normal working day, whereas in temperance countries a lot of alcohol marks the transition from work to play.

An unfortunate upshot of prohibition and guilt is that in ambivalent countries, drink-related acts of violence are commonplace, and even expected. In the dry countries they

---

JAPAN can't be categorised in the above terms. While it is a heavy-drinking country – business negotiations are routinely conducted in bars and restaurants with the consumption of large amounts of alcohol – violence is virtually unknown. Public drunkenness is frequent – and not illegal.

UP to 14 million working days a year in the UK are lost to heavy drinkers phoning in sick (heavy drinkers take off nearly five times as many days as moderate drinkers and teetotallers), lateness due to hangovers, long lunch hours, and afternoon inefficiency and impaired decision-making due to over-consumption at lunchtime.

SOME THINGS DRINK MAKES PEOPLE DO

> 'WANT some pretzels?'
> 'No thanks, we're on duty. A couple beers would be nice, though.'
> – *The Simpsons*

> 'THE biggest problem comes when the Karamajong warriors go on drinking sessions,' Walter Ochero told reporters in Kotido (north-east Uganda), 'because that's when they have most trouble with the zippers. When they get drunk, some of them fail completely to remove their trousers when they want to go to pass piss …'
>
> 'Traditionally, Karmajong men wear a *suka*, or cloth wrap-around. But the army accused them of using the *suka* to conceal weapons and has forced them to wear trousers when they come to town … A square flap over the groin area, fastened with Velcro, is being considered.'
> – *New Vision*, 27 May 2002

are rare and shocking. An Italian unfortunate enough to find himself in an English pub and suddenly to be asked, 'Are you looking at me, pal?' would merely be perplexed, even if the question were in Italian (*Stai guardando a me, stronzo?*). Were a defendant in an integrated society to plead in mitigation that he was pissed at the time of the offence – that it was out of character and the drink talking – would be considered to have compounded his crime.

That almost all integrated cultures drink and yet remain essentially harmonious while a fair proportion of those in ambivalent cultures drink and get aggressive suggests that

DRINK | A USER'S GUIDE

> HAPPY, peaceable drunks were the Papago of Mexico, whose young men painted the soles of their feet red so that when they passed out other people had something to admire.

aggression is a learned behaviour (the English have been learning it a long time – in the 16th century men carried ale-daggers in case of brawls in taverns).

Research among a number of native peoples emphasises the point. A study of 60 small and folk societies found that whereas men get drunk in 46 of them, they get involved in drunken brawling in fewer than half. Among the Bolivian Camba, who regularly down immense quantities of almost pure alcohol and get paralytic, total concord reigns – thick heads, yes, but no thick lips, not to mention no hitting of women, no destruction of property and no being sick in other people's gardens, all the types of social behaviour that many in ambivalent countries regard as the hallmarks of a good night out.

Alco...heroics

> *Then trust me, there's nothing like drinking*
> *So pleasant on this side of the grave;*
> *It keeps the unhappy from thinking*
> *And makes e'en the valiant more brave.*
> – *Charles Didbin*

Throughout history armies at war have drunk to stiffen their resolve. The Vikings downed a toxic ale they called *aul* before

SOME THINGS DRINK MAKES PEOPLE DO

heading into battle, sometimes stripped to the waist. The drunkest – and fiercest – fighters were called 'berserkers', which in Norse means 'bare shirt' and from which we get the word 'berserk'. In the 18th century, Frederick the Great commented that 'many battles have been fought and won by soldiers nourished on beer', but the English had such a liking for gin, which originated in Holland, that they drank that before going into action, drunken bravery becoming known as 'Dutch courage'. Gin was credited with triumphs against the French at Blenheim and Ramillies. Throughout the 19th century the French fuelled their Colonial campaigns with absinthe, and the Cubans in their war against the Spanish colonists carried daiquiri because 'it acted as a good painkiller if they got wounded'. Once informed that General Grant drank whiskey while leading his troops, President Lincoln reportedly replied, 'Find out the name of the brand so I can give it to my other generals.'

There's no lack of examples of defeats being attributed to drunkenness, however – the Battle of Hastings, for example, or the huge Russian losses in World War One, which led Nicholas II to ban the sale of alcohol throughout the empire (and which contributed to the revolution of 1917).

You don't have to be sober to be a hero; in fact it can help not to be. On the night of 4 November 1951 in the Korean War, the Chinese made a surprise attack on the 1st King's Own Scottish Borderers on Hill 355, driving them from their positions. Private Bill Speakman, a man with a bad disciplinary record who is alleged to have been drunk at the time, stuffed his pockets with grenades and charged the enemy,

DRINK | A USER'S GUIDE

> DRUNKEN hunters cut electric power to a third of the population of Kyrgzstan's capital, Bishkek, when they used ceramic insulators on high-voltage lines for target practice. One building that suffered the blackout was a hotel hosting a conference ... on alcohol abuse.
>
> – Press report, 2 March 2002

coming back to refill his pockets. When he ran out of grenades, it's said, he hurled empty beer bottles. Twice wounded, Speakman was awarded the VC.

Emotional baggage not stowed: air rage

A phenomenon that started in the 1990s was air rage – aggression breaking out in passenger planes. The phenomenon is so recent and so many incidents go unreported (a mouthful of abuse, say) that no one is absolutely sure about numbers, but worldwide figures suggest a four- to sixfold increase in incidents.

One thing everyone is sure about, however, is that alcohol is the main cause of air rage. Flying primes people to get drunk. They often fly (and drink) on an empty stomach, exposed to the mild hypoxia of the pressurised cabin, their brains marginally deprived of oxygen by the cost-cutting practice of using recycled air. Add stress and anxiety caused by confusing check-ins, long queues, security checkpoints, delays, strikes, lack of confidence in traffic controllers, shrinking seats and no smoking rules that make the nicotine-deprived distinctly edgy – the list could go on – and even

SOME THINGS DRINK MAKES PEOPLE DO

people who wouldn't normally take a drink think they need one.

None of which excuses the air rage antics of those who thump cabin crew or fellow passengers, grope stewardesses, try to break into the cockpit or punch out the windows, or pretend to be terrorists, have weapons or be about to blow up the aircraft – the latter all very popular wheezes with drunks since September 11. More unusually, a boozed-up banker took off his trousers on a flight from Buenos Aires to New York, defecated on a first-class food trolley and then 'simulated sex with the back of his seat'.

Authorities have been getting tough. In the US, the Federal Aviation Administration has increased the maximum fine from $1,000 to $25,000; in the UK, courts are routinely handing out jail sentences and the government is talking about raising the maximum penalty to five years.

> IN 2001, UK airlines carried 85 million passengers and had notifiable trouble with 100 individuals, while US airlines reported 300 'major incidents'.

> IN May 1999, Ian Bottomley from Witham, Essex, was jailed for three years for injuring three stewards and causing £30,000 of damage on a BA jumbo from Johannesburg to Heathrow. He attacked crew and threatened to kill other passengers after being told to stop looking at pornography on his laptop.

DRINK | A USER'S GUIDE

Airlines now train crew in how to calm down drunks and how to deal with them when they won't. A year or two ago, crew were tying unruly passengers to their seats with headset cords. Now they have proper restrainers. And British Airways for one has introduced a soccer-style yellow card that's issued to offenders warning them about possible arrest. Some US airlines have issued life bans.

Reasonably, the airlines point out that no one twists passengers' arms to make them drink, and it isn't as if tea and coffee, bottled water, soft drinks and fruit juices aren't

---

IN August 2000, a group of 12 drunken Irish tourists flying from London to Jamaica got involved in a 'bar room brawl' after cabin crew refused to serve them more vodka and champagne. The crew enlisted the help of a wrestling team to restrain them and the Boeing 767 was diverted to Norfolk in Virginia, where Patrick Connors and Francis Coyle, from Lewisham in south London, were sentenced respectively to a year's imprisonment, with six months suspended, and three months' imprisonment, with six weeks suspended.

THERE have been several instances where unruly passengers given a tranquilliser by an on-board doctor have died – alcohol can be fatal in combination with other drugs. In 1998 a drunken passenger on a flight from Bangkok to Budapest died after being tranquillised, causing the flight to make an unscheduled stop in Istanbul. After a 13-hour delay it was allowed to continue and, a newspaper report observed, 'The 183 passengers behaved themselves, in spite of their late arrivals and missed connections.'

SOME THINGS DRINK MAKES PEOPLE DO

> BECAUSE of the danger of deep-vein thrombosis (DVT), doctors have recently added their voice to those seeking some kind of legislation – a limit on the number of drinks a passenger should be allowed, say. Most passengers wouldn't take kindly to that: a drink, after all, can make an often less-than-pleasant experience that much more tolerable. A research study carried out by Birmingham University among 1,000 BA Executive Class travellers showed that even the risk of DVT had impelled only 20 per cent to cut back on the boozing – and a quarter steadfastly stated that they wouldn't do so in any circumstances. But, they said, they did take an aspirin and remember to stretch their legs.

available. Of course, selling alcohol is a money-spinner, which the airlines wouldn't deny but, reasonably, they ask, what about personal responsibility?

Sex and drink: double trouble

When booze dissolves inhibitions and judgement, there's virtually no limit to the embarrassing things that people get up to, a high percentage of them sexually motivated. George Best, too well looked after in BBC hospitality before stumbling on to the Terry Wogan television show, ignored the host's amiable questions and lent forward to confide conspiratorially: 'You see, I just like fucking.' Anne Robinson once danced in an alcoholic haze on the bonnet of a car wearing nothing but high heels. Hugh Grant, depressed by the preview of *Nine Months*, the box-office flop that was supposed to make him a Hollywood star, got pie-eyed,

DRINK | A USER'S GUIDE

> WINE comes in at the mouth
> And love comes in at the eye;
> That's all we shall know for truth
> Before we grow old and die.
> I lift the glass to my mouth,
> I look at you, and I sigh.
>
> – W.B. Yeats 'A Drinking Song'

> DRINK to me only with thine eyes,
> And I will pledge with mine;
> Or leave a kiss within the cup
> And I'll not ask for wine.
>
> – Ben Jonson, 'To Celia'

started thinking with his other head (as a previous conquest of Bill Clinton's said of the President's shenanigans with Monica Lewinsky) and got caught in an alley with a hooker – with his pants down.

Sex and drink have been inseparable since the beginning of time. The ancient Greeks and Romans combined wine and fertility in the cult of Dionysus (Bacchus). Their festivals dedicated to the god were characterised by unrestrained sexual behaviour – and the consumption of large quantities of vino – after which the majority of the population calmed down until the next time. And perhaps to a certain extent all of this was a sexual safety valve. Europe in the Middle Ages held similar festivals (even the innocent maypole is a phallic symbol), as certain tribes in Mexico, Cameroon and Peru still do today.

SOME THINGS DRINK MAKES PEOPLE DO

Who knows? Drunken young women flashing their boobs for a laugh outside nightclubs and in Spanish holiday resorts may be obeying a primitive instinct. (By the same token, drunken young men mooning out of car windows may also be involved in a vestigial ritual display – but that's dubious.)

There's no doubt that a certain amount of alcohol hits the G spot. A couple of drinks boost the testosterone in the bloodstream – of both sexes – and perks up the libido.

Along with amorousness alcohol brings a lowering of standards. In a very different age, Peter Finley Dunne wrote: 'There is only one thing to be said in favour of drink and that is that it has caused many a lady to be loved that otherwise might have died single.' Less elegantly, we'd say drink helps ugly women to get sex. But it helps ugly men to get sex too,

---

ALCOHOL, up to the point of no return, has always been considered an aphrodisiac, particularly champagne in recent centuries. At various times different ingredients have been added. The ancient Romans thought that the blood of slain gladiators increased the aphrodisiac kick. According to the 13th-century theologian Albertus Magnus, powdered partridge brain in red wine did the trick. In the 17th century the addition of ants and cinnamon was favoured.

In medieval times, spiced possets (hot milk curdled with ale or sometimes wine) were given to newly married couples when they retired for the night (and again the next morning) to bolster their sexual vigour.

In Nigeria today Guinness is regarded as an aphrodisiac. 'There's a baby in every bottle,' they say – which is not, let's hasten to add, an official Guinness slogan.

DRINK | A USER'S GUIDE

if less often; even drunken women can be more discriminating than men, who just want sex regardless.

Sadly, some women report, men are only able to say 'I love you' when they're drunk.

Attractiveness of sexual partners apart, women are increasingly on the pull. A recent survey in *Cosmopolitan* magazine suggested that 11 per cent of women under 25 had had intercourse with someone they didn't know when they were drunk. Another survey suggests that eight out of

---

ACCORDING to experiments carried out at Glasgow University's department of psychology, after a person has consumed four units of alcohol, their perception of the attractiveness of members of the opposite sex is increased by 25 per cent. Professor Barry Jones called this 'the beer goggle effect'.

DRUNKENNESS can lead to unplanned and unsafe sex – in England 29 per cent of women say they have been so carried away by drink that they haven't used contraceptives. In April 2002 all-women colleges in the US reported a 150 per cent increase in drink-related sexual activity, leading to a steep rise in sexually transmitted disease.

On both sides of the Atlantic there's been disquiet about date rape, after a series of cases in which women have had 'roofies' (Rohypnol) or GHB (gamma hydroxy butyric acid) slipped into their drinks, causing recklessness, disorientation and loss of consciousness. Women are advised: never put your drink down, never accept an 'open' drink from anyone you don't know, avoid punchbowls and watch out for your friends.

SOME THINGS DRINK MAKES PEOPLE DO

> 'CANDY is dandy but liquor is quicker.'
>
> – Ogden Nash

ten 16-to-24-year-olds have been so drunk they can't remember whether they had sex or not.

If the excuse is often one of youth, it's not one that can be made by non-young airline passengers who've taken to having sex with strangers.

There have always been some people who get a buzz out of lavatorial quickies in aeroplanes (welcome to the Mile High Club), just as there have always been others who get a buzz out of doing it in lifts, churches and cemeteries. But generally, it's fair to assume, those involved have known each other, and alcohol hasn't necessarily been a factor. Strangers out of their brains on booze achieving sexual lift-off right there in their cabin seats, sometimes not even under a small airline blanket, is a phenomenon, like air rage, that appeared in the 1990s.

The incident that received the widest publicity brought together business executives Mandy Holt (36) and David Machin (40) aboard an American Airlines 757 en route from Texas to Manchester. The uproar they created, which saw them briefly reunited in court charged with 'indecency, conduct causing alarm and distress, and being drunk on an aircraft', was nothing compared with what probably went on once their spouses got them home.

DRINK | A USER'S GUIDE

> WOMEN appear to be more receptive than men to the possibility of sex after a couple of drinks, but less so thereafter.

> I love to drink martinis,
> Two at the very most.
> Three, and I'm under the table,
> Four, and I'm under the host.
>
> – Dorothy Parker

The story was a gift to a headline writer on British newspaper the *Sun*: MILE-HIGH MANDY GOT RANDY ON BRANDY.

The desire to have sex and the ability to perform can be a close call alcoholwise. Beyond that indeterminate 'few drinks' the genitals of both sexes become numbed and less responsive, and for men, it's worse. The more they drink and the more they think they want sex, the less capable of it they are. In Shakespeare's *Macbeth*, the porter advises Macduff on the effects of alcohol: 'Lechery, sir, it provokes and unprovokes: it provokes the desire, but it takes away the performance … makes him stand to and not stand to.'

The ancient Greeks thought that a falling out between a man and his best friend occurred because for sex the penis had to be hotter than the rest of the body and drunks were hot all over, thus destroying the differential. What happens, in fact, is that alcohol dilates the small blood vessels throughout the body, so less engorgement takes place where it's

SOME THINGS DRINK MAKES PEOPLE DO

needed and the wobbly bits remain steadfastly wobbly. Even more discomforting, a man may find that he remains defiantly erect but unable to ejaculate, a condition that involves him going through the motions with increased desperation (who says men can't fake it?).

A good idea at the time ...

'Oh, honey, I didn't get drunk,' Homer tells Marge, 'I just went to a strange fantasy world.' It's not an unreasonable way of putting it: drunkenness, as most of us have reason to know, is a world where logic can be as skewed as through Alice's looking-glass.

It seemed like a clever wheeze to the two Egyptians in Cairo who'd been hammering whisky all night. They thought they'd avoid paying by jumping into the Nile and swimming to the opposite bank. One mixed more water with his whisky than he intended and didn't make it; the other got stuck with both bar tabs. It seemed funny to three Cambodians in Pnomh Penh to play Russian roulette with an unexploded anti-tank mine as they drank in a café, each in turn downing a shot and then stamping on the 25-year-old piece of ordnance, until one

---

IN August 1999, a 33-year-old computer technician took part in a drinking competition in a hotel bar in Sydney, Australia, which had a 100-minute limit and a sliding points scale ranging from one for beer to eight for spirits. He won, with 236 points (34 beers, 4 bourbons and 17 tequilas) and was taken back to work to sleep it off – which he did, permanently.

DRINK | A USER'S GUIDE

won and all three lost. It seemed a sensible precaution to the plastered Russian security guard in Moscow to get his equally plastered partner to stab him in his bulletproof vest to test whether it would protect him against a knife. It didn't.

Not all drunken escapades send their perpetrators to the big bar in the sky, but the man in Brighton, England, who visited a prostitute and then worried he'd contracted something nasty did get sent to hospital – Accident and Emergency, not the VD clinic: after drinking heavily he tried to eradicate his problem with a bottle of bleach. A youth in Paris found himself on a similar A&E trip. After demolishing the contents of the family liquor cabinet with his friend, he bet he could whip his penis out of dad's model guillotine cigar cutter before the blade fell, and lost by a foreskin.

A policeman in the Philippines shoots himself in the shoulder while opening a beer with the trigger guard of his pistol; a drunk in Upper Hutt, New Zealand, is arrested after wondering what it would be like to have intercourse with a horse ('My client,' said his lawyer in court, 'is very sorry that there was some injury to the animal'); the mashed mayor of a small town in Kentucky, USA, is arrested for mowing the municipal flower beds; a driver in Adelaide eats his under-

---

IN February 2002, the 100-strong St Petersburg Philharmonic, on their way from Amsterdam to Los Angeles, were thrown off a US United Airways flight at Washington for drunkenness. Their behaviour, said a United official, was 'the sort of thing you expect from a heavy metal band, not a philharmonic orchestra'.

SOME THINGS DRINK MAKES PEOPLE DO

pants in the hope they'll absorb the alcohol in his body and help him fool the breathalyser; a one-armed man is stopped in Swansea, Wales, over the limit, driving an unadapted car *and* talking on his mobile in his one hand; a woman arrested for drunk-driving in Argentina calls a friend for a ride home – and he staggers into the police station in such a state that he's booked too …

In 1993, Wendy Northcutt became intrigued by those 'who have improved our gene pool by killing themselves in really stupid ways' and started the Darwin Awards website, which has led on to two best-selling paperbacks. All human (extinct) life is here, not just those who've eliminated themselves through booze, but they're included. Log on to www.DarwinAwards.com for tales of the likes of:

The drunken pair in southern Georgia who one night scattered a herd of deer and isolated a buck so that one of them could jump from the back of the truck and wrestle it to the ground. He did, and got badly gored – and died when his buddy drove over him. When asked by police about the tyre marks on the deceased's chest, he replied: 'How else was I supposed to get the deer off him?'

The North Carolina woman who, with her equally boozed boyfriend, climbed over the fence of an upmarket inn with pillows and blankets so they could sleep on the roof. In the morning he found she'd rolled over more than she knew.

The Pennsylvanian who when bitten by a friend's cobra refused to go to hospital and went drinking instead, only to slough his mortal coil hours later with his last words ringing in his friend's ears: 'I'm a man, I can handle it.'

DRINK | A USER'S GUIDE

> WHEN the music's over
> Turn out the light
> Turn out the lights
>
> – Jim Morrison and The Doors

Northcutt's personal favourite is of a liquored-up Alabama soldier taking part in a spitting contest from the third floor of a building. To give his final spit momentum, he ran at the barrier – and accompanied its trajectory.

✳ A User's Guide 11

THE ROAD TO DRINK-DRIVE

'If you drink, don't drive. Don't even putt.'
— Dean Martin

In ancient Rome it was an offence to be drunk in charge of a chariot. Don't drink and drive made sense even then. In 1872 the English made it an offence to be 'drunk while in charge on any highway or other public place of any carriage, horse, cattle or steam engine'.

But what, when it comes to being in charge of a means of transport, is drunk? In 1927 an Appeal Court judge quashed the conviction of a man whom a jury had found guilty of

'DRINK and drive: we need the business.'
— Tow-truck bumper sticker

DRINK | A USER'S GUIDE

being incapable of driving his car, because he was not 'drunk in what an ordinary reasonable person would consider as such'. One might be inclined to think that the judge was gaga or perhaps not as sober as a judge, but his thinking was in tune with the times. In 1935, the UK Ministry of Transport claimed that only 29 out of 3,297 fatal accidents involving motor vehicles were caused by drink – prompting the British Medical Council to observe that this 'took no cognisance of those persons who had been under the influence of alcohol to such an extent insufficient to attract notice'.

It was another 25 years or so before the world commonly passed the kind of drink-drive laws we have now. This in spite of many pieces of research such as that carried out by Professor John Cohen of Manchester University, who tested three groups of Manchester bus drivers. The first was a control group of sober drivers, the second was given two single whiskies and the third was given six. In the two-shot group, several drivers were confident they could get a 2.5-metre- (8-foot-) wide bus between posts less than 2.5 metres apart. The six-shot group thought they could do better!

You don't drink and drive in Japan – period. Japan is zero tolerant. Sweden isn't as strict in law but is in practical terms:

THE most recent research shows that accident-proneness increases 50 per cent as the blood alcohol level goes up from 10 milligrams per millilitre of blood to 50 milligrams. It doubles at 60 milligrams and quadruples at 80 milligrams. At 100 milligrams the likelihood of an accident increases sevenfold – and at 150 milligrams it increases 25 times.

THE ROAD TO DRINK-DRIVE

> IN November 2001, a man who was so drunk he could not walk was stopped by police in Moenchengladbach, Germany, after he borrowed his dad's electric wheelchair to go for a nightcap. A police spokesman said the man was over the legal drink-drive limit and they had been forced to confiscate the wheelchair after cautioning him.

its limit is set at 20 milligrams of alcohol per 100 millilitres of blood (0.02 per cent) – that's four or fewer ounces of beer, or not much more than a lick of liquor. Most European countries permit a level of 50 milligrams, as do Canada, Australia and New Zealand, but five countries – the UK, Ireland, Italy and Luxembourg – allow 80 milligrams.

Of the US states, until fairly recently only California, Maine, Oregon, Utah and Vermont set a permitted alcohol level as low as that in the UK, but constant pressure from powerful lobbying groups has forced 15 or more other states down to that level from 100 milligrams (0.10 per cent), and a dozen or so others are talking about 60 milligrams (0.06 per cent) or lower, with Washington state considering 20 milligrams (0.02 per cent). If you're under 21, however, you only need a blood alcohol level of 20 milligrams in order to be convicted of driving under the influence, and that's right across the US.

The don't-drink-and-drive campaign took several decades to get its message across in all countries, yet it has saved tens of thousands of lives since its beginning. In Britain in 1979 (the first year of proper records), 1,790 people died in drink-related accidents; across the 1990s the annual

DRINK | A USER'S GUIDE

> MORE than one in three fatally injured pedestrians have been drinking, with over a quarter of them above what would be the legal limit for driving. Between 10pm and 4am, three-quarters of pedestrians killed are 'over the limit' – although there isn't, of course, a legal blood alcohol level for pedestrians.

> 'THE AAAA is a new organisation for drunks who drive. Give them a call and they'll tow you away from the bar.'
> – Martin Burden

toll has been about 500. But 'could do better', remains the verdict. A fifth of the driving public have never heard of blood alcohol concentration, and one in five of those who have (and a quarter of under-30s) have no idea how much alcohol equates to the limit. A recent UK survey showed that a quarter of those interviewed thought they could drink three to five pints of beer and still be below the limit, and a half thought it would take up to five pints to affect their driving ability.

For the sensible, the designated driver scheme has been a lifesaver. In the US and Canada it's credited with reducing drink-driving fatalities by a quarter in the ten years it's been running, and after a slow start the idea is catching on in the UK. Thinking pub chains, restaurants and bars provide a designated driver with free – non-alcoholic – drinks. Many designated drivers on a group night out have been surprised to discover they've had a good time …

THE ROAD TO DRINK-DRIVE

Breathe into this, sir

The first non-portable drink screener was developed in the US in the late thirties, and it's a shame that the name at least didn't stick around – the Drunkometer. The best of its successors was patented in the early fifties – the Breathalyser, which has given us the generic word 'breathalyser' – like Hoover for vacuum cleaner.

Various technologies and devices are in use today, but the one that most drivers are familiar with is the simple hand-held device used by the police. This was introduced into the UK in 1962 – to screams of protest about interference with individual freedom (Minister of Transport Barbara Castle was dubbed Killjoy Castle). Since then, generations of motorists have got used to being pulled over.

A policeman sitting in his patrol car watched a man stagger out of a pub and weave through the car park, trying his key in four or five vehicles. Finally he got into one and kangarooed into the road. The policeman let him drive a few yards, then stopped him.

'I'd like you to take a breathalyser test,' he informed the driver. 'OK,' the man said, 'but I'm sober. I'm the designated decoy.'

MEN are four times more likely than women to drive after drinking. Male drivers involved in fatal crashes are twice as likely as females to be intoxicated. Fatally injured drivers who've been drinking are least likely to have been wearing safety belts.

DRINK | A USER'S GUIDE

Would sir (or madam) kindly blow into the tube? Sir or madam is delighted (bright smile, easy conversation, alert attention), delivers about two litres (3½ pints) of breath (the lungs hold less than a third of the alcohol that's in the blood, so that 35 milligrams of breath equates to 80 milligrams of blood) and breathes a sign of relief if the needle stays on the side of righteousness.

In Britain, where over 2,000 motorists are breathalysed every day, roadside screening is usually taken as proof of drunkenness in the legal sense. In America, it's considered an indicator only and must be supported, often by the roadside sobriety testing we've all seen in the movies.

Breathalysers have advanced from the early plastic bags of solution into which drivers blew and the later devices with solid crystals that proportionately turned green in the presence of alcohol; newer methodologies employ infrared light

---

SOBRIETY tests include the HGN (horizontal gaze nystagmus), the walk and turn and the one-leg balance. HGN (follow my finger) looks for jerky eye movements, which can indicate intoxication. Walk and turn assesses the ability to move in a straight line, walk in a heel-to-toe manner, turn on one foot and walk back, while following instructions (for example, keep arms at sides, walk a fixed number of steps). The one-leg balance is a divided attention task in which the driver is asked to raise one foot 15 centimetres (six inches) off the ground while counting aloud rapidly from 1,001 to 1,030. Sobriety tests are only reliable with a person who is well above legal alcohol limits – probably with a blood alcohol concentration of around 0.15 per cent.

THE ROAD TO DRINK-DRIVE

> MANY US high schools now randomly breathalyse all students attending school proms. The Delaware River Valley Regional High School adopted the policy after more than a dozen students were suspended for arriving drunk at the fall homecoming dance.

and/or electrically charged 'plates' that attract and count the ions of alcohol. One German machine also measures breath temperature. Some give a print-out and most are now the size of pocket calculators.

But when it comes down to it, all breathalysers are calibrated to give a crude pass-fail reading, and if the needle is in the middle, the question is: legally intoxicated or not? In maybe-yes-maybe-no cases, officers make a judgement. If your road use before being stopped was normal, you might well be sent on your way. If it was erratic and you jumped a red light, you'll probably be asked to blow again.

Breathalysing isn't an exact science. Even advanced hand-held devices are relatively cheap and cheerful. More sophisticated equipment does the job more accurately but more tediously – at some location distant from the spot where you were stopped – and also more expensively. The problem from a legal point of view is that the simplicity of roadside testers makes it easy to challenge their accuracy, even though the police follow guidelines about checking their kit, in some forces before each and every use, to ensure the calibration isn't out of whack. In the US, even sophisticated desktop machines have been called into question by defence lawyers who've argued that their clients' readings have been

DRINK | A USER'S GUIDE

> A driver can be asked to give a blood or urine sample – or can demand one – if convinced his or her breath test was wrong. Urine normally contains about 1.3 times as much alcohol as blood. The pass-fail mark in the UK is 107 milligrams of alcohol.

> IN recent years alcohol breath tests have become compulsory in nuclear power plants and are widely used in airline, maritime and other industries.

distorted by electrical 'spikes' caused by cameras, coffeepots, microwaves and radio waves from cell phones.

A perennial argument is that breathalysers measure mouth alcohol as well as lung alcohol, which bumps up a reading – but that's why the police take the precaution of waiting 15 minutes before asking a driver to blow, to ensure mouth alcohol is dispersed. Courts everywhere have also heard pleas that readings have been contaminated by everything from tobacco to mints, asthma inhalers to breath sprays – even denture adhesive.

Every year in the US, at least 10,000 drink-drive cases raise challenges about breathalysers. In the less litigious UK, there are still scores of cases – a Scottish QC called the breathalyser 'an elastic ruler'. Nonetheless, most people think the way breathalysing is conducted is a sensible use of resources, and pretty fair, and the Home Office periodically reiterates its satisfaction with the way breathalysing is conducted – despite occasional embarrassments, such as

THE ROAD TO DRINK-DRIVE

when St Bartholomew's and Royal London School of Medicine showed that one widely used model of breathalyser was giving readings 6–8 per cent too high, which in borderline cases would make a difference.

Three years ago, Canada came up with a way to immobilise drunken drivers, which has spread to the US, Sweden and Australia and is being tried in the UK. The Alcohol Ignition Interlock is essentially a breathalyser, but it's wired into the ignition. Every time the driver gets into the car, he or she has to blow into the machine. If it isn't satisfied that the driver is sober, the vehicle won't start. To prevent cheating, the driver is required to blow at irregular intervals once on the move; an alarm sounds if alcohol has been drunk since the engine was started. Drivers can't get child passengers to trick the device because they can't blow hard enough. A driver could try to persuade a sober passenger to blow – but most, presumably, would refuse. Failed attempts to start the car and attempts at disconnection or any other tampering are stored in the unit and can be downloaded.

Convicted drunken drivers who opt for the Alcohol Ignition Interlock can get their licence back, but they have to pay for installation – about £3,000. The advantages of the device are already apparent to some bus and lorry companies, and taxi firms, who are having them installed in their fleets.

A User's Guide

DRINK, WOMEN AND THE YOUNG

Women and drink

In the 1970s a group of feminists attempted to invade El Vino's, a long-established drinking haunt at the top of Fleet Street – and an exclusively male enclave. The assembled journalists and barristers stopped drinking long enough to beat the feminists back out the door. Across the Atlantic in New York, Chumley's was still proud of its motto: 'Good ale, raw onions and no women'.

Could this be only 30 years ago? Nowadays the drinking environment is as much female as male, women sit in twos and threes in winebars across the land ordering up bottles with aplomb, and crowd into pubs on ladies' night to shout 'Off, off, off!' at the male strippers.

Throughout history the majority of societies (for which

DRINK, WOMEN AND THE YOUNG

read men) have imposed restrictions on women's drinking. In early – and virtuous – Rome, when all wives were subject to their husbands, Cato the Elder claimed that men could inflict the death penalty on their spouses for adultery – and for drinking, the second presumably because it could lead to the first. The elder Pliny related that a married woman was forced by her family to starve herself to death because she'd stolen the keys to the wine cellar.

Few societies have put the block on women drinking at all, but some have limited how much they could drink and almost all have limited what they could drink and the context in which they could drink it – not that all women have always obeyed the rules.

When beer replaced ale, women drank 'small' (weak) beer. When distillations were first introduced, women didn't touch them at all – it took a man to deal with the fiery spirits. Traditionally, men drank out of bigger vessels. Even societies that have a single alcoholic beverage – such as the Lele in

> IN the early centuries of ale, before manufacture became commercially viable, brewing was something that women fitted in with all the other household chores. When the alehouses developed, women were employed to do the brewing; unless widowed they could only hold a licence to run an alehouse under a husband's name. Once beer gained ground in the 16th century and the number of alehouses increased, men moved in to run the new brewing industry, and women were eased out. Only now did the word 'brewer' – for men – grow out of the female 'brewster'.

DRINK | A USER'S GUIDE

> THE male mentality is capable of converting 'a woman's drink' into a 'non-alcoholic' drink: in 1994 a drunk in the Scottish Highlands who drove his car off the road at night insisted in court that he hadn't been drinking – he'd only had a Barcadi and Coke.

Zaire, who drink palm wine – have a weaker, sweeter version considered suitable for women.

Women's drinks are still with us – but now we're talking marketing, not sociology. Most famously in Britain, there was Babycham – Bambi-like cartoon deer standing on what appeared to be a flying saucer – launched in 1953 as 'a drink that embodies the femininity and the style so desired by women'. By the 1990s this sparkling pear wine ('Champagne de la Poire') from Shepton Mallet in Somerset was considered the depths of naffness, but the continuing fascination with retro-chic has apparently got it once again scaling the heights of hipness. Baileys – an Irish liqueur consisting of whiskey and cream – has been a runaway success with women everywhere since its launch in 1974. Apparently a quarter of the cows in Ireland are needed to produce the 50 million gallons of milk it takes to meet Baileys' annual demand.

Australia has just launched the Barrumundi wine brand, aimed exclusively at women and promoted in pastel, cosmetics-like colours. Independent career women may well go for empowerment in a bottle; more significantly, it's women who push the supermarket trolleys.

As to the places where women drink, the El Vino's story may be extreme, but males have habitually protected the

DRINK, WOMEN AND THE YOUNG

drinking environment as their own. For centuries the only women found in drinking places were bawds and serving wenches – though from Elizabethan times onwards, highborn ladies and those a few rungs up the social scale did enjoy the odd bit of slumming. By the 18th and 19th centuries women of the working class on both sides of the Atlantic were drinking in public as readily as men.

If, by and large, women haven't tried to equal men in the drinking department, some women, naturally enough, are capable of hard drinking, such as the respectable woman who astounded Samuel Pepys at a mutual friend's dinner party by knocking back a pint and a half of white wine in a single draught. Kindred spirits were the three female market-stallers in Cheapside who, as the *London Spy*, a late 17th-century precursor of *Private Eye*, related, lost a merchant a sizeable wager through their ability to knock back a few jars.

The merchant had refused a vintner's bid for a consignment of wine but agreed to the wager the vintner proposed to settle the matter – that three women he knew could polish off a hogshead of claret (239 litres/52½ gallons) at a sitting, without spewing, staggering or falling asleep. The merchant didn't think it was possible, but quickly realised he was on a loser when the women turned up after their market closed

---

IN the Reign of Henry VII, ladies at court received a daily ration of a gallon of ale. Some 50 years later, Queen Elizabeth I drank 'large quantities of particularly strong brew'.

DRINK | A USER'S GUIDE

and one of them downed the contents of a two-gallon container without drawing breath, 'just to taste the Tipple'. He wanted to concede and salvage the remainder of the hogshead – which he'd provided – but this angered the women, who declared they'd 'come for a Bellifull and a Bellifull they would have; and they would see the last of it, were it a Mile to the bottom'; and they did, stepping behind a curtain from time to time to make use of the provided chamber pots, and telling tales of their drinking exploits as they drank. One said she'd drunk 20 pitchers of wort out of the tun when she was 16, 'and that it never gave me the wildSquirt'. Another said that before she was married she drank 19 quarts of sack and sugar at Uxbridge Fair 'to oblige young Squire Cuddle, and afterwards Rid Home a Straddle, three miles, upon her Father's Mare without falling'. By five in the morning the hogshead was dry, each of the woman called for a quart of mulled white wine to settle her stomach, and off to the market they went 'to meet their Horses and their

---

HARDLY anyone today, of either sex, would dare to take on the equivalent of 100-plus bottles in a 10-hour stint like the stallholders of Cheapside, but Oliver Reed might have – he could never turn down a challenge, especially when it came to drinking. A man who on the stag weekend before his second marriage purportedly downed 122 pints (who was doing the counting?), Reed died of a massive heart attack in Malta in 1999, where he was filming *Gladiator*, after knocking back ten pints, 12 rums and a couple of whiskies in under three hours – and arm-wrestling sailors from the Royal Navy frigate HMS *Cumberland*.

DRINK, WOMEN AND THE YOUNG

> IN the 18th century, a Highland lady wrote that decent gentlewomen always began the day with a dram.

> IN hierarchical Japanese society, women have traditionally drunk very little. In the last decade the number of Japanese women who drink has jumped to over 60 per cent of the female population.

Drudges, who were to bring in their Commodities, so far from Drunk that they march'd very steadily'.

There was a retreat into respectability after the half-century of the gin craze of the 18th century, which had caused general revulsion particularly in regard to what it had done to women. Now no decent woman went into a pub unescorted. There was something of a breakout during World War Two, but the shackles were back on straight afterwards. That the pub was a male preserve was culturally instituted until the 1950s. A few establishments had women-only snugs – a hangover from Edwardian days – where panels of frosted glass were intended to protect women who entered not just from the sight of the bar but also from the attention of the barman, who had to be summoned by tapping on a hinged panel. Once served, such brave souls were left to drink in a silence that probably felt sinful.

If, as some psychologists claim, men's need to feel dominant over women stems from an underlying insecurity, men in

DRINK | A USER'S GUIDE

> IN the absence of cylindered oxygen and epidurals, 17th- and 18th-century alewives brewed a high proof 'groaning' ale for pregnant women during labour.

> ONE pub chain recently carried out exit surveys with female customers and was pleased to find they'd got most things right. They hadn't, however, anticipated what would come top of most women's wish list: sexy barmen.

the UK – at least some men – have had much to feel insecure about during the course of the 1990s. Women have not only moved onto their territory but their views have radically changed a great deal of the drinking environment itself.

In southern European countries, where alcohol is morally neutral and part of everyday life, most drinking places are highly visible and have open spaces and lots of glass for seeing in and out of – and that, the new British pub-restaurants chains found when they came to reinvent their premises, was what women wanted here. British males might like darkness, confinement, and surroundings so shabby that they could slop their beer without worrying about stains on the carpet, but women wanted panoramic windows so that they could decide from the outside whether they wanted to go in – and once in, they could both see out and be seen. And they wanted more attractive furnishings and decorations, better-lighted corridors and more hygienic toilets. Even the bog standard pub built in other times and limited in its

DRINK, WOMEN AND THE YOUNG

ability to do much about its structure has had to take a lot of this new thinking aboard.

The young and drink

For centuries the young tippled in public houses just like everyone else, if they had the money. Even up to World War One, youngsters were in and out of the public bars – and if they weren't drinking in them were going back and forth with jugs to the tap-room fetching beer for their mothers and fathers.

The 19th-century temperance movement had more effect in America than in Britain, and consequently in turfing the young out of boozers – but not in places like New York, Boston, Chicago and San Francisco, where there were even dives that catered specifically for street gangs, bootblacks

---

IN 1824, 12-year-old Charles Dickens entered an establishment in Parliament Street, London, and ordered 'your very best – the VERY *best* – ale'. This was called the Genuine Stunning. Young Dickens continued: 'Just draw me a glass of that, if you please, with a good head to it.'

CIDER, I will not sip,
It shall not pass my lip
Because it has made drunkards by the score.
The apples I will eat, but cider, hard or sweet,
I will not touch, or taste, or handle more—

– 'A Child's Vow', 19th-century temperance poem

DRINK | A USER'S GUIDE

and newsboys. Some such places carried on during Prohibition, serving up questionable 3-cent whiskies.

Temperance and Prohibition together gave the US a more nervous attitude to alcohol and the young, from which it has never really disengaged. In legal terms, the US maintains the strictest youth drinking laws of any Western country, with the highest legal minimum drinking age (21) and some state laws that verge on the lunatic – in Missouri anyone under drinking age who takes out household rubbish

---

UNDER current British laws, children of any age can go into parts of pubs that are set aside for meals or as family rooms; over-14s can go into a pub unaccompanied by an adult but can't be served alcohol; 16-year-olds can buy and drink beer or cider (but not spirits) if they are having a meal. In Northern Ireland nobody under 18 can enter a pub.

At least 18 countries have a minimum drinking age of 18. Six have a national minimum age of 21: Russia, China, Egypt, Honduras, Samoa and, of course the US. Three Canadian provinces set a minimum age of 18, the rest of 19. In Japan the minimum age is 20, in Italy and Malta it's 16.

The age at which young people can legally purchase alcohol varies widely. In some cantons of Switzerland, it's as young as 14. In Norway, beer and wine can be legally bought and consumed by 18-year-olds, but the minimum age for buying spirits is 20. Some countries, including Greece and Indonesia, legislate on the legal age for purchasing alcohol but have nothing to say about consumption.

Curious fact: the UK is the only country in which the minimum age for consuming drink at *home* is laid down – five, with parental consent.

DRINK, WOMEN AND THE YOUNG

> IN some European countries ID cards are mandatory and can be used as proof of age. In the UK many feel that an ID card system would be invasion of privacy, though, for the purposes of legal drinking ages, there is a voluntary card scheme operated in pubs and clubs. In the US, driving licences are generally used as ID, but this is not all that useful where drink is concerned, as people can legally drive years before they can legally drink.
>
> In June 2002 in Australia, boys who forged driving licences so they'd be allowed into pubs overlooked one small detail: their photographs showed them wearing school uniform.

containing a single empty alcohol container can be charged with illegal possession.

But there's nothing like telling people not to do something to ensure that they go out and do it. Sobriety societies on many US campuses are the latest anti-drinking pressure groups, but the young still drink – 10 million 12- to 20-year-olds, according to a recent US survey, seven million of them bingeing (survey-speak for five or more drinks in a session).

But the figures in the UK are higher – studies indicate that fewer than one in ten 13-year-olds *haven't* tried alcohol and half of those aged 13 to 16 binge. The young in Britain, including young women, are the biggest young drinkers in Europe, and Spain, Italy and Greece complain that the Brits have exported youthful binge drinking, like football hooliganism. Some of their youngsters are copying British youth, who they've seen whooping it up in Ibiza, Ayia Napa, Ios, Faliraki and other foreign spots.

DRINK | A USER'S GUIDE

> ACCORDING to recent research, middle-class British children turn to drink because of exam pressure and high expectations from parents. Didn't the poet Philip Larkin write, 'They fuck you up, your mum and dad …'?

The British generally shrug their shoulders at youthful drinking (while avoiding city centres late on a Saturday night). They weren't censorious when Prime Minister Blair's under-age son Euan was found on his hands and knees in Leicester Square or when under-age Prince Harry was caught drinking to excess at private parties and at a pub near dad's country home. Booze has ever been a rite of passage.

✱ A User's Guide

ALCOHOL, CHURCH AND STATE

🍺 Booze and belief

> *'A barrel of wine can work more miracles than a church full of saints.'*
> – Italian proverb

Early Christians and Jews shared the same view of alcohol as the Arab world. Alcohol was A GOOD THING. Only later, with the birth of Islam, did most of the Arab world decide otherwise and Christianity become assailed by some doubt.

> 'GOD was an alcoholic. He created the world when he woke up drunk.'
> – Peter Cook

DRINK | A USER'S GUIDE

The Bible and the Jewish Talmud warn against overdoing the sauce ('at the last it beeth like a serpent and stingeth like an adder') but make ample reference to its virtues and, it's fair to interpret, its use as an opiate for those caught between life's rocks and hard places ('Give beer to those who are perishing, wine to those who are in anguish; let them drink and forget their poverty and remember their misery no more'). Jesus drank alcohol ('For John the Baptist came neither eating bread nor drinking wine, and you say, "He has a demon." The Son of Man came eating and drinking, and you say, "Here is a glutton and a drunkard"' – Luke 7:33–34), turned water into wine at Cana, and, as the parable of the new wine into old bottles at least equivocally shows, didn't disapprove of a drop.

According to the early church, to despise alcohol was heresy, and heaven as a kind of open-all-hours pub has always had its attractions. The pre-Christian Anglo-Saxons saw heaven as a place where the living might be able to drop in for a quick one with departed friends; and the Vikings, like the followers of Orpheus, saw it as a place for one long piss-up, with ale streaming endlessly from the udder of a mythic goat named Heidrun. The 11th-century Irish saint, Bridget, pictured paradise with a lake of beer from which the heavenly

---

'THE fact that a believer is happier than a sceptic is no more to the point than the fact that a drunken man is happier than a sober one.'

– George Bernard Shaw

ALCOHOL, CHURCH AND STATE

> IN the 6th century, the abbot of the monastery on Caldy Island off the north Wales coast fell down a well in a spirituous rather than spiritual state and was killed. As a result an ecclesiastical ruling set 30 days' hard penance for a monk who got drunk and 40 days for priests and deacons.

host supped for all eternity (hadn't St Patrick 600 years earlier set about Christianising the Irish with his personal brewer in tow?).

Emerging from a wine-drinking culture and at first spreading through other wine-drinking cultures, the early church not only used wine sacerdotally but had no problem with its followers using wine in its untransubstantiated state. It was less sure, once it started to evangelise the world's beer drinkers, that beer was OK. Beer equated with paganism and produced pagan drunkenness, which was a godless kind of drunkenness. Among the converted Germanic peoples the church forbade beer – and hailed wine drinking as a sign of conversion.

With the centuries, this twitchiness disappeared, and the upper echelons of the clergy took to downing bellyfuls of both beer and wine. In the 8th century the English-born monk, the Venerable Bede and the Welsh-born Boniface, 'the Missionary of Germany', both complained about the boozing of the bishops. Take a charitable view, though: alcohol was seen as a food, remember, and the prelatic types had to keep up their strength for the thirsty work of rooting out sin.

In many a monastery they were going at it hammer and tongs in the drinking department. While most monasteries

DRINK | A USER'S GUIDE

> AS church buildings proliferated in the Middle Ages and required upkeep, fetes known as 'church ales' were held to raise funds. The church tolerated a lot of social licentiousness in the name of God's glory. Some 'church ales' went on for three days. In the 13th century, at one in Wiltshire, England, bachelors who could still stand up were allowed to go on drinking for nothing.

either made wine or brewed – and had large parts of their vast domains given over to viticulture or grain growing – some did both. Later came the distillation of liqueurs, a monastery specialism. Like wine and beer, liqueurs required sampling – a monastery's reputation was at stake, after all. Notwithstanding religious observance, life inside the monastery walls was a lot jollier than outside. In England, even the humblest monk expected his tankard of ale on the refectory table when he came in from a hard early morning's praying.

Clergy outside the monastic fraternity also lived better than the parishioners who supported them; 'the Good Creature of God' – booze – was a cherished member of their flock. 'If die I must, let me die drinking in an inn,' a Welsh clergyman called Walter Map wrote 800 years ago.

Drunkenness was, of course, a sin, but it was expiated by penances doled out to the clergy at any level by higher ecclesiastic authority and by the parish priest to the laity. It was only after the Protestant Reformation weakened the church's power that, from 1552 in England, drunkenness became a matter for civic punishment.

ALCOHOL, CHURCH AND STATE

The Reformation emphasised an idea that wasn't new and wasn't altogether welcome: moderation. Drink made one of the moving spirits, the Frenchman John Calvin, very hot under the clerical collar; the German Martin Luther (who liked a drink, mostly beer, naturally) had bigger issues on his mind – and he had a sense of humour: 'According, if the devil should say, "Do not drink", you should reply to him, "On this very account, because you forbid it, I shall drink, and what is more, I shall drink a generous amount." Thus one must always do the opposite of that which Satan prohibits. What do you think is my reason for drinking wine undiluted … if not to torment and vex the devil, who made up his mind to torment and vex me.'

The Puritans took the moderation ethic to colonial America; while strong threads of it still run through the country, it quickly lost wide observation, even among the clergy; the conventions of hospitality meant that they accepted a drink at every house

---

IN the 16th century the rector of Lymington became so drunk at a fair that he was put in the town stocks. In the 17th century a 'drunkard's cloak' commonly replaced the stocks as a punishment for drunkenness – a tub that had holes for the arms to pass through.

'SORROW can be alleviated by good sleep, a bath and a glass of wine.'
– St Thomas Aquinas

DRINK | A USER'S GUIDE

call and were frequently seen to stagger home. At a celebration of a minister's ordination in New England in 1785, 80 people knocked off 30 bowls of punch before the ceremony, and the 68 who came back for dinner disposed of a further 44 bowls, plus eight of brandy, 18 bottles of wine 'and a quantity of cherry rum'. Four years later, in the year of Washington's inauguration, the first bourbon distillery was set up in Georgetown, Virginia (later Kentucky), by a Baptist minister, the Rev Elijah Craig.

The broad church today has a relaxed attitude to drink, with the Catholic Church being the most relaxed of all – understandably, given its long history of association. While drunkenness still registers a two or three on the sin Richter scale, the Catholic clergy nevertheless have a reputation for enjoying a ball of malt – indeed, the words 'whisky' and 'priest' have been known to occur in conjunction.

There are Christian denominations, however, that preach total abstinence, including the Methodists and Baptists, Quakers and Mormons, Seventh Day Adventists and Jehovah's Witnesses, Christian Scientists and Salvationists, who all see alcohol as the torrent likely to carry drinkers down the chute to hell.

In the view of some, Paul's exhortation to use wine 'for thy stomach's sake' means (going by the words that follow, 'and

---

IN his 1869 book *The Beer of the Bible*, anthropologist James Death, who was also the head brewer of the Cairo Brewery in Alexandria, suggested that manna from heaven, which fed the Israelites in the desert, was *wusa*, an Arabic bread-based beer.

ALCOHOL, CHURCH AND STATE

'YOUR Ushers and Communion Preparers will rejoice at how easy and mess-free it is to fill large quantities of communion cups. This machine can actually fill as many as 240 cups per minute! For more information about how your church can obtain one of these amazing devices, fill out the form below and a Rapid-Fill Communion Wine Dispenser representative will contact you.'

– US advert

'A practical joke took an odd turn last Sunday at Kingston Lutheran Church in Lewisville, Texas, after someone spiked the communion wine with large doses of Viagra.

'"I suspected something was wrong when I noticed many of the men squirming in their seats," said Pastor Larry Barnes. "It was a nice day outside, and at first I thought they were just anxious to get out of here."

'"My husband started rubbing my leg in a rather sensual manner," said Mrs Tom Kerr, long-time member of the church. "He grabbed my hand and put it in his lap. I wasn't sure what to think."

'Things took a turn for the worse when nine-year-old Tim Sutter stood up and shouted, "Look, my pee-pee is stiff just like Mr Roberts said it would be some day."

'At this point, attention turned to Arthur Roberts of Dallas, daycare director for the church, who attempted to flee the service but was stopped by other members. He fell to the floor and started crying out, "Oh God, what have I done?", over and over. He then proceeded to give a full confession of his sexual activities with the young Sutter boy.

'Several members of the church thought that the practical joke was an act of God, not one played by some prankster.'

– News report

DRINK | A USER'S GUIDE

> 'THE pallbearers carried the coffin into the chapel – then carried the vicar out because he was too drunk to continue.'
>
> – *The Times*, 1994

thine often infirmities') that it should be rubbed in like embrocation. And some turn their face from any suggestion that the Bible condones booze. In their interpretation, Jesus didn't drink wine, nor did he turn water into wine at the marriage feast at Cana; what he drank and what he transmuted the water into was grape juice, not *fermented* grape juice. 'Every man at the beginning doth set forth good grape juice; and when men have well drunk then that which is worse: but thou hast kept the good grape juice until now.'

Doesn't seem to chime, does it?

Authority's ambivalence

The law in most lands has always had an uneasy relationship with drink. When it lets things rip, it risks letting the populace get paralytic. When it tightens the screws too much, it risks riot. And though governments don't like it, they need drink – the national cash box depends on taxing it.

Curtailing availability has always had its uses – one Roman emperor, Domitian, ordered the destruction of half the vineyards, a ploy that also occurred to the Egyptian caliph, Hakin. Mogol head honcho Genghis Khan made it illegal to be drunk more than three times a month, and he

ALCOHOL, CHURCH AND STATE

didn't even have a breathalyser to help him. In 10th-century England, King Edward ordered the drinking vessels – which in those days passed from person to person – to have levels marked with pegs (from which the expressions 'gone a peg too low' and 'take [someone] down a peg or two' derive). During the 20th-century years of attempted Prohibition, Sweden, Finland, some Canadian states and the US state of Ohio tried to control drinking by issuing individuals with ration books, a measure that, improbably, lasted from 1919 to 1955 in Scandinavia, and, even more improbably, six years longer in Canada.

WHEN things were going badly for Britain during World War One, the blame fell on the munitions factory workers, whose drinking, the teetotal Home Secretary David Lloyd George said, was doing more damage to the war effort than the German submarines. The government effectively cut off the supply of whisky by introducing legislation that forbade the sale of any less than three years old. It also drastically reduced the strength of beer – to conserve stocks of barley for bread making, it said – and restricted malting so that heat and power could be given over to the munitions factories.

IN Russia's long history, only Mikhail Gorbachev has made any serious attempt to tackle the national problem of alcohol abuse. He increased the price of vodka by 50 per cent, declared all-out war on illegal producers and had public drinkers arrested. State alcohol sales in Moscow fell by over a third in 18 months. With liberalisation – and the abolition of the state alcohol monopoly – the anti-drinking laws fell apart.

DRINK | A USER'S GUIDE

The law has generally tried to give the drinker a fair shake – a German beer law of 1466 stipulated that brewers 'shall sell no beer to the citizens unless it be three weeks old', though the authorities were less concerned about visitors: 'To the foreigners they may knowingly sell younger beer.' The ancient Sumerians were harsh: the code of King Hammurabi, dating back to about 1720 BCE not only specified prices and quality standards of beer but also prescribed punishment by drowning for overcharging.

Increasing taxation on alcohol to pay for war or its consequences is a common theme of history – the levy on beer was 20 cents before the American Civil War and two dollars after it – and when a government is strapped for cash for any reason, as America was after the Great Depression: Franklin Roosevelt openly stated that the reason for bringing Prohibition to an end wasn't to chop off gangsterism at the knees but because he needed a liquor tax to raise $3.3 billion for his public works programme. Taxation has also often been used as a blunt instrument against excess, as happened during the English gin epidemic – when the genie had been let out of the gin bottle by the opposite measure of deliberately keeping taxes low.

NEW York state still operates the 17th-century puritan 'blue law' that forbids the sale of liquor or wine on Sundays. Twenty-three other states have reformed their legislation. According to a survey based on 2001 figures, Sunday sales in New York would generate additional taxes of $70 million and 2,000 new jobs annually.

ALCOHOL, CHURCH AND STATE

> A government that as often as not chose to turn a blind eye was forced into action by a pamphlet penned by a London magistrate, Henry Fielding, author of the novel *Tom Jones*, and by the famous print *Gin Lane*, by William Hogarth, which showed a woman so drunk that she wasn't aware of her baby falling from her arms into the basement of a gin house. Fielding wrote: 'Should the drinking of this poison be continued at its present height during the next 20 years, there will be very few of the common people left to drink it.'

In the late 17th century barring French alcohol imports was one-half of English tactics to stiff the French; the other was giving the people gin in replacement. To make it attractive, the government levied a gin tax of two pence a gallon – compared with the four shillings and nine pence levied on strong beer. The country made whoopee – more whoopee than the government wanted. The government should have seen it coming. Not only did it hang a 'special offer' sign on gin, it did so without closing a legal loophole – a Channel Tunnel-sized loophole – that made it illegal to sell beer or cider without a licence but didn't require a licence for the sale of hard liquor. Soon, not only were there 9,000 gin 'shops' in London alone – one in ten houses – but gin was being hawked by barbers and tobacconists, grocers and chandlers (general provision stores), barrowboys and peddlers.

The government whacked the gin tax up to five shillings – which only put respectable sellers of branded gin out of business. More legislation introduced heavy fines for illegal sales, and yet another Act forbade anyone from selling gin without a

£50 licence. Everyone ignored the law (five licences were sold in seven years). Next, the distillers were prohibited from retailing, which knocked government revenues so badly that the distillers were let back into the market again. And on the sorry saga see-sawed into the next century, until the Duke of Wellington as Prime Minister removed all taxes on beer and permitted anyone to open a beer shop – another 'special offer' sign that turned the nation back towards its traditional bevy.

Yet there were more emphatic influences at work now: a series of failed harvests meant that no grain could be spared for distilling; the temperance movement was on the march, when it wasn't on its knees praying; the owners of the emergent factories were urging action because they needed a sober workforce; and the novel idea had occurred that alleviating the misery of the urban poor just might be a better way to go. As Tony Blair almost certainly would have said, had he been around: 'Tough not just on drinking, but on the causes of drinking …'

✳ A User's Guide   14

OH, NO YOU DON'T!

🍺 Temperance and Prohibition

> *'The only Irish known to R.M. Smyllie was whiskey, which he drank from a hand covered in a white glove, a consequence of a promise to his mother on her deathbed that he would never touch a drop again.'*
>
> – Declan Kiberd

You wouldn't have messed with Carry Nation. She stood 1.83 metres (6 foot) tall, weighed over 76 kilograms (12 stone) and carried a hatchet when she broke up saloon bars from San Francisco to New York. She was arrested over 30 times for her 'hatchetations', lectured incessantly against the demon drink, and sold souvenir hatchets to pay her fines and to fund a refuge in Kansas City for the wives of alcoholics.

Carry Nation was a one-woman vigilante group who didn't belong to the late 19th-century temperance movement. But

DRINK | A USER'S GUIDE

> 'I AM only a beer teetotaller, not a champagne teetotaller; I don't like beer.'
>
> – George Bernard Shaw

> AT the beginning of the 20th century, the American apple crop was so wholly devoted to cider that temperance reformers chopped down great orchards.

many women of all classes did, on both sides of the Atlantic, praying outside saloons and public houses with clergymen, middle-class men of conscience and respectable working men from the trade unions.

Time has cast the reformers in a faintly comic light of holy-roller do-goodery, but, arms linked in America with the Anti-Saloon League, they put up the first trenchant opposition against the squalor, vice and violence that excessive drinking had brought about.

The gin epidemic in England, when men and women had sold their clothing and furnishings, their tools of trade, even their children, to raise cash for liquor, had gone. But gin was still a problem, and other cheap spirits had spread. People who didn't know where their next meal was coming from crammed into every boozer. At the height of the gin epidemic, the British had been drinking 19 million gallons of gin; by the 1870s they were drinking 26 million gallons, distillations various.

OH, NO YOU DON'T!

In the big cities of America, social conditions were just as dreadful as in Victorian England; small wonder that the 'dangerous classes' or 'surplus population' sought refuge in the bottle or the glass. In the low-class dives of New York's Bowery, which had names like the Flea Bag, the Hell Hole, the Dump and the Morgue, solace wasn't even in glasses but in thin rubber tubes, attached to barrels stacked behind the bar and from which for three cents a customer could drink all he wanted until he had to stop for a breath.

The temperance campaigners mostly relied on prayer and the power of persuasion, but in America they weren't above a bit of strength-in-numbers intimidation to make establishments break open their casks and pour their booze into the gutter; nor, in England, were they above scaring heavy imbibers into signing a pledge to give up drink, telling them that if they didn't mend their ways they'd eventually combust spontaneously. By 1900 it was estimated that a quarter of Americans were card-carrying abstainers.

The temperance movement made inroads among the English well-to-do and middle classes, but it had nothing like the same impact among working people as it did in the States. In Ireland, however, the tub-thumping Father Matthew is said to have won 75,000 to the cause.

THE artist George Cruikshank – whose father Isaac had died an alcoholic – was instrumental in persuading people to join the temperance movement, writing a series of books on the subject. The titles were not subtle: *The Bottle*, *The Drunkard's Children*, *The Worship of Baccus*.

DRINK|A USER'S GUIDE

The movement's initial aim was to wean drinkers off spirits and get them back on to beer or cider, but as crusading got up a head of steam its determination became to stamp out all alcohol.

One potent illustration of the extent to which the movement turned around America's attitude to drink is a famous

---

AT first those who signed the pledge had two choices: moderation, or total abstention, which was marked on their card with a 'T' for total — from which 'teetotal' derived.

'On the wagon' dates from around 1900 in the US and refers to the horse-drawn water vehicle that once sprayed down the dust.

IN 1916, in an attempt to hold off Prohibition, August Busch, the second member of his family to guide the Anheuser-Busch beer empire, built the Bevo Mill (a replica of a Dutch windmill) between his estate and the brewery, serving a brew called Bevo, which contained less than half of one per cent alcohol. No one cared for it, and when other companies tried to market other 'near beers', under names like Yip, Vico, Quizz and Hoppy, drinkers spurned them. One critic wrote that 'such a wishy-washy, thin, ill-tasting, discouraging sort of slop might have been dreamed up by a Puritan Machiavelli with the intent of disgusting drinkers with genuine beer forever'.

When Prohibition did arrive, drinkers turned to bootleg, and all but the most powerful breweries were driven out of business. Anheuser-Busch had to turn to other production lines, including truck bodies and refrigerated cabinets, to stay alive.

OH, NO YOU DON'T!

> HUNGARY'S 1919 attempt at Prohibition, brought in by the government when it created a Soviet republic, lasted 133 days. The measure got thrown out in the counter-revolutionary coup.

engraving of Washington celebrating the founding of the union. Prints from the engraving made in 1848 show him glass in hand; prints made in 1876 from a re-engraving had lost the glass – and the decanter on the table was hidden under a hat.

In the US, temperance shaded into Prohibition – nine US states had effectively taken the pledge before 16 January 1920, when Americans woke up in a country that was officially dry.

Legislative attempts at total Prohibition have been made in many lands down the ages; all have ended in failure – but none as resounding as America's. It's unknown or forgotten that Finland, Norway and Canada also introduced Prohibition, and did it a year earlier. The Canadians threw in the towel in 1927; the Norwegians and Finns held on for over 13 years, only a few months less than the Americans, but they never attracted the world's attention, because, unlike their fellow prohibitors, they didn't turn Prohibition into a farce.

In social terms, the temperance movement had as profound an effect on Britain as it did on America. It stopped, for instance, the traditional practice of paying out workmen's wages in pubs late at night – which had obvious consequences; payments were moved to non-alcoholic surroundings of one kind or another and took place at or before

DRINK | A USER'S GUIDE

> 'ABSTAINER: a weak person who yields to the temptation of denying himself a pleasure.'
>
> – Ambrose Bierce

> *ANIMAL Farm* is a parody of communist Russia, but also a warning about the totalitarian state – and alcohol is the symbol of corruption and greed. Jones loses his farm because he's a drunk. One of the seven rules drawn up by Napoleon the pig is that 'No animal shall drink alcohol to excess' – but when he starts doing so himself, he changes the rule.

breakfast, giving women a chance to get hold of the loot. In the bigger scheme of things, the movement empowered women and was a significant factor in the fight for the vote – on both sides of the Atlantic drinking places had been a centre of political activity from which women were excluded; and in America votes were routinely bought with liquor.

But the temperance movement didn't succeed in moving the British government towards Prohibition, though Lloyd George toyed with the idea when he became prime minister in the middle of World War One. A Swedish–Norwegian scheme allowing municipalities to buy up local alcohol outlets and manage the trade was piloted in Carlisle (where 100 outlets were reduced to 19) and was considered a success, but tentative plans to extend the scheme created such a hullabaloo that it went no further. Anyway, all this had less to do with prohibitionary intent than wartime jitters.

OH, NO YOU DON'T!

Many Americans naively believed that Prohibition was going to be the answer to all the nation's ills; so certain were they that in some places they even got rid of their jails. They quickly got them back again – and the federal penitentiaries, which went into Prohibition with 4,000 criminals banged up in them, came out of it with over 26,000. New York went into Prohibition with 15,000 legitimate saloons and came out with 20,000 illegal speakeasies – 200,000–500,000 nationwide, no one knows.

What America had done was swap bands of marching women for gunmen carrying violin cases. Capone made $60 million a year; the Detroit bootlegger Chester Le Mare made an alleged $215 million in a single year. In the endemic climate of corruption and backhanders, 800 federal agents were dismissed for taking protection money from the

> CAUGHT between a rock and a hard place, the US government allowed the vineyards to market fruit juices to prevent them going out of business – which provided a ready source for making illicit hooch. So did their dried raisin cakes. Salesmen made it clear than on no account must a jug of juice made from raisin cakes be left for 21 days in a warm place because it might ferment ...

> BOOTLEGGERS were originally the traders who hid bottles of liquor in their kneeboots to sell illegally to the Indians.

speakeasies, and for bribery and redirecting seized consignments of booze back onto the market. More than 1,000 innocent bystanders died in shootouts.

The irony of the saga is that before prohibition was unleashed, alcohol consumption in America was on the way down. Back in 1830 it had peaked at 18 litres (4 US gallons) of absolute alcohol per capita per annum; by 1900 it had halved; and in 1920 it was at an all-time low of 1.46 gallons. By the time Prohibition was dismantled on 5 December 1933, consumption had marginally risen, to 1.63 gallons per person per year.

The hangovers from Prohibition

Parts of America, notably the south and west, gave Prohibition popular support; most states that remain dry are found here, although anyone who thinks a dry state is dry is wet behind the ears.

That states are casuistically designated wet or dry is just part of Prohibition's legacy: so is the myriad of mildly schizophrenic drinking laws, such as the universal one that liquor carried in the street must be in a brown paper bag (or sack, as the Americans say). There are states (Utah) that don't have

> UNDER the Pennsylvania Dram Shop Act, anyone who injures him- or herself after being served while visibly intoxicated can sue the drinking establishment. If he or she is injured by someone else who is visibly intoxicated when served, he or she can again sue.

OH, NO YOU DON'T!

> 'WHEN I read about the evils of drinking, I gave up reading.'
> – Henny Youngman

watering holes open to the public and others (Kentucky – which doesn't make bourbon any more) where, theoretically, you can be put in the slammer for five years for sending a gift of alcohol to a friend. There are states where by law the interior of public drinking places must be visible from the street and others where that is illegal; and there are states where food is available where drinks are served and others where it is illegal to serve food and drink together. In Vermont a customer can't have more than one poured drink in front of him at a time (no drink and chaser, then). Some states stipulate that anyone drinking must be seated, others that they must stand at a bar – though anyone standing in Texas who takes more than three sips of beer is, technically, committing an offence.

And you wonder why so many Americans drink Coca-Cola.

Islam, Koran, interpretation

Dodgy place for a Muslim to be caught drinking, Saudi Arabia. One hundred lashes is the punishment under shari'a Islamic law. A third offence and a death sentence can be imposed; Saudi has around 200 public beheadings a year and some of those are drinkers.

The Koran is usually cited as justification for three-strikes-

and-you're-out retribution, but that's highly suspect reasoning. The Islamic good book prescribes execution for adultery, the murder of a Muslim and deserting Islam, but says nothing of the kind about drinking – and on that score is no more or less equivocal than the Bible. Whereas *sura* (chapter) 2:219 ('In them [alcohol and narcotics] is great harm and some benefits for human kind. But the harm of them is much greater than their benefits') ostensibly forbids drink, *sura* 16:67 ('And among fruits you have the palm and the vine, from which you get wine and healthful nutriment: in this, truly, are signs for those who reflect') presumably takes the opposite view. Islam's answer to this dichotomy is that, as the *suras* are in reverse order to that in which Allah revealed them to Muhammad, the earlier ones are abrogated by the later. But that raises the question as to why Allah, in his omnipotence, didn't say what he meant in the first place.

In his early years Muhammad had nothing against sensible drinking, but during an eight-year exile in Medina, 250 miles from Mecca, there was a bit of a punch-up one night after dinner, when the company had settled down to taking a drop or two, and a Meccan recited an insulting verse about the Medinites. He got biffed on the head with a large meatbone. Muhammad was so horrified that he sought guidance from Allah – and came back with a blanket drinking ban that had them pouring wine into the gutters like people in twenties' America.

Islam, of course, draws not only on the Koran but also the Hadith – the much worked-over collection of stories about the Prophet's life and what other people said he said – and

OH, NO YOU DON'T!

> 'ELEVEN things are unclean: urine, excrement, sperm, blood, a dog, a pig, bones, a non-Muslim man and woman, wine, beer, and the perspiration of a camel that eats filth.'
> – Ayatollah Khomeini

> 'I am so holy that when I touch wine, it turns into water.'
> – Aga Khan III

other authorities; and Islam is big on interpretation, which is bad news for a 'you're nicked' drinker in Saudi, which makes hard-nosed interpretations – but you can't blame Muhammad for that. What he said and stuck to was that paradise flows with wine – reminiscent of early Christianity's thirst for the afterlife. A fundamentalist view is that the wine in the Koran is non-alcoholic – reminiscent of fundamentalist Christians' denial of the existence of wine in the Bible.

Fundamentalists of all stripes do have a way of disappearing up their own fundamentalism.

'To drink is a Christian diversion/Unknown to the Turk or the Persian', Congreve neatly but inaccurately rhymed. Before Muhammad in the 7th century, the Arab world was renowned for heavy drinking. And for centuries after him many Arabian dynasties found alcohol and religion compatible bedfellows – Turkey's vast empire carried on boozing as if nothing had happened and was notorious for its drunkenness. It was a similar story in Syria, Mesopotamia (now Iraq) and Persia (Iran). When Persia was overrun by the Arabs in the very century of the Prophet, they appreciated the quality of its wines and didn't interfere as the people went about tending their vineyards, which included the vineyards of Shiraz and which gave the world one of its most famous grape varieties. In the 11th century the poet Omar Khayyam waxed lyrical in the *Rubaiyat* about 'a loaf of bread, a jug of wine, and thou'; 300 years later his fellow Persian, Hafiz, sought to quench his desire for women with wine.

Only in the last few centuries has an upsurge in Islamic conservatism – largely as a backlash against westernisation – brought a complete block on booze. But westernisation continues – and observation of abstinence in all Islamic countries is beginning to be more honoured in the breach than in the observance.

'Religions change, but beer and wine remain.'
– Anonymous

A User's Guide 15

OH, YES WE DO!

Prohibition? What Prohibition?

Prohibition ordered Americans not to drink. Before you could say 'make mine a double', tequila was pouring over the border from Mexico, whisky was coming across the lakes from Canada in fast boats and rum was arriving from the Caribbean. Bigger vessels under foreign flags heaved to outside the three-mile limit with liquor from Holland and Belgium to be transferred to smaller craft under cover of darkness. In 1923 US customs officials seized 134 vessels, and in 1924 they seized 236, but the smugglers were running them ragged, like waterborne Keystone Kops.

With their long, broken coastlines – and with Denmark just a hop across from Sweden – the Scandinavian Prohibitionists didn't stand much of a chance either. Isolated at the top of Europe, Finland might have been expected to do better, but

DRINK | A USER'S GUIDE

little Estonia, a prolific producer of booze, was only 80 kilometres (45 miles) away over the Gulf of Finland.

Prohibition in the US began with the government getting a quick taste of what was to come: in the first three months half a million dollars' worth of liquor was stolen from bonded depositories. More legitimate liquor walked out the door through medical prescription. Every medical practitioner was allowed to fill 100 prescriptions for medicinal whiskey in any three-month period. In 1927, 1.8 million US gallons of whiskey were issued this way and an increased volume the following year, when doctors were estimated to have trousered a dishonest $40 million. (*They* said prescription pads were either stolen or forged.)

A lot more people than usual apparently took communion during Prohibition. In 1922, 2,139,000 US gallons of wine for ecclesiastical use were booked out, a figure that two years later was 2,940,700 – an increase of over 800,000 US gallons.

On top of the genuine booze that flooded into the US or was siphoned off from legitimate sources, there were illicit stills and fermentors almost everywhere; if hardly on the scale of the racketeers, many respectable bankers, farmers, spinster aunts and college kids with chemistry sets had a little something bubbling away in a bathroom or

---

A bunch of medical students in 1920s London showed crusading Prohibitionist William Eugene 'Pussyfoot' Johnson what they thought about his attempt to talk England dry – they dragged him from the lecture platform. Pussyfoot lost an eye in the melée.

OH, YES WE DO!

> MOTHER'S in the kitchen washing out the jugs,
> Sister's in the pantry bottling the suds,
> Father's in the cellar mixing up the hops,
> Johnny's on the front porch watching for the cops.
>
> – Prohibition song

cellar. In 1921, agents seized 95,933 pieces of equipment, large and small.

Prohibition was never going to be more than a finger-in-the-dyke exercise, as history should have counselled.

It was ever thus ...

Attempts to ban, curb or exorbitantly tax booze have inevitably resulted in riots, smuggling and a rush to make poteen.

On Christmas Day 1661, the English government levied a tax of four pence a gallon to restrict whiskey distilling in Ireland. Poteen production began on Boxing Day. The government rarely got its tax because most of the stills were off in the hills – a century later at least a third continued to be. After the union of the English and Scottish parliaments in 1707, ever-increasing taxes sent the Scottish stills the way of those of the Irish. By the end of the 18th century, 10 Scottish distilleries were licensed; thousands weren't and they didn't become so until an Excise Act of 1823 made distilling legally profitable again. Illicit whisky was smuggled into Glasgow and the big cities from the surrounding countryside in tin pots attached to the hoops under girls' skirts.

DRINK | A USER'S GUIDE

> THE problem for poteen makers was making the malt. They would leave a sack of grain in a stream to soak, then take it home to dry under the bed. When they fired up in bog or glen, they hoped the small plume of smoke that arose from the bothy wouldn't give the game away to the custom men or the soldiery.
>
> Illicit distilling has disappeared from Scotland, but is a way of life in Ireland, especially in Galway, and the old copper still has given way to the Burco boiler, which is cheap to run and twice as efficient.

> IN 1808, William Bligh (he of *Bounty* mutiny fame) who'd become governor of New South Wales, was run out of town by the officers of the New South Wales Corps after he stifled the colony's rum traffic.

There was an object lesson in America's own backyard if the government of 1920 had wanted to heed it. One hundred and twenty-nine years earlier, George Washington had declared a tax on bourbon – and thousands of whiskey makers had taken up arms and only been quelled by 15,000 soldiers. As a result, a large number of them took their stills to the woods, and indeed to this day some remain out there along the Appalachian Trail and the Cumberland Gap.

The illicit stills are still in use in Sweden, 200 years after the government there tried to stamp them out (and quickly withdrew the reform when the peasants revolted). An estimated 180,000 people were making aquavit then; 100,000 are making it now. The Swedes don't figure high up in the world drinking league, but they're determined drinkers – in

OH, YES WE DO!

the days of rationing books, those who'd had their book withdrawn for abuse still managed to get their hands on supplies, to the despair of the authorities. They're dedicated drinkers in Norway, too, where 35 per cent of the booze in the country comes from 'clandestine sources' – this despite the most draconian anti-alcohol laws in Europe: state-run package stores reminiscent of communism, a tightly controlled issue of liquor licences to cafés, limited sales hours (10am–9pm), no advertising, tough punishment for transgression and taxes three times higher than in Britain.

Since the introduction of the single market on one side of Europe and the collapse of communism on the other, there isn't anywhere that doesn't have illegal traffic in alcohol to contend with, and that includes Britain, where evasion of tobacco and alcohol taxes is thought to cost the Treasury £1.2 billion a year (alcohol accounting for 'only' £215 million).

Most revenue is lost to organised villainy with warehouse set-ups for distribution to no-questions-asked pubs and shops; some is lost to Jack the Lad opportunists who flog their gear from plastic bags in boozers, at markets, at car boot sales and at pop festivals. No one is against a crackdown on such trade. But the government has run into trouble with the way it's

RETURN TO SENDER

After Canada decreased taxes on tobacco in 1994, criminal organisations either switched to, or intensified their involvement in, contraband booze. Canadian tax on spirits is typically 83 per cent, twice the US level – which makes smuggling an attractive proposition.

DRINK | A USER'S GUIDE

treated the general public nipping over the France or Belgium on 'booze cruises' to do a little stocking up. In direct contravention of EU open-border rules, Britain set artificial limits on what an individual could bring back – and anyone with more was automatically regarded as being guilty of smuggling unless they could prove that what they had was for personal use – impossible unless they drank and smoked everything on the spot. Penalties have included confiscation of vehicles – 10,000 in 2001–2, hundreds of which have been crushed.

The High Court has ruled that customs must return confiscated goods and vehicles, or pay compensation in lieu, and ordered them to stop pulling trippers over for random searches, but the scenario is still playing out. It isn't over till the fat lady stops singing and pours herself a drink after the performance.

Eastern (broken) promise

> 'Many Arab states are struggling with a growing rate of alcohol and other drug addiction.'
> – Christian Science Monitor, *21 August 2002*

Whatever Islam decrees, alcohol is available throughout the Islamic world from Morocco to Indonesia. How many

---

SAUDI customs guards recently arrested two men with a donkey on their way into the kingdom from Yemen. The donkey was carrying a large quantity of fish – and 35 bottles of spirits.

OH, YES WE DO!

> GOVERNMENT inspectors in Sharjah, one of the seven United Arab Emirates, have ordered shops to get rid of their stocks of non-alcoholic beer after finding out that the bottles were fermenting in storage.

> A bottle of branded Scotch costs $200 on the Saudi black market, a price many of the large expat population is willing to pay. But more have their own sophisticated stills for making *sidiqui* – moonshine. The unwritten rule for expats is that drinking takes place behind closed doors. Getting caught bringing alcohol into the country can be punished with 80 lashes. In April 2002, a Briton who ran an underground drinking club was sentenced to 800 lashes and eight years in nick; he was also fined £400,000.

Muslims drink is an open question, but – whatever the risks – it seems that numbers are increasing. There's even an alcohol problem in some Muslim countries.

On the surface, those in the Arab peninsula appear to adhere most strictly to abstinence, but even in Saudi Arabia rich Saudis bring in booze from more tolerant neighbouring states, especially Bahrain (only a causeway away) and Jordan, where it's openly on sale. Expats and frequent travellers tell of caches of liquor behind false walls and doors in luxurious homes, and princes of the royal house visiting London gambling clubs don't exactly bother hiding their partiality for the sauce.

Across Islam, the gap between official conviction and the popular mood is widening, leading at times to sudden fierce periods of zealotry, though not against those powerful enough to defend themselves.

DRINK | A USER'S GUIDE

> DRINKING alcohol at weddings and parties is becoming increasingly common among Uzbek women, according to the Tashkent newspaper *Savdogar*. 'It is not a good sign that that some women drink as much vodka as men,' says the paper. 'About 10–15 years ago it was unusual to hear about women drinking alcohol, but now it has become an ordinary thing.'

If you're looking for a symbol of the ambivalence in Islam's relationship with alcohol, look no further than the Murree brewery, which legally brews and distils beer, vodka, gin, rum, brandy and whisky – in Islamic Pakistan, where punishment for drinking can be whipping and imprisonment.

The brewery was started over 130 years ago to keep British troops in the subcontinent in good spirits (and became enclosed by Pakistan's borders when the state was created out of India in 1947); today it ostensibly does the same job for the 3 per cent of Pakistanis who aren't Muslims. That 3 per cent are allowed to drink, though they must fill out an application declaring their religion, profession and father's or husband's name. Until recently, Christian Pakistanis also had to provide a letter from a priest saying it was all right for them to drink.

As virtually everywhere in Islam, Pakistan has a thriving black market in booze, as does next-door India, where many Muslims, and Hindus (who form the majority of the population), drink.

According to Hindu scripture, drinking is one of the five heinous crimes (Manu, mythological founder of the human

OH, YES WE DO!

race considered the only atonement was for the drinker to be branded on the forehead). Half a century ago, the ascetic Mahatma Gandhi gave prohibition of alcohol the weight of the law. Prohibition didn't become universal until 1977 – and lasted only two years except in the state of Tamil Nadu, which held on for 21 years longer. Today Tamil Nadu is 'semi-dry', with a rarely enforced rationing system – the restaurants don't bother asking to see permits. The states of Karnataka and Maharsashtra are awash in smuggled booze, and Goa – for centuries under the influence not of the British but of the equally hard-drinking Portuguese – is reputed to be India's hardest-drinking state.

Indians who can't afford the black market make their own booze from many fruits, but distilling coconut is most common. In Iraq and Iran they usually use dates and pomegranates. Since the Gulf War the Iraqi leader has found it expedient to project himself as a devout Muslim and as part of a 'faith campaign' has banned restaurants from selling alcohol, but Iraq remains secular in outlook – the veil is less common there even than in Jordan and Egypt – and many people enjoy a drink or two. In even more secular Iran the supermarkets in the richer suburbs do brisk under-the-counter trade, pizza parlours sell Fanta laced with vodka and

BUDDHISM disapproves of alcohol and advises followers to refrain. Sikhism isn't against it (but forbids tobacco).

DRINK | A USER'S GUIDE

> ACCORDING to the British Foreign Office, Saddam Hussein had been buying a weekly average of 10,000 bottles of alcohol, mostly Scotch, for the Iraqi military and political elite, paying for it with food and medicine delivered under international aid programmes.

> SHAREEF would appear to have the world at his Nike-clad feet. He is bright, articulate and popular with his peers at Guildhall University, east London. He's plugged into the information age, studying for an MA in financial markets and information systems, and after two years working for the Financial Services Authority he has experience in the workplace.
>
> But Shareef, 26, has discovered that life as a practising Muslim in Britain is not that straightforward.
>
> 'When I first started working at the FSA we had a team meeting in the pub. Someone asked me, "What do you want to drink?" I said, "Orange juice" and they all started laughing. When they stopped laughing someone said, "Right, what do you really want to drink?"'
>
> – *Guardian*, 18 June 2002

in the alleyways the young buy beer from Holland and Australia and vodka from Azerbaijan – with one eye out for the religious police.

The Islamic revolution that for a couple of decades had Iran in the grip of the ayatollahs appears to have lost out to an older desire. And in the Koranic colleges, the mullahs ... mull.

✱ A User's Guide 16

ALCOHOL ADULTERATED, BOOZE BLACK MARKET

'The brewers have gotten the art to sophisticate beer with broom instead of hops, and ashes instead of malt, and (to make it more lively) to pickle it with salt water.'
– Nathaniel Knott, Advice of a Seaman, 1634

Alcohol has always lent itself to scamming or, if you prefer, taking advantage of a marketing opportunity. In Roman times the scammers added bitter almonds to wine to give it the semblance of age; in Restoration London they favoured litharge (a compound of lead) or cider to give a bit of pizzazz. When the price of malt rose steeply at the beginning of the

DRINK | A USER'S GUIDE

19th century, English brewers turned to cheap colouring agents including molasses, elderberry juice and Spanish liquorice – and less scrupulous one used opium and tobacco. Throughout the century, consignments of beer, wine and spirits, which were usually moved by canal, got 'tapped' along the way, the stolen portions being replaced with water. That was a scam not unknown to stevedores in the dockyards of Britain until containerisation put a stop to the practice.

Wine scams still happen. In 1973 a pillar of the French wine establishment was caught passing off wine from the less desirable Midi region as the more desirable Bordeaux. In 1985 Austria's wine producers were found to be adding antifreeze to give body and sweetness to wines made from thin and acidic harvests (and the Austrian wine market still hasn't recovered from the loss of public confidence). In the past few years there have been serious frauds in Italy, America and Australia – methods ranging from faking labels, caps and

---

IN 2001 Berlin was overrun by fake beer. 'Beer bandits' nicked barrels from breweries, filled them with homebrew and sold them on to restaurants. According to the newspaper *Bild*, one in five glasses drunk in the Berlin area was 'no name' beer.

IN 1419, Londoner William Harold was sentenced to the pillory for an hour for 'contrefetying of old and feble spynissh wyn for good and true Romeney, in the parish of seynt Martyns in the vyntry'.

ALCOHOL ADULTERATED, BOOZE BLACK MARKET

> UNTIL now there's been no method of analysis to distinguish one wine from another, but scientists at the National Institute of Agronomic Research in Montpellier are perfecting one — using the same DNA technique as is used on human tissue.
>
> One company that's already embraced DNA profiling is Australia's BRL Hardy, which has impregnated the tamper-proof labels on its premium Eileen Hardy Shiraz with DNA taken from its 100-year-old vines.

corks to filling bottles that once contained a great wine with something more humble. Claims abound of vintage wines being routinely topped up with younger plonk. One sommelier is known to offer a mix 'n' match service that can inflate a bottle's worth by tens of thousands of pounds.

In 2001, in an upmarket scam of breathtaking audacity, three London companies offered cases of Château Lafite 1996 as an investment that, they said, would provide 'head-splitting' returns — and in a way they weren't lying: the same premier cru that they offered for £4,000 could be had from other merchants for about half that sum. The companies were closed down.

The have-I-got-a-bargain-for-you-John merchants of 300 years ago found the spread of distillation a boon, and nothing's changed there. By the 18th century's gin epidemic, a lot of what was being sold on the streets was alcohol diluted with alum, turpentine and sulphuric acid. During American Prohibition, denatured alcohol was washed to rid it, with luck, of its poisonous additives, and just-out-of-the-still whiskey was aged with an electric needle.

DRINK | A USER'S GUIDE

> NO one knows how many people were poisoned to death during the gin epidemic. During Prohibition, an estimated 35,000 Americans were killed by bootleg liquor, some of which contained not only antifreeze but also benzene, camphor and embalming fluid. Not for nothing was it dubbed coffin varnish, rot gut, tarantula juice, sheep-dip and strike-me-dead.
>
> Some drinkers died and many were made seriously ill because they believed the story that alcohol in antifreeze could be made safe by filtering it through a loaf of bread. The soaring death rate in Moscow today is partly attributed to dangerous moonshine, in which aviation fuel is a common ingredient.

The authorities have always struggled against the street entrepreneurs, even the Scots in the Middle Ages and they had the death penalty for adulterating whisky – a punishment most Scots, no doubt, think should never have been rescinded.

A User's Guide

PRODIGIOUS DRINKING

National characteristics

Excessive drinking is like venereal disease – every nation blames some other nation for giving it to them. The English blamed the Dutch for making them drunkards, the Germans blamed the French, and the French blamed the Italians. Who said that blame culture was a modern phenomenon?

All nations throughout history have mistrusted foreign drinking habits; the ancient Greeks despised the Thracians and the Macedonians because of their excess. The 17th-century English were fond of making lists of national characteristics to show how much better they were than other nations and, naturally enough, found others bigger drunkards.

The much-travelled Englishman Fynes Moryson visited Germany in the 17th century and found 'drunkenness as their almost sole vice'. In Denmark, the 'Danes passes (if it be possible) their neighbour Saxons in the excesse of their drinking'. Poles were 'as stout drinkers as the Germans', among the Swiss 'drunkenness has much patronage even among the best sort' and 'Nederlanders use lesse excesse in drinking than the Saxons, but more than other Germans'.

It all comes down to which end of the telescope you're using. The Swiss Thomas Platter visited London in the same century and thought he'd never seen so many taverns and drunks. In the previous century, Rabelais, a Frenchman, wrote 100 years earlier about being 'drunk like an Englishman'. Two centuries later, Verlaine, another Frenchman, found the English as 'noisy as ducks, eternally drunk'.

Some Englishmen, at least, thought their fellow countrymen sots. 'The only plagues of London are the immoderate drinking of fools and the frequency of fires,' wrote William Fitzstephen, secretary to Thomas à Becket in the 12th century. Four hundred years later, in *Othello*, Shakespeare has Iago (a Venetian) say of his relish for elbow bending: 'I learn'd it in England, where indeed they are most potent in potting: your Dane, your German, and you swag-bellied Hollander ... are nothing to your English.' And, to paraphrase what follows, your English drinks your Dane into unconsciousness, sees off your 'Almain' without breaking sweat, and waits for your Dutchman to do what Billy Connolly describes as 'the Technicolor huey' before filling them up again.

Would Shakespeare's audience have been appalled at this? Certainly not the men. They would have preened. Men do – because down the centuries men of almost every nation have assumed the same contradictory view: foreigners get drunk; we hold our liquor (and if sometimes we don't, it isn't

PRODIGIOUS DRINKING

> 'NO matter what they say, a woman will always be impressed by the amount a man can drink.'
> – Advice given to rookie bartender Tom Cruise in the film *Cocktail*.

drunkenness). Ambivalence is the name of the drinking game. And machismo. In most of South America, in Cuba, the West Indies and the south-east Asian republic of Laos, men are expected to drink heavily and still walk, talk and comport themselves without impairment. In Nigeria, the more a man consumes and remains apparently sober, the more respect he gains.

Taking things a little bit further, the Russian who didn't help finish the vodka when the bottle was opened – and who didn't do it downing his shots in one – would be thought effeminate, and in Paraguay a man who didn't drink at all would be labelled not just effeminate but also cowardly, degenerate and stupid. You can't say there aren't British and American males who don't also think along these lines.

But, along the beer–wine fault line, attitudes aren't as entrenched as in the 19th century, when an English author felt sure enough of his readership to opine: 'Beer, then, is predominantly the drink of those branches of the white races of mankind ... the energetic, and progressive and colonizing people who for the last five hundred years have been the social, industrial and political leaders of civilization as we now see it'; and a French physician, Professor Henri Babinski, wrote: 'The long-time use of wine has certainly contributed to the formation and development of fundamental qualities of the race [the French]: cordiality, frankness, gaiety, which differentiate them so profoundly from people who drink beer.'

The intemperate 18th century

Let other mortals vainly wear
A tedious life in anxious care,
Let the ambitious toil and think,
Let states or empires swim or sink,
My sole ambition is to drink.

– Anonymous, 18th century

It's hard to believe the amount of alcohol the upper classes knocked back in the 17th, 18th and 19th centuries, or the amounts of food that accompanied at least some of it. The well-known 18th-century drunk Theodore Hook excused his drinking by saying: 'When one is alone, the bottle does come round so often.'

In the 18th century, the most intemperate in English history, dinner usually began between 4 and 5pm and guests were 'up to the chin in beef, venison, geese and turkeys; and over the chin in claret, strong beer and punch'. After four or five hours, when the ladies retired, the gents got in two or three hours of steady drinking, pausing only to relieve themselves in chamber pots concealed inside the drawers of the sideboards. 'One has no kind of concealment and the practice strikes me as most indecent,' the son of the French

PRODIGIOUS DRINKING

philosopher De La Rochefoucauld wrote home in 1784. Supper was at nine, with port, brandy and more punch. Throughout the proceedings a servant was on hand specifically to untie the cravats of those who keeled over, to prevent them from choking.

It was much the same story in America at the time. There, too, excessive drinking was a way of life. Businessmen and auctioneers sealed bargains with a drink. Judges interrupted court to drink. It was common for men on a long journey by horse or carriage to drink a quart of hard liquor at each stop – and on a 113-kilometre (70-mile) trip there could be eight stops.

The English aristocracy hadn't been exactly abstemious in the reign of Charles I – even the elephant in the royal menagerie at the Tower of London drank wine. But once 11

(GENTLE)MEN BEHAVING BADLY

Charles Sackville, Earl of Dorset, got so hammered in the Cock in Bow Street, Covent Garden, that, urged on by his cronies, the rakes Sir Charles Sedley and Sir Thomas Ogle, he swaggered onto the first-floor balcony and exhibited himself naked to passers-by. According to Pepys, he 'acted all the postures of lust and buggery that could be imagined, and abusing of Scripture … preached a mountebank sermon from that pulpit, saying that there he hath to sell such a powder as should make all the cunts run after him – a thousand standing underneath to see and hear him. And it being done he took a glass of wine and drank the King's health.' When the trio urinated on the assembly a riot broke out. Brought before the Lord Chief Justice, they were each fined £2,000.

years of Cromwellian puritanism were out of the way and Charles's son, Charles II, was on the throne in 1660, they really began to party (and it can be said that the partying was only really halted by World War One).

They'd really got into their stride by the 1800s, when it was quite normal for a couple of friends to finish off as many as 10 bottles of burgundy and champagne over a meal. One pair of chaps locked themselves in a room with a hogshead of claret (worth mentioning again: 52.5 imperial gallons, 63 US ones) and saw it away in a week, as well as an unspecified number of bottles of cherry brandy. The chamber pots would have been overflowing if the contents hadn't been defenestrated. Prodigious drinking was so common that four- or five-bottle-a-day men weren't regarded as exceptional, and the Lords Panmure, Dufferin and Blayney were known as six-bottle men.

Port was chiefly to blame for making Englishmen drop like flies (though Samuel Johnson, a port man who, his biographer James Boswell noted, polished off 36 glasses in one evening session, lived to the age of 75). It was to the heavier Portuguese plonk that they turned when imports from France were prohibited; their faces rapidly became the colour of their tipple, their bellies sagged and their extremities were in

> ASKED if he'd finished three bottles of port without assistance, the 18th-century Irish politician Sir Hercules Langrishe replied, 'No, not quite that. I had the assistance of a bottle of Madeira.'

PRODIGIOUS DRINKING

> FROM the Middle Ages up to World War One, working men routinely drank on the job – drink was thought to bolster stamina. In the 17th and 18th centuries men downed as much as four gallons of beer or cider a day – employers put barrels in the fields or on the docksides.
>
> Labourers started the day with a quart or more of beer or cider, and if the supply ran out during working hours would sometimes quit. US workers had a similar arrangement – though there, farmhands expected the hard cider to be fortified with drams of rum.
>
> In Brittany today when any collective farm work is done, bottles of red wine litter the edges of the fields. A farmer known for a lack of generosity finds labour hard to hire.

an agony of gout, but they kept going, stout fellows. Lord Torrington wrote to a friend in 1793, boasting that he drank three pints of port and half a pint of brandy every day without doing himself any harm, but eventually could manage nothing but snail tea and soon joined the Lords Panmure, Dufferin and Blayney.

Gin did for the working classes what port did for their social betters. 'Drunk for a penny, dead drunk for two pence,' enticed the gin shops across London, adding, 'clean straw for nothing' – the 18th-century equivalent of the club's chill-out area. For 20 years, at the height of the gin craze, many people drank two or three pints of gin a day, the streets were littered with bodies and thousands chilled out permanently – one in eight deaths were attributed to gin, and the death rate exceeded the birth rate. No wonder the stuff was popularly called 'a kick in the guts' or 'strip-me-naked'. An inept

DRINK | A USER'S GUIDE

> IN 1900 it was calculated that Schuylkill County, Pennsylvania, produced 230,000 barrels of ale, beer and porter, which it consumed, along with 20,000 imported barrels – an average annual consumption of over 47 barrels for every man, woman and child.

> DURING the reign of King William III, a garden fountain was once used as a giant punch bowl into which went 560 gallons of brandy, 544 kilograms (1,200 pounds) of sugar, 25,000 lemons, 20 gallons of lime juice and 2.3 kilograms (5 pounds) of nutmeg. The barman rowed around in a small boat attending to guests.

government failed to sort the situation out – perhaps because there was almost as much drunkenness inside Westminster as without.

Parliamentary drunkenness was nothing new. The first Scottish Parliament at Edinburgh after the Restoration was known as the 'Drunken Parliament'. The historian Gilbert Burnet commented, 'It was a mad, warring time, full of extravagance; and no wonder it was so, when the men of affairs were almost perpetually drunk.' When Queen Anne ruled alone after her husband William's death in 1702, she dismissed Harley, Earl of Oxford, from his post as Lord Treasurer because he was always so pissed she couldn't understand what he said, and whatever the subject, he made it up as he went along.

It was parliamentary business much as usual in the age of the gin epidemic. The Whig Prime Minister, Sir Robert

PRODIGIOUS DRINKING

Walpole, was a drunk, set on the path as a boy by his father who poured him a double portion of wine and told him, 'Come, Robert, you shall drink twice while I drink once, for I will not permit a son of mine in his sober senses to witness his father's intoxication.' The Tory leader Lord Bolingbroke was another – he sat up whole nights drinking and wrapped a wet napkin around his eyes in the morning while he was driven to his official business.

Pitt the Younger (who at his peak daily drank six bottles of port, two of Madeira and one or two of claret – a six-bottle-plus man) carried on the prime ministerial tradition later in the century. He often made speeches when puddled and frequently ducked behind the Speaker's chair to throw up – not that Cornwall, the Speaker, would have noticed: he kept a mug of beer by him which was constantly replenished, and he was usually asleep.

Of Pitt's successors, in the 19th century came Lord

THE bill for the celebration party for the 55 drafters of the American Constitution was for 60 bottles of claret, 54 bottles of Madeira, 22 bottles of port, 8 bottles of whiskey, 12 beers, 8 bottles of hard cider and 7 large bowls of punch.

'IT just shows, what any Member of Parliament will tell you, that if you want real oratory, the preliminary noggin is essential.'

– P.G. Wodehouse

DRINK | A USER'S GUIDE

> THE Palace of Westminster today has 19 bars, where 30,000 pints of beer are drunk a year and the annual spend is £2 million.

Melbourne, a brandy drunk (who was in a stupor throughout Victoria's coronation) who also addressed the House the worse for wear; and, in the 20th century, Herbert Asquith, a wine drinker with no head for it who in 1911 was so drunk he stayed slumped on the front bench during an important debate, unable to rise at all. That was unforgivable. Politicians may talk rubbish but you don't expect them to keep quiet.

Toasts and other excuses

> *Let the toast pass;*
> *Drink to the lass;*
> *I'll warrant she'll prove an excuse for the glass.*
> — *Richard Brinsley Sheridan – the playwright*
> *who got drunk while his theatre burnt down*

When William of Orange was newly enthroned and was entertained by Lord Brooke at Warwick Castle, a cistern containing 120 gallons of punch was drained dry by the company many times, so often did they drink the king's health. Some toasted until they collapsed. Some collapsed in stages, carrying on toasting on their knees.

PRODIGIOUS DRINKING

In the centuries of excess, the toasting was as prodigious as the drinking – there were even toasting clubs where every drink taken was in response to a toast and anything under 30 toasts was a pretty poor evening. In Georgia, to the south of Russia, drinking is still all done in toasts – a graduation ceremony, for example, demands 'a feast of 20 toasts'.

In medieval times, when so much wine had deteriorated by the time it arrived in England, the practice was to drop a piece of toasted bread in the cup to draw the astringency. In the

> WHEN they converted to Christianity, the Vikings stopped toasting their gods – and toasted the saints instead.

> THE best-known drinking song in opera is Sigmund Romberg's from *The Student Prince*: Drink, drink!/ Let the toast start!/ May young hearts never part!/ Drink! Drink! Drink!/ Let every true lover salute his sweetheart!
>
> **Some other operatic tributes to booze:** 'Libiamo ne'lieti calici' (from Verdi's *La Traviata*), 'Vedi! Le fosche notturne' (Anvil Chorus from Verdi's *Il Trovatore*), 'La donna è mobile (from Verdi's *Rigoletto*), 'Inaffia l'ugola! (Iago's drinking song from Verdi's *Otello*), 'Il segreto per esser felice' (from Donezetti's *Lucrezia Borgia*), 'Viva il vino spumeggiante' (from Mascagni's *Cavalleria Rusticana*), 'Champagner hat's verschuldet' (from Johann Strauss's *Die Fledermaus*), 'Votre toast je peux vous le rendre' (Toreador Song from Bizet's *Carmen*), 'Beer's no doubt a gift' (from Smetana's *Bartered Bride*).

DRINK | A USER'S GUIDE

reign of Charles II, a certain beau pledged a noted beauty in a glass of water taken from her bath, whereupon another roisterers cried out that he would have nothing to do with the liquor, but would have the toast (that is, the lady). A term was born.

The toast dates back into unrecorded history. In their turn, Greeks and Romans, Jews and Saxons, raised a libation to their gods, rulers, each other and the outcome of their actions; in every culture the toast was a gesture of good faith or friendship.

The merit of the words that accompanied the toast were their brevity and sometimes their wit, a point lost on the windy 18th and 19th centuries, which turned the toast into a speech – the toasts at the thirteenth reunion of the Army of Tennessee in 1879 were of such length that by the time

---

TIME was when everyone drank from the same vessel – the two-handed loving cup. While the drinker stood to drink, so did a companion called the 'defender', to guard his back against sword or dagger. In his turn, the defender drank, his back guarded by a third companion, and so on. The custom is symbolically observed at Lord Mayor's banquets. When individual goblets became the drinking norm, the practice became to make the toast with the other arm extended to show that there were no concealed weapons.

The reason for the much later clinking of glasses is obscure: the explanation that it symbolised the ringing of the church bell – a warder-off of evil – is hard to believe. The simple suggestion that drinking is a sensory experience and that the clink just added sound to sight, smell and taste seems likely.

PRODIGIOUS DRINKING

> 'THE Americans are a funny lot; they drink whiskey to keep them warm; then they put some ice in it to keep it cool; they put sugar in it to make it sweet; and then they put a slice of lemon in it to make it sour. Then they say "Here's to you" and drink it themselves.'
>
> – B.N. Chakravaty

> ONCE kept waiting by a courtier, Elizabeth I asked where he'd been and was told he'd been drinking her health. 'I always do badly when people are drinking my health,' she said testily. Phyllis Diller was expressing a similar thought when she said: 'Health is what my friends are always drinking before they fall down.'

Mark Twain replied to the fifteenth, it was already 3.30 in the morning.

Now, by and large, the toast is limited to formal occasions and brevity is once again preferred (though you'll be lucky to get through life without attending a do where some fool gets carried away with his own dreadful rhetoric – and, what's more, he'll have it written down). But all those 'chin-chins', 'bottoms up', 'here's mud in your eye' and 'down the hatches' are folksy echoes.

Since the time of Elizabeth I, the royal toast has been a cherished piece of Royal Navy tradition and (since the reign of George III) is unique in being drunk sitting down. As Prince Regent and Lord High Admiral, George cracked his skull against a beam of a ship as he rose to drink his father's health – and swore (probably in more senses than

DRINK | A USER'S GUIDE

> THE royal toast isn't drunk in regimental messes in the Light Infantry, a privilege first conferred on the 32nd as an honour for their defence of Lucknow, and later on the 85th, after some of its officers protected the unpopular George IV from being mobbed by rioters outside the Theatre Royal in Brighton.

> IN Korea the toasting glass is never refilled until it's completely empty, whereas in Japan the glass is constantly refilled so it is never empty. Russians used to smash toasting glasses into the fireplace because to drink from them again was thought to dilute the toast. At Jewish weddings spilling a drop of the toast is considered bad luck.

one) that when he became king, he'd cut out the standing up, and he did.

The royal toast wasn't always loyal – the Jacobites, who wanted the return of Bonnie Prince Charlie, held their glass over a fingerbowl so that their toast was to the 'true' king 'over the water' (in France). The defiance became so blatant at the coronation of George III that fingerbowls were banned at every dinner he attended.

Historically significant as the toast is, it's only an element in humankind's drinking rituals, from christenings to wakes and all stops in between: birthdays, passing an exam, getting a new job, getting engaged, getting married – and, of course, the hen and stag nights proceeding it that invariably find the prospective groom tied to a lamppost without his trousers.

PRODIGIOUS DRINKING

THE ancient Greeks had many drinking games, the most popular of which, *kottabos*, involved hitting a disk with drops of wine. The Romans usually went in for seeing who could down the most without stopping or survive bouts lasting days. Wild Russians liked to stand on the ledges of upper-floor windows while they downed a bottle of spirits (Pierre Bezuhov drinks a bottle of brandy in *War and Peace*), which might be classified not as a game but as an extreme sport.

Some drinking games still follow the Roman model; others are more inventive, all involving the drinking of forfeits for failure to accomplish given tasks – thus ensuring that dedicated players become rat-arsed.

Entire websites are devoted to drinking games – one lists over 360 of them.

Six of the best sites: www.geocities.com/Television City/Set/7200/drinking.htm, www.webtender.com/handbook/games/, www.barmeister.com/games.html, www.barnondrinks.com/games, www.necbeer.com/fun/games, www.angelfire.com/ca/drinking games/

There really is no end to humankind's ingenuity in finding excuses for a piss-up. Let's drink to it.

> *'Here's to us that are here, to you that are there, and the rest of us everywhere.'*
>
> – Rudyard Kipling

World drinking league

Who, today, are the hardest drinkers? The Russians? The Germans? What about the Scots and the Irish?

DRINK | A USER'S GUIDE

When it comes to alcohol abuse, the Russians are out there on their own (booze accounts for 500 deaths per 100,000 people, and 40 per cent of men and 17 per cent of women suffer from alcoholism – World Health Organisation figures); but the Germans are only in danger of relegation from the drinking league, and the Scots and Irish drink less than the English. Australia, New Zealand and the US (like Britain overall) are middle-order abusing nations. The reason why Germany, the US, Ireland and Scotland aren't higher up the league is because all have a high percentage of teetotallers – one in three in Germany compared with one in ten in the UK. Drinking carries great cultural weight in all four countries, of course, which means that those doing the drinking have to do a lot of it to maintain their countries' mid-league positions.

When it comes to alcohol consumption as distinct from alcohol abuse, the story is somewhat different. In the last two health-conscious decades the per capita consumption in most Western European countries, America and Canada has dropped by a quarter or more. In France, it's halved, in Italy it's fallen by a third. Between 1950 and the mid-1980s the UK doubled its consumption, but has remained pretty steady since. France still heads Western Europe at 10.6 litres of pure alcohol per capita, followed by Germany (10.4), Spain (10.1), Italy (8.9) and the UK (7.5). The US comes in slightly ahead of the UK at around 8 litres, which is about 1½ litres ahead of Japan.

But Russia heads the consumption table today, its intake risen threefold since pre-communist days and now around 18 litres of pure alcohol – which translates into 38 litres of

PRODIGIOUS DRINKING

100-proof vodka. Before we get sanctimonious, it's worth noting that in 1984 that was the intake of Luxembourgers, then the big hitters in the world drinking league.

Outside Europe the country with the biggest drink problem is Japan, where consumption has risen fourfold since the war and alcohol-related illness is rife. Accurate figures are difficult to come by because the Japanese find the whole issue so distasteful that they tend to pretend it doesn't exist.

Why abuse and consumption – other than in Russia – don't correlate is culturally based. In countries that qualify as 'Mediterranean', consumption has traditionally been part of everyday life in a way, alien elsewhere, that simply doesn't lead to abuse. In countries like the UK, Australia and the US the drinking is frequently bingeing – and 14 units on a Saturday night just ain't the same as two units a night across seven nights of the week.

✱ A User's Guide — 18

DISASTROUS DRINKING

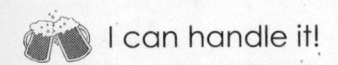

I can handle it!

> *'I drink no more than a sponge.'*
> – *Francis Rabelais*

What's the difference between a drunk and an alcoholic? Dylan Thomas said an alcoholic was somebody you didn't like who drank more than you – which, by definition, would stop a lot of alcoholics being defined as alcoholics.

The alcoholic has to have another drink; the drunk doesn't … necessarily. You might hesitate to use the term 'alcoholic' in relation to Aunt Maude who collapsed after two Christmas ports and lemon, but at the moment she was hauled out of the fireplace she was 'a drunk' (though the indefinite article unfairly suggests a continuing condition, so it would maybe be fairer simply to say she'd been drunk or, more euphemistically, tipsy). In the morning Aunt Maude will reach for the

DISASTROUS DRINKING

Andrews. The alcoholic – who may feel equally awful – will reach for the tipple of the night before.

Of course, the alcoholic was once only an occasional drunk, a social drinker who then moved up a gear to heavy drinking and finally to 'alcohol dependence' – the term preferred these days to what most of us go on thinking of as alcoholism. The downward path is insidious, from drinking for fun, to drinking to get drunk, to drinking to feel 'normal'. 'First the man takes a glass,' runs a Chinese saying, 'then the

---

'IT only takes one drink to get me drunk. The trouble is, I can't remember if it's the thirteenth or fourteenth.'

– George Burns

'I must have a drink by eleven, it's a deed that must be done. If I can't have a drink by eleven, I must have eleven by one.'

– Source unknown

BLOOD ALCOHOL CONCENTRATION
0.03–0.12 per cent: euphoria
0.09–0.25 per cent: excitement
0.18–0.30 per cent: confusion
0.25–040 per cent: stupor
0.35–0.50 per cent: coma
0.45 per cent+: death

glass takes a glass, then the glass takes the man.' In the UK, one in five men and one in ten women are drinking between the 21/14–50/35 demarcation lines that indicate safe levels of drinking, and 1½ million men and ½ million women are drinking beyond them – which is about where the glass takes the man. Or woman.

I can't handle it!

'If the headache would only precede the intoxication,' as Samuel Butler said, 'alcoholism would be a virtue.'

Much research shows that with practice and commitment anyone can become an alcoholic, but some people have a head start.

Drinking problems tend to run in families: 'Drunkards beget drunkards,' Plutarch observed 2,000 years ago. Individuals with an alcoholic father have at least twice the chance of becoming an alcoholic themselves (the general consensus, but Danish research puts the chance at four times). Buster Keaton, Raymond Chandler and Michael Barrymore are cases in point; Charlie Sheen followed dad Martin – both now recovered alcoholics – and Ben Affleck followed dad Tim, who has also put his demons behind him and now works as a substance abuse counsellor. Having two heavy-drinking relatives increases the odds of an individual following in their unsteady footsteps by at least three times.

Studies with identical twins indicate that if one has a drink problem there is a 70 per cent chance that the other will have one too, whereas with non-identical twins the odds drop to

DISASTROUS DRINKING

> A Roman general was known as such a drunk that when he hanged himself after a defeat in 281CE his soldiers jested there hung a tankard, not a man.

> 'OH, Lisa, you and your stories. "Bart is a vampire." "Beer kills brain cells." Now, let's go back to that ... building ... thingee ... where our beds and TV ... is.'
> – Homer Simpson

32 per cent. This isn't conclusive evidence that genes are involved, but scientists are convinced that they are. Understanding of what is and isn't involved is limited, but the recently completed human genome-mapping project will probably advance our knowledge dramatically within the next five years.

Neurophysiological tests with groups of subjects with and without a family history of alcoholism show that at moderate doses of alcohol, where both groups attained equivalent blood alcohol concentrations, those with alcoholic luggage rated themselves significantly less intoxicated. Alcoholics have what scientists term 'stunted' brainwaves. The P3 spike of electrical activity in their brain, which tells the rest of the cerebral nervous system to calm down after a 'surprise' – a bright flash, a sudden noise or, in this context, a drink – is smaller than in other people, and the smaller the spike, the more severe the alcoholism.

A couple of key chemicals are involved. One is dopamine,

DRINK | A USER'S GUIDE

> BINGE drinkers who die have usually had more than 20 drinks in under two hours.

part of the brain's reward circuit, which causes the euphoria that accompanies sex, good food, exercise – and drinking. In alcoholics the alcohol takes over the reward process and the cognitive centre can't override the pleasure centre's demands. This is because alcoholics produce less serotonin, a critical neurotransmitter that controls mood, emotion, learning, memory, sleep and pain – and the message 'enough' doesn't get through.

Some people just don't have a stop light.

Predisposition apart, scientists accept that alcohol dependence is a nature/nurture thing. Anyone who's divorced, poor, unemployed and has no family ties – and who, it goes without saying, is partial to a drop – has the risk factors piled up against them.

Heavy drinkers on the slide into dependence could blame their liver for keeping up with them and aiding and abetting their increased intake and their tolerance to it. Those with a genuine talent for alcohol seem to have a supra-efficient liver: many break down alcohol at twice the rate of moderate drinkers. And they function with as much as 800 milligrams of alcohol – that's 40 standard drinks – in their bloodstream, enough to put most of us on our backs, some perhaps permanently. Until the later stages of their

DISASTROUS DRINKING

addiction, 80 per cent of alcoholics hold down jobs and in most circumstances appear normal (like Henri Paul, Princess Diana's last driver in Paris).

To fool most of the people most of the time, alcoholics need cunning. The English novelist Malcolm Lowry, whose semi-autobiographical novel *Under the Volcano* follows an out-of-control alcoholic into the abyss on the last day of his life, hid bottles up the chimney. Before he pulled back from the edge, Michael J. Fox used to suggest to his wife that they have a bottle of wine, he'd go into the kitchen to open one, quickly polish it off, then return innocently with another. Errol Flynn filled the flower vases in his room with booze and ate oranges on set, for the vitamin C, he said, but really for the vodka that he'd injected into them with a syringe.

AN alcoholic will ultimately drink anything with alcohol in it. It was said of the 18th-century London librarian Richard Porson 'that he drank everything he could lay his hands upon, even embrocation and spirits of wine intended for the lamp'. The playwright Sheridan was known to drink eau de cologne if nothing else was handy; Van Gogh drank whatever he cleaned his brushes in.

If alcoholics are well off, they're not faced with stark choices, other than in extremis. Those who are down and out frequently drink methylated spirits (in the UK nicknamed 'blue' or 'jake') or surgical spirit ('white' or 'surge'), often mixed with cider or lager to make it palatable. Both contain alcohol produced from wood (methyl alcohol) – a poison that's a fast track to oblivion. An estimated 1,000–2,000 alcoholic vagrants sleep on the streets of London.

DRINK | A USER'S GUIDE

> DRUNKS often die from inhalation of vomit – Lowry, sixties rock 'n' wailer Janis Joplin, Jimi Hendrix, Jim Morrison of the Doors.

> HOLLYWOOD'S addiction problem has reached epidemic proportions according to Fireman's Fund, which insures more than half the films shot in the US. A fifth of productions have stars or directors with alcohol (or drug, or both) 'issues'.
>
> But the problem has brought job opportunities – for celebrity babysitters. The entertainment – and sports – industries now advertise for 'sober companions'. They're rather like minders, except they protect the clients from themselves. Most use gentle persuasion, good example and distraction; some are able to dictate who the star can talk to, while others insist that the star joins them in meditation or prayer sessions – or accompanies them to Alcoholics Anonymous. Sometimes it takes three SCs to watch one determined star, each working an eight-hour shift.
>
> A successful sober companion can pull in as much as $5K a week.

Alcoholics have to be inventive. The unnamed star of a recent big-budget Hollywood movie told producers that he'd sorted out his alcohol problem but, despite being under the constant eye of a 'sober companion', still managed to be constantly drunk; he was discovered to be paying a blonde, who everyone took to be his girlfriend, $7,000 a day to bring him booze in Evian water bottles – more vodka. Yet more inventive was country singer Tammy Wynette's husband

DISASTROUS DRINKING

George Jones, who, when she confiscated his car keys, took the lawn mower on a two-mile drive to the nearest bar. More inventive still was the inveterate abuser Ozzy Osbourne, one-time lead singer of the British heavy metallers Black Sabbath. When his wife hid his clothes to stop him going out, he hit LA in her Laura Ashley maternity dress.

'An illness of unknown cause'

The Egyptians, Greeks and Romans warned against the dangers of drunkenness and, as each culture progressed, forgot what they said. The historian Gibbon conjectured that generalised drunkenness was a cause of the collapse of the Roman Empire.

Because it was safer than water, and bucked you up no end, the corollary, as far as the Middle Ages were concerned, was that alcohol was good for you; they were there well ahead of Guinness. The belief was so strongly embedded in Western thought that even in the 19th century the medical profession by and large considered drunkenness to be a vice and a civic rather than a physical problem. Admittedly there was no internet for doctors to surf and pull down the conclusion of earlier practitioners, such as the Persian Muhammad

---

IN the Elizabethan period Sir Walter Raleigh cautioned against too much alcohol, 'for it transformeth a man into a beast, destroyeth natural heat, deformeth the face, rotteneth the teeth, and to conclude, maketh a man contemptible, soon old, and despised'.

DRINK | A USER'S GUIDE

Rhazes, who a full eight centuries before had written 'Great damage is done by wine when it is abused and used regularly to get drunk. Delirium, hemiplegia, paralysis of the voice, croup, sudden death, acute illness, pains in the ligaments, as well as other illnesses that would take too long to list, attack the heavy drinker.' But you might have thought that doctors would have believed the evidence of their own eyes – the hospitals were overflowing with people wrecked by booze and four out of five patients in the new, specialised mental hospitals were there from the same cause.

THE inebriated boulevardier, his nose shedding as much illumination as the lamppost to which he clings, is a stock cartoon figure. Yet 'boozer's nose' is a calumny on 10 million sufferers in the US and over two million in the Britain, mostly men; many of them drink only modestly or not at all. Drink doesn't cause the condition – though, once it appears, it increases enlargement of blood vessels in the skin.

Rosacea is a disorder that typically shows up after the age of 30 (Bill Clinton) and has been known throughout the ages. It can develop into rhinophyma, in which bulbous growths appear on the nose and may extend onto the face. A boozing companion of Nero, a cobbler called Vatinius, had rhinophyma, and a wine glass named after him that became popular had four drinking spouts, each of which was said to match his bulbous hooter. W.C. Fields had the condition, which sometimes caused bleeding through his make-up.

Unconnected to R&R, alcohol often causes the capillaries in the heavy drinker's cheeks to break, resulting in what is known as 'grog blossom', which sounds more attractive than it generally looks.

DISASTROUS DRINKING

But the mainstream medical profession stubbornly maintained that drunkenness was 'an illness of unknown cause'. Eventually, when the evidence to the contrary became overwhelming, doctors blamed everything on distilled drink (spirits) – and exempted beer, cider and wine as being 'hygienic'. It wasn't until World War Two, when France and Germany called up most able-bodied men, examined them and related their physical condition to their drinking habits, that what should have been as plain as a pikestaff had to be faced: spirits might be much stronger, but people who drank 'hygienic' beverages drank an awful lot more of them. Once strength and volume were taken into account, in the final analysis an alcoholic drink was a drink was a drink.

The French for a time were very reluctant to admit this in its entirety. They were prepared to say white wine was more toxic than red, that it lacked red's 'fortifying qualities' – but they wouldn't hear a word against *vin rouge*.

From the late 19th century drunkenness increasingly ceased to be seen as a vice – whose resolution, therefore, was will power – and became an illness. Doctors everywhere rushed to provide a cure. America took a disciplinary approach, creating institutions rather like prisons where the inmates wore clothes 'of such pattern as may be prescribed', subsisted on bread and butter and oatmeal gruel, and had their addiction forcibly treated. Continental Europe wasn't keen on going that route, but Britain followed enthusiastically, Home Department regulations laying down the use of the strait waistcoat for men and handcuffs and ankle straps for women. Some alcoholics never again made it into the outside world.

DRINK | A USER'S GUIDE

> THE Third Reich proposed sterilising alcoholics on the grounds that they were morally degenerate.

Well-heeled drunks everywhere took themselves off to sanatoria with well-stocked libraries, played golf, went on accompanied country walks and ate well, the while submitting themselves to therapies that included electric stimulation, strychnine injections and hot (or cold) baths.

The decline in drinking resulting from the Great War in Europe and Prohibition in America killed off the fervour for institutionalised treatment. It was a drain on the public purse – and fewer and fewer middle-class drunks in the private sector were willing to sign away a year of their life for treatment, which the sanatoria demanded.

Such treatments had not been a roaring success. But this left the way open to medical men everywhere, and they continued the search for the definitive answer with zeal. Psychoanalysis, hypnotism, aversion therapy, oxygen under the skin – they all had advocates. So did the administration of everything from calcium, to adreno-cortical extract, to the patient's own serum laced with alcohol. The American doctor Leslie E. Keeley's worthless patent, The Double Chloride of Gold, sounded so impressive that it launched 118 clinics. One of the daftest 'cures', presented in the sixties by a Dr Shilo, was a bizarrely specific regimen of 231 lemons over 29 days. Quite the most horrific – even including brain surgery and electroconvulsive therapy adminis-

DISASTROUS DRINKING

tered in such large doses that recipients were left completely and sometimes permanently confused – was devised in the late sixties by an American group led by Dr C.H. Farrar. They injected patients with suxamethonium, swiftly gave them a glass of booze before the drug induced total paralysis that also shut down their lungs, and then resuscitated them, with the warning that what they'd experienced was what would happen if they ever drank.

Most alcoholics who wanted to end their addiction wisely kept themselves out of doctors' hands and tried the self-help support offered by organisations like Alcoholics Anonymous.

Help!

> *'Have you heard about the Irishman who joined Alcoholics Anonymous? He still drinks but under a different name.'*
>
> *– Aubrey Dillon-Malone*

Today, anyone who's anyone who has a drink problem goes to Alcoholics Anonymous, though – as the worst of celebrity excesses appear by some inverse law to take place in public – being anonymous for them it isn't. But AA pulls many

---

WOMEN are more likely than men to start drinking heavily in later life. Male drinking patterns are defined early.

celebs through their addiction, just as it does many other alcoholics who do remain anonymous.

Started in the US in the thirties, AA – credo: 'Alcohol – not a disgrace but a disease' – is for anyone with the bottle (sorry) to stand up in front of a bunch of fellow addicts and admit their addiction. With luck, members help each other to stay sober.

AA membership doesn't involve the signing of a lifetime pledge but centres on the idea of being sober 'just for today' – and taking every day one at a time. The organisation doesn't monitor or attempt to constrain anyone's behaviour, nor does it dispense drugs or offer psychiatric treatment, which it leaves to the drying-out clinics. Its 12-step programme is embarrassingly religious for many drinkers – six of the 12 steps mention God – but the first is the most important: the individual's admission of powerlessness over alcohol.

AA's gospel has spread to 150 countries, the worldwide membership is steadily moving towards 2 million and there are nearly 90,000 group meetings a week. The Western country with the fewest AA groups per capita is Portugal, with 0.6 groups per million population; the highest is Iceland with 800 per million – even though Portugal consumes two and a half times as much booze.

'THE difference between a drunk and an alcoholic is that a drunk doesn't have to attend all those meetings.'

– Arthur J. Lewis

DISASTROUS DRINKING

NOT all alcoholics need detoxification, but many do. Clinics wean them off the booze in a planned way – for the badly addicted sudden abstention could cause death (which isn't even true of marijuana). Individual counselling follows, or group therapy, usually in groups of half a dozen or a dozen. An extension includes psycho-drama, in which individuals act out roles relevant to their problems, principally to help them become aware of the gap between their self-image and the way others see them. There are usually physical workouts. Typically, a cleaned-up alcoholic without major problems [sic] can be on the street in 30 days.

In a few severe cases addicts are prescribed disulfiram (Antabuse), a drug that deliberately blocks the ALDH enzyme, preventing the body from breaking down any alcohol imbibed and leading to a build-up of acetaldehyde poisoning. The theory is that the alcoholic will be afraid to drink because of the side effects. Some aren't. A few have died as a result.

According to the World Health Organisation, which has conducted clinical trials around the globe, so-called brief interventions are a successful therapy for many problem drinkers. By a combination of changing some of their drinking to low-level beverages, alternating what they drink with soft drinks, and having a drink-free day, even hard drinkers can cut their intake by up to a third.

MEN with alcohol-related problems outnumber women 10 to 1, but women are three times more likely to seek help.

DRINK | A USER'S GUIDE

> MOST clinics tie into AA's 12-step programme. The Betty Ford Center is the world's most famous institution for the treatment of alcohol dependence. The Smithers Alcoholism Rehab Unit at St Luke's Roosevelt Hospital in New York has a big reputation – novelists John Cheever and Truman Capote both fetched up there. 'The Devil's Island of alcoholic clinics,' Capote called it. Promises, in Malibu, which sorted out Charlie Sheen, Christian Slater and Ben Affleck, and at least tried with Robert Downey Jr, is now highly fashionable. Promises, incidentally, will match a client with a suitable sober companion or sobriety minder, for a fee (check it out on www.promisesmalibu.com).
>
> In the UK, the place for celebrity detox is the £500-a-day Priory, which has treated everyone from the Marquess of Blandford and Caroline Aherne to singer Sinead O'Connor and actress Emily Lloyd.
>
> The Salvation Army operates more rehab centres worldwide than any other organisation, including more than 200 specialised units in English-speaking countries.

Statistically, not all members, anonymous and non-anonymous, are winners in the sobriety stakes, and AA releases no information on success rates – it doesn't keep membership records for a start. But enough voices have sung its praises to indicate that the fellowship offers at least a chance of salvation to people already doing their drinking in the last-chance saloon.

DISASTROUS DRINKING

To drink or not to drink: that is the question

Not drunk is he who from the floor
Can rise alone and still drink more
But drunk is he, who prostrate lies,
Without the power to drink or rise.

– *Thomas Love Peacock*

Must the recovered alcoholic remain TT if he or she wants to stay in the recovery position? It seems a simple question, but to ask it is to walk into the middle of a medical row.

From the early 19th century doctors had no doubt that once an alcoholic always an alcoholic, and the only cure was abstinence – total abstinence. For AA it's an article of faith. But in the early sixties the respected dean of the Institute of Psychiatry at the world-famous Maudsley Hospital in London published a paper claiming that seven out of 93 diagnosed addicts had returned to normal drinking not, as the editor of the *Quarterly Journal of Studies on Alcohol* put it, 'for any ridiculously insignificant 30-day period', but for a minimum of seven years and as many as 11 years.

Since then, the research and more like it that questioned the total abstinence stance has been accused of inadequate

---

'A man is never drunk if he can lie on the floor without holding on.'
– Joe E. Lewis

DRINK | A USER'S GUIDE

protocols, even of falsifying data and recruiting subjects who weren't out-and-out, dyed-in-the-wool alcoholics.

Common sense suggests that an alcoholic isn't likely to be able to return to acceptable social levels of tippling. Many a celebrity has cleaned up his or her act, attended AA ('I am Famous Person [name as appropriate] and I am an alcoholic') and then, after a period of abstention, fallen off the wagon. Charlie Sheen was in and out of rehab for 10 years before seemingly coming good – mind, he added drug addiction and sex addiction to alcohol addiction, so he didn't make his life easy. Yet some prodigious drinkers, after sustained foreswearing of alcohol, appear able to return to it. Buster Keaton was for years a severe drunk who got DTs and was locked up in a sanatorium. After he quit, for the rest of his life he allowed himself one beer every evening, without a problem. Years of dedicated boozing cost Peter O'Toole a large section of his intestines through alcohol-induced pancreatitis and he turned TT. This was in the seventies, but now, though his fractured digestive system keeps him on an invalid's diet, he indulges himself from time to time 'with a drop of red wine, sometimes a little beer' and the odd bottle of champagne.

AN addiction to champagne put the composer Robert Shumann in the nuthouse for a while. The Restoration dramatist Nathaniel Lee drank himself into Bedlam, where he declared: 'They said I was mad: and I said they were mad: damn them, they outvoted me.' When he was better he was let out, but on the same day 'he drank so hard, that he dropped down in the street, and was run over by a coach'.

DISASTROUS DRINKING

> **Some films featuring alcoholics:** *The Lost Weekend, The Bad and the Beautiful, Room at the Top, Who's Afraid of Virginia Woolf?, Abigail's Party, When a Man Loves a Woman, Withnail and I, Days of Wine and Rose, Leaving Las Vegas.*
>
> **Best comic on-screen drunk:** Lee Marvin in *Wandering Star* – or perhaps his horse.
>
> **Films in which alcohol all but plays a supporting role:** *Casablanca* (champagne), *The Big Sleep* (Marlowe incessantly drinking brandy or rye), *The Great Gatsby* (wine and champagne – though Jay Gatsby's fortune comes from bootleg). And there's alcohol in the ultimate feel-good movie, *It's A Wonderful Life* – the drunken bar that would have existed if George hadn't lived, and in which Clarence the angel asks for mulled wine!

And he, too, hasn't fallen back into his old ways (O'Toole's fellow hellraiser, the recently deceased Richard Harris, who walked away from alcohol about the same time, kept away). Were Keaton and O'Toole alcoholics according to the strictest definition? Is being alcohol dependent something that you simply either are or aren't? Perhaps it's not surprising that the 'yes-they-can-no-they-can't' issue remains unresolved.

Recovered alcoholics who find the idea of staying alive more attractive than going for a drink don't go for a drink. But, God, some sometimes *yearn*. 'None of the joys I've had since – like receiving comedy awards or having my own TV show – have matched the white-heat of being drunk,' the comic Frank Skinner says. Skinner, who from the age of 14 until his late twenties began the day by drinking sherry before

DRINK | A USER'S GUIDE

> AN alcoholic who is denied alcohol – which may happen if he or she is hospitalised for some reason – is likely to suffer delirium tremens, the dreaded DTs. As well as physical distress and uncontrollable body movements, the alcoholic, who may already be prey to hallucinations, may see terrifying sights and feel horrible things. The belief that insects are crawling over the skin is common.

> 'I feel sorry for people who don't drink. They wake up in the morning and that's the best they're going to feel all day.'
> – Dean Martin

he got out of bed, still wonders whether alcohol will drag him back, even though the four-day benders – the vomiting, the bed-wetting, the drinking straight from the tap because he couldn't hold a glass, the calls to his doctor because he thought he was dying – are 16 dry years behind him.

Anne Robinson, the winking question mistress of television's *The Weakest Link*, has no truck with alcohol's siren call. She hasn't had a drink for 23 years and only too vividly remembers how hard it was just to wash or brush her teeth – and she had the shakes for 10 years after giving up. Alcoholics Anonymous saved her and she still goes every week, 'because it helps to remind me that I'm only a drink away from being a drunk'.

DISASTROUS DRINKING

Who's doing the abusing – you or it?

Keith Waterhouse's play, *Jeffrey Barnard Is Unwell*, is based on the life of a drunken journalist, once sacked from the tipsters' paper *Sporting Life* for throwing up on the Queen Mother's shoes at Ascot, who wrote a column for the *Spectator* from his bar stool in Soho. The title comes from the tactful line that the magazine used to insert when Barnard was too pissed to deliver. Peter O'Toole played the lead and Barnard liked him – O'Toole could match him drink for drink. Barnard was less taken with Tom Conti, who later played the role – not a big drinker, Conti.

A year or two later Conti was having a meal in Soho and sitting a couple of tables away was an old man with white hair who looked like a skeleton with skin stretched over it. He kept staring at Conti, who didn't realise it was Barnard until he asked someone who it was. Alcohol ages, as Anne Robinson notes. In her autobiography she writes of a terrible moment when her ex-husband and daughter wait for her at a station. They see what they think is an old woman shuffling towards them and it's Anne. Aged 35.

> AMERICAN jazz musician and actor Dexter Gordon was found by film studio doctors to be a diabetic – and to have virtually no liver. And his everyday blood alcohol concentration was eight times higher than the drink-drive limit and should have killed him. Yet Gordon never appeared drunk and had no trouble remembering his lines. He was 67 when he died.

DRINK | A USER'S GUIDE

'IN the 1980s, Graham Mason, who has died aged 59, was the drunkest man in the Coach and Horses, the pub in Soho where, in the half-century after World War Two, a tragicomedy was played out nightly by its regulars.

'His claim to a title in bibulous misbehaviour was staked against stiff competition from Jeffrey Barnard and a dedicated cast of less celebrated but formidable drinkers.

'Mason was a fearsome sight at his most drunkenly irascible. Seated at the bar, his thin shanks wrapped around the legs of a high stool, he would swivel his reptilian stare around behind him to any unfortunate stranger attempting to be served and snap: "Who the f— are you?"

'Sometimes this prompted a reaction, and on one occasion a powerful blow to the head sent Mason flying, with his stool, across the carpet. Painfully clawing himself upright, he set the stood in place, reseated himself and, twisting his head round again, growled: "Don't you ever do that again."

'At lunchtime he would walk through the door of the Coach and Horses still trembling with hangover, his nose and ears blue whatever the weather. On one cold day he complained of the noise that the snow made as it landed on his bald head.

'Unlike his friend Barnard, though, Mason did not make himself the hero of his own tragedy. His speciality was the extreme. In one drinking binge he went for nine days without food. At the height of his consumption, before he was frightened by epileptic fits into cutting back, he was managing two bottles of vodka a day …'

– Obituary notice of the former BBC News and ITN reporter, *Daily Telegraph*, 15 April 2002

DISASTROUS DRINKING

Greater ravages than ageing – physical or mental – await. Two years before his death (in 1994, aged 54), progressive occlusion of the arteries leading to gangrene had cost Barnard a leg – not, by then, that he was very often able to stand on both legs anyway. But it didn't cost him his sense of humour – he placed a personal ad, which read, 'diabetic, alcoholic amputee seeks sympathy fuck'. Novelist Ernest Hemingway's alcohol-induced problems included hypertension, kidney and liver disease, oedema of the ankles, high blood urea, mild diabetes mellitus, recurrent muscle cramps, chronic sleeplessness and paranoia.

Most long-term alcoholics eventually lose their awesome capacity for booze. Where once they seemed to have hollow legs, they now get smashed at the smell of the proverbial

---

ONE in 60 people in the UK is estimated to be an alcoholic, one in 25 is dependent on alcohol to greater or lesser extent (the rate for drug dependence is one in 50). One in four hospital beds in both Britain and the US are occupied by someone with an alcohol-related illness. In the UK in 1994–5, 28,000 hospital admissions were due to alcohol dependence or the toxic effects of alcohol. Between 1996 and 2000, £24 million was spent in the UK on transplants for people suffering from alcohol-related damage.

Alcohol is the fourth leading cause of death among British and American men. Across the EU and the more developed European states it accounts for eight deaths per 100,000. But in a group that includes Russia, Ukraine, Hungary, Latvia, Lithuania and Estonia, the toll is one in three.

DRINK | A USER'S GUIDE

barmaid's apron. And they're suddenly keeling over in the street. What's happened is that, after years of fire-fighting duties, their ultra-efficient liver – which has kept going even when three-quarters of it was destroyed – has thrown in the towel.

Cirrhosis – which carried off at least two bibulous British monarchs (George IV and William IV) and the composer

> MORE from the dark side: in two-thirds of murders, either the victim or the perpetrator has been drinking; three-quarters of non-fatal stabbings are drink-related. Those with a drink problem are calculated to be up to 80 times more likely to kill themselves, and 65 per cent of suicides have been drinking.
>
> Alcohol is a factor in 40 per cent of domestic violence cases and 23 per cent of child neglect calls to national helplines.

> CIRRHOSIS is the end of the line in liver damage terms. The organ has reached the point where it's no longer able to regenerate itself. It may still have pockets of live tissue, but most of it is now fibrous and non-functioning – an alcoholic's liver can have shrunk to one-third of its healthy size and look as hard and knobbly as a tramp's boot. It can no longer process the blood that until now has been passing through it, however sluggishly and inefficiently. And now the blood, which has to make it back to the heart, forces a path through the veins, draining the upper part of the intestine. Unfortunately, the veins, which aren't made for the job, ultimately swell and twist under the strain, causing bleeding and even fatal haemorrhage – which is what took Jack Kerouac off the road permanently.

DISASTROUS DRINKING

Beethoven among many, many others – is incurable. If the alcoholic can stop drinking the liver's function may improve and thereby prolong life expectancy.

Sex, drink – and more physiology

Heavy long-term drinkers, male and female, pay more than a temporary price in terms of their sexuality. The punch-drunk libido finally spends most or even all of its time on the canvas. It happened to Kingsley Amis, who started having therapy but lost interest, just like his libido, because cutting down on alcohol was demanded. Still, he got a novel (*Jake's Thing*) out of it.

Further down the line, things can get worse. Female abusers lose the inability to achieve orgasm and ultimately their external genitalia shrivel; they also suffer menstrual and hormonal problems. Male abusers suffer testicular atrophy and shrinkage of the penis. Females may develop male characteristics but males may develop female ones and these can be more pronounced, including a rounding of body shape and gynaecomastia – enlargement of the breasts. This occurs because the Leydig cells in the testes, under alcoholic assault, produce less and less male-defining testosterone and the damaged liver can't metabolise the predominantly female hormone, oestrogen, which circulates naturally. High blood-alcohol levels also damage the boozer's semeniferous tubes so that his sperm count plummets, and his remaining sperm show abnormalities, reduced motility (they're just not enthusiastic swimmers any more) and a loss

DRINK | A USER'S GUIDE

of sense of direction. Alcohol has made the sperm lose the will to live – or more accurately, fight for it.

According to a text on sexual debility, 'a chronic alcoholic is eight times out of 10, sexually speaking, a eunuch'. There are exceptions, as in everything else. Errol Flynn continued boozing and bedding with bravura to the last. The autopsy

---

YOU DON'T HAVE A PROBLEM ... DO YOU?

Agree or disagree with the following statements:

1. The bottle says 20 standard drinks but you only manage to get five out of it.

2. When there's no booze in the house you try the empties, just in case.

3. You go to the loo to be sick – and take your drink with you.

4. You can't remember what you drink but it doesn't matter – you always have what's above the second optic from the left.

Now answer these serious questions:

1. Have you ever thought you ought to cut down on your drinking?

2. Have people annoyed you by criticising your drinking?

3. Have you ever felt guilty about your drinking?

4. Have you ever had a drink first thing in the morning to steady your nerves or get rid of a hangover?

These four questions are used in screening interviews for alcohol dependence. Yes to two or more and you've got a problem.

DISASTROUS DRINKING

> ACCIDENT and emergency departments in a number of UK hospitals now ask arrivals who they think might be alcohol abusers – those who've fallen, tripped or collapsed; those who have head or facial injuries; and those who have non-specific stomach problems, chest pains or psychiatric symptoms – a series of questions designed to find out their alcohol consumption. If it's more than eight units a day for a man or six for a woman, once or more a week, they're referred to a specialist alcohol worker.

said he had the organs of an 80-year-old man and he was only 49; and, no, the report didn't specify that.

According to research, six units a day every day is enough to set the ball rolling.

Or perhaps that's atrophying.

How much alcohol over and above the recommended levels drives the individual drinker into the downward spiral? Who knows? Beyond the recommended levels you're drinking in the twilight zone.

'Long quaffing maketh a short lyfe,' the 16th-century English dramatist John Lyly wrote. Modern medical interventions often pull disintegrating alcoholics back from the brink (of snuffing, not of drinking) so that they can go on drinking a while longer. Some alcoholics achieve a normal lifespan against the odds. The forties are still often the time of last orders (down-and-out drinkers die on average at the age of 42). William Pitt the Younger, hard-drinking twice British Prime Minister between 1783 and 1806, was dispatched from the dispatch box at the age of 46. Rabbie Burns died at

DRINK | A USER'S GUIDE

> 'I'M told I'm slowly killing myself. That's okay, I'm in no hurry.'
> – Robert Benchley

> 'I can manage on one liver.'
> – Homer Simpson

37 of alcohol poisoning, which also did for the Welsh poet Dylan Thomas at the age of 39, though the autopsy report called it 'insult to the brain'. He ended his life in a New York bar, on his knees, telling some unknown young woman: 'I have just drunk 19 straight whiskies. I think that's the record. I love you.'

The average timescale on which the drinker is shunted from social drunk to alcoholic to (literally) dead drunk is 10 years. Some manage to put it off for 25; others make it in five.

It's your call. *Call*. Not shout.

The good news for 90 per cent of alcoholics who haven't yet developed cirrhosis is that, remarkable organ that it is, the liver will recover – within as little as three weeks of abstinence.

A User's Guide 19

FAMOUS DRINKERS

'Women, Protestant pastors and Jews do not get drunk.'

– Immanuel Kant

The first drunk was Noah, who planted a vineyard after the Flood and, the Old Testament tells us, 'got drunk'. Were his young vines quick-growing because they were enriched by what he had to shovel out of the ark?

Drunkards lurch across the pages of history ancient and modern, rulers and leaders, artists, composers and writers, sportsmen and celebrities, all helped along the path to alcohol abuse, not just by predisposition but by power or status, and stress, the great alcoholic catalyst.

Often, celebrities are also impelled not just by sheer indulgence but also by the fear of waking up one morning and finding that their public sees *them*, not their manufactured persona (though for modern celebrities 'line them up' is more

DRINK | A USER'S GUIDE

> IF the lovable Dick ('Hello, Mary Poppins') Van Dyke and the astronaut Buzz Aldrin, a modern-day superhero, can become alcoholics, anyone can.
>
> You could fill a book with celebrity and known-names drunks. Sample (leaving out names mentioned elsewhere): John Barrymore, Dean Martin, Laurence Harvey – and the English traitors Burgess, Maclean, Philby and Blunt. Sample: Edith Piaf, Mary Pickford, Judy Garland, Joan Crawford, Tallulah Bankhead, Rita Hayworth, Isadora Duncan.

> STUDY after study shows that sportsmen are more likely than those who don't play sports to become binge drinkers. Like sports, drinking involves risk-taking and the desire to push at boundaries, psychologists say.
>
> One of the most colourful drunks in any sport came from a relatively sedate game, cricket, in the shape of the Yorkshire slow left-arm bowler Bobby Peel, who played for England between 1884 and 1896. Regularly bowled over by drink during matches, he was once suspended by his county captain, Lord Hawke, for 'bowling at the pavilion in the belief that it was the batsmen'. He was finally sacked – while batting with Hawke he peed on the pitch.

likely to mean little white lines than a row of glasses). Sportsmen, who enjoy the camaraderie of a drink in victory or defeat, find it all too easy to replicate their addiction to training in their drinking; and 'creatives' (to use an advertising industry coinage) often get addicted because alcohol so

FAMOUS DRINKERS

magically sparks their creativity (and so tragically becomes indistinguishable from it).

Inebriated rulers and leaders

Dionysius the Younger, tyrant of Sicily, has been called the worst drunkard of all time – his binges sometimes went on for six months. But there are many claimants to the crown, none better than Alexander the Great.

Alexander may have been the golden hero of myth when he was sober, but he wasn't during his frequent marathon drinking sessions. During one, he burnt the Persian capital of Persepolis on a drunken whim; during another, he killed one of his best friends with a spear. Those around him stayed nervous until he lapsed into unconsciousness, a state in which he could remain for days.

He died, at the age of 32, as a result of a fearsome drinking competition with an adversary called Proteas. Alexander called for a two-*chous* (around 6.8 litres/12 pints) cup of wine and drank his health. Proteas took the cup, polished it off – and called for a refill. Alexander tried to meet the challenge, couldn't make it and fell back on his cushion.

> POPE Benedict XII (1334–42) drank so much that the expression 'drunk as a pope' was popular in his lifetime.

DRINK | A USER'S GUIDE

Every country has had its share of alcoholic monarchs. The English had Henry VIII (a golden hero in his youth who became a bitter drunk as his health and his love life deteriorated), William IV and, before him, George IV, a lush from his youth, who found it necessary (if also fairly easy) to get blind drunk on his wedding night to be able to face sleeping with the obese and sweaty Caroline of Brunswick.

The hard-drinking Russians have had appropriately hard-drinking heads of state, including Peter the Great, Ivan the Terrible and the Empress Catherine, who was so shot-away during an assassination attempt that she didn't even know she'd been fired at. With communism came Josef Stalin, a solitary drinker who, when asked why he sent comrade Leon Trotsky into Siberian exile, snarled: 'He drank the wrong kind of whisky.' The whisky Stalin drank was the best – single malt – as were the Napoleonic brandies and the vintage capitalist wines. Often he was carried to bed, beating his servants with a walking stick and accusing them of stealing his liquor. After communism came Boris Yeltsin, who, once tanked up on vodka, danced (sort of) with pretty girls, tottered off podiums, fell down aircraft steps and on one occasion was so drunk he

---

EDWARD Mutesa II was the *kabaka* or king of the ancient kingdom of Buganda. When Uganda was formed in 1962 and the kingdom became part of it, 'King Freddie', as he was known, became the country's first president. A party animal, King Freddie was ousted by Idi Amin and fled to England. He died from acute alcohol poisoning (coroner's report) in a Bermondsey council flat in 1969.

FAMOUS DRINKERS

> THREE of those who've occupied the White House have been drunks: Franklin Pierce (called 'the hero of many a well-fought bottle'), Andrew Johnson and Ulysses S. Grant. Lyndon Johnson and Trickie Dickie Nixon were, shall we say, heavy drinkers.

couldn't get out of the bed on his jet, with the Irish president waiting on the tarmac.

If Stalin was an alcoholic, and Franklin Roosevelt wasn't – though he liked martinis and on occasion liked them so much he had to be carried to bed, like Stalin – there's debate about whether the third of the triumvirate of Allied leaders in World War Two, Winston Churchill, was or wasn't.

He certainly liked to drink. As a young man, when he went to cover the Boer War for the *Morning Post*, he took 36 bottles of wine, 18 bottles of 10-year-old Scotch and six bottles of vintage brandy to the front line. Throughout his long life he had a glass of whisky always by him, drank a bottle of champagne at lunch and often another at dinner, 'and buckets of claret and soda in between'. He was also known to knock off a quart of brandy of an evening and was fond of gin. And martinis, very dry – it has been said that the martini named after him is made by looking across the room at a bottle of vermouth while pouring gin.

But Churchill didn't nurse a bottle like an alcoholic, and his serious drinking was mostly done at meals, making the effects less deleterious than would otherwise have been the case; well into his eighties his blood pressure was an enviable 140 over 80. No one ever reliably saw him the worse for

DRINK | A USER'S GUIDE

wear, not even Labour MP Bessie Braddock, who once said to him, 'Winston, you're horribly drunk' and got the famous riposte, 'Bessie, you're horribly ugly, but I shall be sober in the morning.'

Churchill was without doubt a formidable user. But an alcoholic? 'No alcoholic could drink that much,' said Professor Warren Kimball of Rutgers, who edited the Winnie

---

CHURCHILL has provided almost as many quotes about drink as W.C. Fields. A selection:

'Remember, gentlemen, it's not just France we are fighting for, it's champagne!' – Said during World War One.

'I am easily satisfied with the best.' – Said of his favourite champagne, Pol Roger; he gave the name to his race horse.

'When I drink from a bottle I'm happy. When I drank from a half-bottle I'm not happy but Clementine [his wife] is happy. To make us both happy, I will drink imperial pints.' He didn't, much.

'I must point out that my rule of life prescribed as an absolutely sacred rite: smoking cigars and also the drinking of alcohol before, after, and if need be during all meals and in the intervals between them.' – Said during a lunch with the Arab leader Ibn Saud, when he heard that the king's religion forbade tobacco and alcohol.

'During the war I consumed German wine but I excused myself that I was not drinking it but interning it.' – Said after World War Two.

'I have taken more out of alcohol than alcohol has taken out of me.' Which may say it all.

FAMOUS DRINKERS

C and Franklin D correspondence and who, like most historians, has rejected the idea. Others aren't so sure. Churchill's drinking, to use a phrase he applied to Russia during the war, remains a riddle, wrapped in a mystery, inside an enigma.

For the record: Hitler was teetotal.

Writers: the drinking prize

A number of artists – Van Gogh, Toulouse-Lautrec, Utrillo and the paint-spattering Jackson Pollock, who finally spattered his car around a tree – have hit the bottle. So, too, have composers – Beethoven, Mussorgsky – and at least one lyricist – the dwarfish Lorenz Hart, the small half of Rodgers and Hart before alcohol killed his talent (and soon after, him) and Rodgers became half of Rodgers and Hammerstein. But writers have made boozing almost de rigueur.

Many people have tried and failed to make a living out of drinking, but writers have come closest. According to a 15-year study carried out by Nancy Andreasen, a professor of psychiatry at the University of Iowa, 30 per cent of well-known writers are alcoholics, compared with 7 per cent of the general population.

Poets tend to be intense drunkards – something, no doubt, to do with the intensity of the poetic form – so much so that one of their number, John Berryman, said that Randall Jarrell was the only poet he knew who never drank.

Gore Vidal once said that teaching had ruined more American writers than alcohol, which is funny, because so many American writers give creative writing classes, but

DRINK | A USER'S GUIDE

> **Novels featuring alcoholics:** *The Tenant of Wildfell Hall*, Anne Brontë; *The Ginger Man*, J.P. Donleavy; *Under the Volcano*, Malcolm Lowry; *Ironweed*, William Kennedy; *Brideshead Revisited*, Evelyn Waugh; *The Honorary Consul*, Graham Greene; *Post Office*, Charles Bukowski; *The Lost Weekend*, Charles Jackson; *The Disenchanted*, Budd Schulberg; *Hangover Square*, Patrick Hamilton; *Here's Luck*, Lennie Lowers; *A Fan's Notes*, Frederick Exley; *A Disaffection* and *How Late It Is, How Late*, James Kelman; *Age of Iron*, J.M. Coetzee.
>
> **Non-fiction featuring alcoholics:** *The Grass Arena*, John Healy; *Ham on Rye*, Charles Bukowski; *Blessed*, George Best.

untrue. When it comes to ruining writers' lives and, in the final analysis, diminishing their talent, alcohol has no equal.

Of the seven Americans who've won the Nobel Prize for literature, four – novelists Sinclair Lewis, William Faulkner and Ernest Hemingway, and dramatist Eugene O'Neill – were all alcoholics, and a fifth, John Steinbeck, probably was too.

Without looking for shades of differences between alcoholic, heavy drinker and binger, other abusing American wordsmiths – from a long, long list – include Edgar Allan Poe, Herman Melville, Jack London, Jack Kerouac, Scott Fitzgerald, Stephan Crane, John O'Hara, O. Henry, Tennessee Williams, Raymond Chandler, Dashiell Hammett, Sherwood Anderson, Truman Capote, Charles Bukowski, Robert Lowell, Dorothy Parker, John Cleever, John Carver, Terry Southern and Stephen King – who knew he had a problem when he was getting through 'a case of 16-ounce tall-

FAMOUS DRINKERS

boys a night' (6.8 litres/12 pints) and turned out the blockbuster *Cujo* that he 'barely remembered writing'.

Ireland has produced its share of literary boozers, given the size of the place (and ignoring those sitting at scores of bars, talking about writing the great Irish novel but too busy boozing to try). James Joyce is the most famous of them – a fall-down drunk of whom a friend nevertheless said, 'Joyce gets drunk in the legs, but not in the head.' Most boisterous is Brendan Behan, who (like Welsh poet Dylan Thomas) turned his alcoholism into a kind of music-hall act ('When I arrived in Canada I saw a sign, "Drink Canada Dry", so I've started'); he once killed a horse by getting it drunk. Among English literary boozers – Thomas Hardy, Evelyn Waugh, Anthony Burgess, Kingsley Amis, to name a few – Malcolm Lowry is the one who possibly matches Behan as a roaring boyo. Peter Ackroyd is currently England's most colourful drinking author. A man who can imbibe with the passion that

---

FRENCH brandy and brandy liqueur were William Faulkner's tipples, rather than the local corn mash whiskey. He dedicated *As I Lay Dying* to 'Dr Cointreau, the translator'.

UPTON Sinclair, author of scores of novels, was a rabid teetotaller. In the fifties he wrote *The Cup of Fury*, listing all the authors he'd known who had a drink problem ('never has anybody gotten so blind drunk as Sinclair Lewis') to warn young people against the evils of alcohol.

DRINK | A USER'S GUIDE

he writes – four preprandial Scotches followed by two bottles of wine washed down with a brandy, a lunchtime interviewer typically reports – he finished his biography of London, had a heart attack, and is said to be in constant negotiation with his physicians about how much they'll let him have.

Writers live and work inside their heads. They work alone. They make their own hours. Blankly facing a blank page, or the word processor's winking cursor ('ready when you are'), writers may need a drink and take it, and they're mostly the worst of kind of drinker – the solitary drinker.

Not that, at first, most do it while they write, and some keep drinking and writing apart even when they're fully signed up to alcohol dependence – Kingsley Amis's study was almost as full of empties as books but, as his second wife Elizabeth Jane Howard noted, he never drank until he finished work (and, in the beginning, at least, he did try to be helpful domestically – when they moved house, while she packed and carted the boxes, he polished off the half-empty bottles in the cabinet to save her extra effort). Jack London refused to touch a drop until he'd done his thousand words for the day, when he allowed himself 'a pleasant jingle'. Then he had another 'jingle' after dinner. Finally, though, he drank in order to be able to write at all. Jean Stafford, the respected novelist once married to poet Robert Lowell, in the beginning sipped sherry as she wrote and at the finish binged through treatment, a heart attack and a stroke, 'barely able to draw a sober breath' and unable to finish a book she had been working on for 20 years. Hemingway drank and wrote, a few beers at first but then the kind of consumption he transcribed

FAMOUS DRINKERS

> 'THE story goes that I first had the idea for THHGTTG while lying drunk in a field in Innsbruck.'
>
> – Douglas Adams, author of *The Hitch-Hiker's Guide to the Galaxy*

to the characters in his novels – Jack Barnes and Brett Ashley in *The Sun Also Rises* put away three martinis before lunch and five or six bottles of red wine during it. After he was told to cut down on his boozing, Hemingway tried to hold himself to three whiskies before dinner, but he couldn't do it and soon was lacing his tea with gin at breakfast and swigging throughout the day.

The *British Journal of Addiction* concluded that drunken authors turn out their best work when they're sober, which is hardly a surprise. Some take the cure and leave the bottle alone: Cheever, Carver, Walter Travis – who might not be regarded as one of the greats (he wrote *The Hustler* and *The Man Who Fell to Earth*) and who suffered a 17-year gap between books because of booze. Some alcoholic writers quickly succumb to their excesses, leaving their literary reputation untarnished. Some, like Behan, go on, their stuff getting less and less good to the bitter end. 'I'm not a writer with drinking problems,' he joked, 'I'm a drinker with writing problems.' A few, who couldn't take it any more, ended it: London, with an overdose of morphine, Hemingway with a bullet in the brain. Hart Crane jumped off a cruise ship into the Caribbean, preferring that kind of drink to get him than the other.

There don't appear to be famous alcoholic scientists. Alcohol interferes with logical thinking.

DRINK | A USER'S GUIDE

Alcoholic career openings

If you don't have a literary talent but are attracted to a job offering alcoholic perks, consider hotels and catering, the shipping industry, or the military, all with opportunities for above-average mortality from cirrhosis. It's the access to cheap or free booze, of course, as well as often-lengthy periods of 'downtime' in which there's little else to do but drink. The two jobs that have more alcoholics than any other are radio officer and catering supervisor.

Other high-risk occupations include those involving a lot of socialising or unsocial hours and those in which, like writing, you work unsupervised. Particularly at risk are journalists, senior businessmen (expenses/business accounts) – and doctors. According to the BMA, one in 12 doctors abuses alcohol and/or other drugs.

I don't mind if I do ...

What the famous drink is often stated in such a way as to suggest that they drank nothing else. Queen Victoria's favourite tipple was said to be malt whisky mixed with claret, but she liked champagne too, and port. Princess Margaret's favourite was said to be Old Grouse whisky, but she drank a great many other drinks, including martinis (her party trick was to name the brands of vodka in them). Charles de Gaulle's favourite drink was said to be brandy, but he got the taste for gin while he was in exile in England (though he tried never to talk about it).

FAMOUS DRINKERS

> THE celebrated British artist Francis Bacon was fond of champagne, which he consumed at his favourite boho Soho drinking club and at the Colony Room. His favourite saying was, 'Champagne for my real friend and real pain for my sham friends.'

The point is, almost everyone likes different drinks at different times in different circumstances – and the drink drunk very occasionally may give more pleasure than the 'favourite' tipple. And people have different tastes at different times of their life. Had James Joyce and Ernest Hemingway died early, they would both have gone down as beer drinkers (Hemingway was partial to Tusker lager when big-game hunting in Kenya; he also appeared in an ad for Balantine Ale), but the middle-aged Joyce's favourite was white wine (Swiss Fendant) and the middle-aged Hemingway's was whatever was left in the last unemptied bottle.

Anyone – if there has been anyone – who stuck to one drink all his or her life might reasonably be accused of a lack of imagination. That couldn't be said of the Queen Mum. Was gin her favourite tipple? It was often reputed to be. But she was more than partial to a triple Dubonnet and gin splash, and to German Blue Nun – she got through a case of that a fortnight.

Whatever she drank, she evidently thought it was good for her, and as she made it to a year beyond the century, that can't be gainsaid. Let's, in this instance, not raise the issue of moderation.

✱ A User's Guide 20

IT'S GOOD FOR YOU, HONEST!

'If you resolve to give up smoking, drinking and loving, you don't actually live longer; it just seems longer.'
– Clement Freud

Alcohol has probably given humankind more pleasure than anything except sex. Alcohol has probably given humankind more pain than anything except sex.

If a jaundiced view about alcohol might indicate that cans and bottles should carry government health warnings like cigarettes, it's important to emphasise: alcohol is good for you. ALCOHOL IS GOOD FOR YOU – for further emphasis.

In moderation, that is. IN MODERATION – and perhaps that message should be in even bigger letters.

According to research, any kind of alcohol at or below the recommended male–female 3/2 unit level:

IT'S GOOD FOR YOU, HONEST!

- has a significant protective effect on the heart, strengthening coronary arteries and reducing fatal heart disease by at least 40 per cent compared with non-drinkers;

- prevents strokes;

- reduces the likelihood of late-onset diabetes;

- cuts the risk of gall-bladder problems;

- improves sperm count; and

- boosts cognitive functioning, especially among the elderly.

Wine is the beneficial beverage par excellence. It has always rightly been regarded as an aid to digestion (in fact, it helps the production and flow of gastric juices that break down food in the stomach – and recent research shows that it kills salmonella, shigella and e-coli, the causes of food poisoning). But red wine offers even more protection that white, having more flavonoids – the antioxidant compounds that combat free radicals, which cause cell damage and orchestrate the ageing process. The French diet is high in saturated fat and yet France has the lowest rate of coronary disease of any developed country other than Japan, thanks, it's believed, to red wine. Recent research published in the *British Journal of Cancer* promotes red wine as a defence against cancer (one of its molecules is converted by an enzyme in the body into an anti-cancer agent). This has been

DRINK | A USER'S GUIDE

augmented by even newer research carried out in Spain, which shows that the antioxidant polyphenols in red wine inhibit the growth of prostate cancer cells – by encouraging them to 'commit suicide' by a process known as apoptosis.

Yet another Spanish trial found that people who drank 14 glasses of red wine a week had 40 per cent fewer colds than those who drank none. White wine was half as effective – beer and spirits had no benefit.

Beer, however, has only belatedly entered the good-for-you camp. A study conducted in the Australian town of Dubbo among 2,805 men and women found that men who drank 21 glasses a week had a 60 per cent lower risk of death than non-drinkers, as had women who drank up to 14 glasses. A study of the drinking habits of 87,000 nurses, published in the *New England Journal of Medicine*, found that beer reduced the risk of heart attack and brain thrombosis by 50 per cent. Further research in Holland indicates that the vitamin B6 in beer prevents the build-up in the body of the dangerous chemical homocysteine.

Six years ago the World Health Organisation concluded that even one alcoholic drink every second day was an aid to

---

HEALTH concerns have fuelled an extraordinary wine boom in Japan, where consumption has trebled, making the country the largest export market by value for wines from both Bordeaux and California.

One French producer claims that the Japanese ambassador has told him that salarymen are 'drinking a glass of claret at breakfast, along with their vitamin pills'.

IT'S GOOD FOR YOU, HONEST!

> ACCORDING to a new study on female alcohol use and blood pressure, young women who consume two or three alcoholic drinks a week are much more fun to do research on than women who do not consume alcohol.
>
> The report, published in the Archives of Internal Medicine, studied patterns among 70,000 nurses between the ages of 25 and 42. Dr Eric Shinauer, who headed the study for Harvard's School of Public Health, put the findings in perspective. 'Alcohol, 70,000 nurses and us,' he said. 'Is that cool or what?'
>
> Shinauer and his colleagues conceded that their initial grant was to study salt consumption. However, upon reflection, they decided that adjusting the parameters would dramatically heighten their interest in the research.
>
> One of Dr Shinauer's colleagues, Dr Chandra Palava, bristled at the suggestion that researchers should also study the effect of alcohol on young men. 'Jesus, we're not gay,' he said.
>
> – SatireWire.com

good health, giving an increase in HDL cholesterol – the good cholesterol. Subsequently, several studies suggested that the benefits of moderate drinking only kicked in for men once they were over 40 and for women once they were past the menopause, and the anti-drinking lobby made as much as it could of this. More recent findings suggests that there are advantages for much younger people; one study found that young women who drink two or three units of alcohol a week have a lower risk of developing high blood pressure.

DRINK | A USER'S GUIDE

> THE US National Institute of Health funded one study on alcohol use – and then refused to publish the findings because they were 'socially undesirable'. The study concluded that moderate drinkers are less likely than non-drinkers to suffer heart disease. The US Bureau of Alcohol, Tobacco and Firearms – a department whose very name seems to equate guns and drink as public dangers – acts as the nation's policeman to ensure that no evidence of alcoholic health benefits is published, and it bans the word 'refreshing' from any description of alcoholic beverages. California may be one of the world's big wine producers but it can't advertise to sell its products.
>
> The respected American Council on Science and Health has backed moderate consumption and has urged policy makers to take this into consideration when they evaluate regulatory and educational approaches to drink.

Curiously, official medical opinion in the US refuses to recognise that alcohol can have any health advantages, despite the plethora of worldwide findings including those of its own researchers. Obsessive about lowering cholesterol levels, which are associated with coronary artery disease, the US medical profession may be, but it won't allow that alcohol might have a part to play in this – though the evidence for it is more conclusive than for the most potent cholesterol-reducing medications. America is scared of opening the door to alcohol abuse – a hangover (so to speak) from its Prohibition mentality.

Hard-drinking Americans drink like hard drinkers everywhere, but in a country where ordering a glass of wine with lunch can cause a lull in conversation and your companion to

IT'S GOOD FOR YOU, HONEST!

slip you an Alcoholics Anonymous card under the table, far more Americans drink less than is healthy – at least as drink and health are equated outside the American medical establishment – than drink so much that it is harmful. The Bible Belt, where less alcohol is drunk than anywhere else in the US, is referred to by many doctors as 'Stroke Alley'.

As long ago as 1826, the first life assurance company was set up to deal solely with non-drinkers, offering lower premiums on the assumption that non-drinkers were healthier. That's now accepted not to be the case. Moderate drinkers are the healthy ones – and they live on average 15 years longer.

✳ A User's Guide

AFTERWORD

A Thought For the Road

Face it: people drink. They may drink less than at any time in the last 300 years – the three-martini lunch in America and the two-carafe one in Britain are no longer everyday occurrences and corporate shindigs (the office party excepted) are now more likely to serve up juice and bottled water than alcohol.

But people drink.

Archaeological and documentary evidence shows that individually and collectively booze meets a deep-seated need in a way that nothing else comes near. Humankind seems to be hotwired to drink – 'Man, being reasonable, must get drunk; the best of life is but intoxication,' Lord Byron wrote. There's even research to suggest that humankind has a predisposition to getting hammered, at least occasionally. And getting hammered occasionally is almost as universal an experience as drinking.

Moralists, ministers (temporal and religious), medical practitioners and mirth-makers will never let the drinker

AFTERWORD

'IF you mean whiskey, the devil's brew, the poison scourge, the blood monster that defiles innocence, dethrones reason, destroys the home, creates misery and poverty, yea, literally takes the bread from the mouths of little children; if you mean that evil drink that topples Christian men and women from the pinnacles of righteous and gracious living into the bottomless pits of degradation, shame, despair, helplessness, and hopelessness, then, my friend, I am opposed to it with every fiber of my being.

'However, if by whiskey you mean the oil of conversation, the philosophic wine, the elixir of life, the ale that is consumed when good fellows get together, that puts a song in their hearts and the warm glow of contentment in their eyes; if you mean Christmas cheer, the stimulating sip that puts a little spring in the step of an elderly gentleman on a frosty morning; if you mean that drink that enables man to magnify his joy, and to forget life's great tragedies and heartbreaks and sorrow; if you mean that drink the sale of which pours into our treasuries untold millions of dollars each year, that provides tender care for our little crippled children, our blind, our deaf, our dumb, our pitifully aged and infirm, to build the finest highways, hospitals, universities, and community colleges in this nation, then my friend, I am absolutely, unequivocally in favor of it.

'This is my position, and as always, I refuse to be compromised on matters of principle.'

– Noah S. 'Soggy' Sweat, Jr

stray far from their cross hairs. It's a fact of life. Raise a glass to them all. Raise a glass to whomever and whatever you like. But remember that health is what we most commonly drink to and while alcohol punctuates life from cradle to

DRINK | A USER'S GUIDE

> THE horse and mule live thirty years
> And never know of wine and beers.
> The goat and sheep at twenty die
> Without a taste of Scotch or rye.
> The cow drinks water by the ton
> And at eighteen is mostly done.
> The dog at fifteen cashes in
> Without the aid of rum or gin.
> The modest, sober, bone-dry hen
> Lays eggs for noggs and dies at ten.
> But sinful, ginful, rum-soaked men
> Survive three-score years and ten.
> And some of us, though mighty few
> Stay pickled 'til we're ninety-two
>
> – Charles Duffy

grave, you don't want to bring the two together more quickly than needs be.

Good health! • A votre santé! • Alla tua salute!
Banza!i • Egeszsegedre! • Gan bei!
Iechyd da i chivri! • I sveikata! • Kan pei!
Kwa afya yako! • L'chaim! • Na zdrowie!
Op je gezonheid! • Prosit! • Santé!
Salud! • Skål! • Slainthe is saol agat!
Stin ygia sou! • Terveydeksi! • Viva!
Yam sing! • Za vashe z-dorovye! • Ziveli!

INDEX

1st King's Own Scottish Borderers 151–2

A

absenteeism 148
absinthe 25, 108–11
abstinence 255–6
accident and emergency departments 265
accident-proneness 166
Ackroyd, Peter 275–6
Adams, Douglas 277
Adams, John 99
Addison, Joseph 137–8
advertising 31, 52, 54–5
Aeschylus 144
Affleck, Ben 242, 254
Affleck, Tim 242
Aga Khan III 207
agave 112–13
age limits, and drinking 182–3
aggressive behaviour 147–50, 152–5, 262
Aherne, Caroline 254
airlines 152–5, 159, 162
  air rage 152–5
Albert, Prince 124, 139
alcohol dehydrogenase (ADH) 5, 7

alcohol dependence 241, 261, 264
Alcohol Ignition Interlock 173
Alcoholics Anonymous (AA) 246, 251–4, 256, 258
alcoholism 240–66
  famous drinkers 267–79
  prevalence 261
  ravages of 259–63
  reformed alcoholics 255–8
  sex and 263–6
  therapy 249–54
alcopops 124
aldehyde dehydrogenase (ALDH) 5, 253
aldehyde dehydrogenase (ALDH) gene 8
Aldolphus, Gustavus 56
Aldrin, Buzz 268
ale 39–40, 43, 44
alehouses 125–7, 129, 136–8
Alexander the Great 269
Alfred, Duke of Edinburgh 14
Allah 206
Allen, Woody 4, 31
ambivalent/dry/temperance countries 147, 148–50
American Airlines 159

American Bar, The, The Savoy, London 143
American Council on Science and Health 284
American War of Independence 138
Americano 122
Amis, Kingsley 3, 263, 275, 276
analgesia 27
Andreasen, Nancy 273
Anheuser-Busch 42, 54, 112, 200–1
animal drunkards ix–x, 146
Animal Farm (Orwell) 202
Anne, Queen of England 230
anti-drinking propaganda 192–3, 195–6
 see also prohibition; temperance movement
antioxidants 281–2
antiseptic properties of alcohol 27
aphrodisiacs 157
aqua vitae/eau de vie 24
Aquinas, St Thomas 189
Aristophanes 2, 126
armagnac 88, 89–90
Arnold, Tom 121
Asahi 55
Asquith, Herbert 232

B

B&B 117
Babinski, Henri 225–6
Babycham 176
Bach, J.S. 56
Bacon, Francis 279
Baileys 176
barley 41
Barnard, Jeffrey 259, 260, 261
Barnes, Larry 191
Barrumundi wine brand 176
Barry, Dave 18, 57
Barrymore, John 131
Barrymore, Michael 242
Bastille xii
Beauvoir, Simone de 142
Becket, St Thomas à 125, 224
Bede 187
beer 39–57, 225–6
 alcohol 29–30
 bluffing connoisseurship 35, 36
 'brewed under license' 49
 calorific value 56
 and the church 187
 decline in popularity 51–5
 early production 20, 21, 22, 23
 hangovers 15
 health benefits 24, 282
 imported 40
 ingredients 39–41
 light 53
 names 45
 nutritional value 27–8

INDEX

pasteurisation 46
recommended allowances 10–11
and religious beliefs 32
return to tradition 46–51
strong 42
temperature 44–6
beer bellies 55–7
beer goggle effect 139
Beethoven, Ludwig van 263, 273
Behan, Brendan 141–3, 275, 277
Belloc, Hilaire 140
Benchley, Robert 266
Benedict XII, Pope 269
Benedictine 117
Berocca 16
Berryman, John 273
berserkers 151
Best, George 155
Beth Israel Deconess Medical Center, Boston 56
Betty Ford Center 254
Bevo 200
Bible 186, 192
Bierce, Ambrose 89, 132, 202
binge drinking 183, 244, 268
Bingley Arms, The, Leeds 130
Bismarck, Otto Eduard Leopold, Fürst von 124
bitters 25, 115

Black Sheep Brewery, Yorkshire 48
Black Tower 74
Black Velvet 123, 124
Blackstrap 99
Blair, Euan 184
Blair, Tony 184, 196
Blandford, Marquess of 254
Blatz beer 31
Blayney, Lord 228, 229
Bligh, William 212
blood alcohol concentration (BAC) 6, 166–8, 170, 241
blood tests 172
Bloody Mary/Maria 122, 143
Blue Nun 74
Bolingbroke, Lord 231
Bollinger, Lily 82
Bombay Sapphire 38
Bond, James 121
Boniface, St 187
bootleggers 203–4
booze cruises 213
'boozer's nose' condition 248
Boston tea party 58–9
Boswell, James 141, 228
bottles 47, 78–9
Bottomley, Ian 153
bourbon 88, 96–7, 190
Bow, Clara 121–3
Braddock, Bessie 272
brainwaves 243
brandy 87–91

DRINK | A USER'S GUIDE

bluffing connoisseurship 36
fortified wines 91–4
heating 89
medicinal properties 25, 26
nosing 89
pomace brandies 90
production process 86, 87–8
Braunstein, Richard 2
breathalysers 169–73
'brewed under license' 49
brewing 40–6, 175
brewpubs 135
Bridget, St 186–7
British Airways 154, 155
British Broadcasting
 Corporation (BBC) 155
British Medical Association
 (BMA) 12, 278
British Medical Council 166
Brooke, Lord 232
Brown, George 4
Buddhism 217
Budweiser 47, 53, 54
Budweiser Budvar 36
Bullock, Sandra 121
Bull's Blood wine 69
Burden, Martin 168
Bureau of Alcohol, Tobacco
 and Firearms (US) 284
Burnet, Gilbert 230
Burns, George 241
Burns, Robbie 265–6
Busch, August 200

Butler, Samuel 242
Byron, Lord 25, 286

C

Cabernet Sauvignon 64
Caldwell, Erskine 132
calories 29, 56
calvados 86, 90, 91
Calvin, John 189
Campaign for Real Ale 47
Campari 115
cancer prevention 281–2
cans 47
Capital Brewery, Middleton 53
capital punishment 205–6
Capone, Al 203
Capote, Truman 254
careers, alcoholic 278
 see also famous drinkers
Carling Red Cap Ale 31
Carlsberg 54
Caroline of Brunswick 270
Carousel, The, Circus Hotel,
 Las Vegas 142
Carver, Raymond 277
Casanova, Giovanni Jacopo 44
casiri 32
Castle, Barbara 169
Catherine de Medici 115
Catherine the Great 50, 270
Catholic Church 190
Cato the Elder 175
caudle 24–5

INDEX

Chakravaty, B.N. 235
champagne 5, 25–6, 77–82, 123–4, 256, 279
Chandler, Raymond 242
Chardonnay 64
Charles I, King of England 227
Charles II, King of England 139, 140, 228, 234
Chartreuse 117
Chase, Chevvy 121
Château de Laubade 36
Château Lafite 63, 221
Château Mouton-Rothschild 71
Chaucer, Geoffrey 145
Cheever, John 254, 277
Chesterton, G.K. 140
chichi 32
Chivas Regal 36–7
Chopin vodka 37
Christianity 185–92, 207, 233
Chumley's, New York 142–3, 174
'church ales' 188
Churchill, Clementine 272
Churchill, Winston 23, 101, 271–3
cider 21, 29–30, 58–61, 99, 181, 198
cirrhosis 262–3, 278
clear drinks 14
Clicquot, Nichole-Barbe 80
Clicquot, Phillipe 80
Clinton, Bill 156, 248
cock ale 25
cocktails 118–24, 143
Coffey, Aeneas 86
cognac 36, 88, 89–90
Cohen, John 166
Cointreau 116
Coleridge, Samuel Taylor 144
communion 210
Conan Doyle, Arthur 140
Condon, Eddie 13
congeners 103
Congreve, William 207
Connemara 36–7
Connery, Sean 31
connoisseurship, bluffing 33–8
Connolly, Billy 224
Connors, Patrick 154
Conti, Tom 259
Cook, Peter 185
corks 82–4
corkscrews 83
Corpse Reviver 123
Cosby, Bill 121
Coward, Noel 9
Coyle, Francis 154
Craig, Elijah 190
Crane, Hart 277
crisps 27
Cristal Champagne 82
Cromwell, Oliver 130, 138
Crowther, James 130
Cruikshank, George 199

293

DRINK | A USER'S GUIDE

Cruikshank, Isaac 199
currency, use of alcohol as 22

D

daiquiris 122, 123–4
Dali, Salvador 31
Daniels, Billy 131
Darwin Awards website 163
date rape 158
de Gaulle, Charles 278
death, drunken 161–4, 166–9, 244, 246, 265–6
Death, James 18–19, 190
deep-vein thrombosis (DVT) 155
Deer Park Inn, Newark, US 131
Degas, Edgar 111
delirium tremens (DTs) 258
depressive qualities of alcohol 4
Descartes, René xiii
designated driver schemes 168
Diana, Princess of Wales 245
Dickens, Charles 55, 140, 182
Didbin, Charles 150
Dietary and Nutritional Survey of British Adults 57
Diller, Phyllis 235
Dillinger, John 132
Dillon-Malone, Aubrey 251
Dionysius the Younger 269

Dionysus (Bacchus), cult of 156
distillation 85–7, 114
disulfiram (Antabuse) 253
Domitian 192
Doolittle, Eliza 105
dopamine 243–4
Dos Reales Anejo 38
Dove, The, London 140
Downey, Robert, Jr 254
Drambuie 116
drink-driving 165–73
drinking games 237
drinking places 125–43
    American 128–30, 131–2, 133–4, 135, 141
    ancient 130–1
    common 129–36
    entertainment 133
    famous 140–3
    Irish 135, 136
    signs 136–40
    for women 176–7, 179–81
Drunken Parliament 230
drunkenness 4, 144–64, 188
    see also alcoholism
Dufferin, Lord 228, 229
Duffy, Charles 288
Dunne, Peter Finley 157
Dutch courage 151
Dylan, Bob 143

INDEX

E

E&J Gallo 68
Eagle and Child, The, Stow-on-the-Wold 130–1
Edgar, King of England 125
Edward I, King of England 193
Edward VII, King of England xi, 95
El Vino's, Fleet Street 174, 176–7
Elizabeth I, Queen of England 177, 235
Elizabeth, Queen Mother 279
enemas, vodka 104
English Civil War 138, 139
Erskine-Brown, Claude 34
ethanol 8–9, 16
ethnicity 8–9
Excise Act 1823 211

F

family drinking problems 242–3, 244
famous drinkers 267–79
Farrar, C.H. 251
Faulkner, William 274, 275
Fawlty, Basil 84
Federal Aviation Authority 153
fermentation 43–4
Fielding, Helen 17
Fielding, Henry 195
Fields, W.C. 3–4, 7, 29, 84, 248, 272
films 257
Finch, Peter 46–7
Fireman's Fund 246
first-pass metabolism 7
Fitzgerald, F. Scott 142
Fitzstephen, William 224
fizzy drinks 5
Flanders, Ned 61
flavourings 47–8
Fleming, Ian 121
Flynn, Errol 245, 264–5
Ford, Henry 131
fortified wines 91–4
Fox, Michael J. 245
Franklin, Benjamin 43, 128
Frederick the Great (of Prussia) xi, 151
Frederick II, Holy Roman Emperor 89
French Paradox 75, 281
French Revolution xii, 117
Freud, Clement 280
Freud, Sigmund 111
fundamentalism 207

G

Gabor, Zsa Zsa 31
Gandhi, Mahatma 217
gender differences 7–8, 251, 253
genetics, drinking problems 242–4
genever 106–7

DRINK | A USER'S GUIDE

George III, King of England 58–9, 235, 236
George IV, King of England 235–6, 262, 270
GHB (gamma hydroxy butyric acid) 158
Gibbon, Edward 247
gin 105–7
   bluffing connoisseurship 38
   Dutch courage 151
   epidemic 127, 195–6, 198, 229–31
   prohibition 118–19
Gin Alexander 122
gin shops/palaces 127, 195
glass clinking 234
Glenfiddich 97
Gluck, Malcolm 76
Goodman, Benny 31
Gorbachev, Mikhail 193
Gordon, Dexter 259
Grant, Hugh 155–6
Grant, Ulysses S. 271
Grant, William 97
Greeley, Horace 58
green fairy 108, 111
Greene, Graham 140
Groening, Matt 45
'grog blossom' 248
Guinness 27, 44, 49, 157, 247
Guinness, Arthur 42
gumption 59
Gwynne, Nell 140

H

Hadith 206–7
Hafiz 208
hair of the dog 11–12, 16–17
Hakin 192
Hammurabi, King 194
Handel, George Frideric 56
hangovers xii, 3–4, 7, 11–17
Harley, Earl of Oxford 230
Harold II, King of England xii
Harris, Richard 257
Harry, Prince 184
Hart, Lorenz 273
Harvey Wallbanger 122
Hastings, Battle of xii, 151
Hawke, Lord 268
Hazlitt, William xi
health
   benefits of alcohol 280–5
   dangers of alcohol 259–63
   see also death, drunken; medicinal qualities of alcohol
heavy drinking 177–9, 223–39
   see also alcoholism
Heeley, H.S. 83
Heinhold's First & Last Chance Saloon, Oakland, Calif. 132
Hemingway, Ernest 2, 111, 123–4, 140, 142, 143, 261, 274, 276–7, 279
Hendrix, Jimi 246

INDEX

Henry II, King of England 72–3, 74
Henry II, King of France 115
Henry VII, King of England 177
Henry VIII, King of England 73, 270
Henry, O. 142
Henshall, Samuel 83
heroics 150–2
Hinduism 216–17
history of drinking 18–37
Hitler, Adolf 273
Hogarth, William 138, 195
Hollywood 246
Holt, Mandy 139–40
Home Office 172–3
Homer 2
Hook, Theodore 226
Hooper's Hooch 124
Hopper, Dennis 41
hops 39–40
horizontal gaze nystagmus (HGN) test 170
'house of call' establishments 132
Howard, Elizabeth Jane 276
Hussein, Saddam 218

I

Ibn Saud 272
ID 183
illicit booze 203–4, 209–18
  see also scams
immobilisation techniques 173
India Pale Ale (IPA) 50–1
inns 127–8, 137, 138
inventive ingredients 32–3
Irish coffee 96
Islam 185, 205–8, 214–18
Ivan the Terrible 270

J

Jack Daniels 96–7
James I, King of England 139
Japanese drinkers 8–9
Jarrell, Randall 273
Jarry, Alfred 111
Jefferson, Thomas 43, 63
Jesus Christ 186, 192
Jim Bream Whisky 31
John the Baptist 186
John Barleycorn, Chicago, Ill. 132
Johnson, Andrew 271
Johnson, Lyndon 271
Johnson, Samuel 2, 88, 127, 141, 228
Johnson, William Eugene 'Pussyfoot' 210
Jones, Barry 139
Jones, George 247
Jonson, Ben 156
Joplin, Janis 246
José Cuervo 113
Joyce, James 141, 275, 279

DRINK | A USER'S GUIDE

Judaism 8, 30, 185–6, 236
Julius Caesar 21

K

Kant, Immanuel 267
karaoke 133
Keaton, Buster 242, 256, 257
Keeley, Leslie E. 250
Kerouac, Jack 142, 262
Kerr, Mrs Tom 191
Kersch, Gerald 12
Keynes, John Maynard 77
Khan, Genghis 192–3
Khayyam, Omar 208
Khomeini, Ayatollah 207
Kiberd, Declan 197
Kimball, Warren 272–3
King, Stephen 274–5
Kipling, Rudyard 11, 237
Kirin 55
kirsch 90
Knott, Nathaniel 219
Koran 205–8
Korean War 151–2
Kosher drinks 30
Kristofferson, Kris 121
Kulmbach Brewery, Bavaria 42

L

labour 180
lager 43, 45–6
Langrishe, Sir Hercules 228
Larkin, Philip 184
Laroche, Michel 84
Lawrence, D.H. 72
Le Mare, Chester 203
Lee, Nathaniel 256
Les Deux Magots, Paris 142
L'Esprit de Courvoisier 89
Lewinsky, Monica 156
Lewis, Arthur J. 252
Lewis, Joe E. 255
Lewis, Sinclair 274
Liberace 31
Light Infantry 236
Lincoln, Abraham 142, 151
liquers 114–17, 121, 188
liver 244, 262–3, 266
Lloyd, Emily 254
Lloyd George, David 193, 202
London, Jack 132, 276, 277
Longfellow's Wayside Inn, Sudbury, Mass. 131
Louis Roederer 81
Lowell, Robert 276
Lowry, Malcolm 245, 275
Luther, Martin 56, 62, 189
Lyly, John 265
Lynch, David 41

M

Macallan, The 36–7, 97
McDonald's Restaurants 148
McGillin's Ole Ale House 131
Machin, David 139

INDEX

machismo 225
Mackeson stout 26
Mackinnon family 116
McQueen, Steve 143
McSorley's Old Ale House, New York 131, 142
Madeira 91
Magnus, Albertus 157
Makers Mark 36–7
malt 41
Manet, Edouard 111
Map, Walter 188
Margaret, Princess 278
Margarita cocktail 111, 122
Martin, Dean 165, 258
martinis 119, 121–2
Marvin, Lee 257
Marx, Harpo 31
Mason, Graham 262
Mateus rosé 74
Mathew, Father 199
Maugham, Somerset 142
Maurisco grapes 92
Maximilian I, Count 41
mead 20–1
medicinal qualities of alcohol 23–7, 60
Melbourne, Lord 231–2
men
  drinking capacity 7
  drinking patterns 251
  drinking problems 251, 253, 263–5

recommended allowances 10
Mencken, H.L. 119–20
Mendelssohn, Oscar 123, 124
Merlot 64
Merman, Ethel 131
mescal 112, 113
methanol 16
methylated spirits 245
microbreweries 47–50
Miller Life 53
Mills, John 41
Ministry of Transport (UK) 166
Mitchell, Joseph 134
moderation 280–5
Moët & Chandon 81
molasses 99
monks/monasteries 73, 114–17, 187–8
Morland, George 138
Morris, Allan 102
Morris, William 140
Morrison, Jim 164, 246
Mortimer, John 34
Moryson, Fynes 223–4
Moulton, David 44
Muhammad 206–7, 208
Mulder, Fox 51
mulled wine 75
Muller, Antoine 80
multivitamins 15, 16
murder 262
Murree brewery 216
Mussorgsky, Modest 273

DRINK | A USER'S GUIDE

N

Nash, Ogden 159
Nashe, Thomas 145
Nathan, George Jean 2
Nation, Carry 197
National Institute of Health (US) 284
Negroni 122
Nelson, Horatio 101
Nero 248
Nicholas II, Tsar of Russia 151
Niven, David 31
Nixon, Richard M. 271
Noah 267
Northcutt, Wendy 163
nutmeg 75
nutrition 15–16, 23–4, 27–9

O

oak 87–8
Ochero, Walter 149
O'Connor, Sinead 254
Ogle, Sir Thomas 227
Old Absinthe House, The, New Orleans 142
Old Angus scotch 31
Old Ferryboat Inn, Holywell, Cambridgeshire 130
Old Tart 69, 70
O'Neill, Eugene 274
opera 233
Orange Fizz 122

Osbourne, Ozzy 247
O'Toole, Peter 256–7, 259

P

Pabst 42, 47
Palava, Chandra 283
pale ale 50–1
Panmure, Lord 228, 229
Parker, Dorothy 160
Parliamentary drunks 230–2
Patrick, St 187
Paul, Henri 245
Paul, St 190–2
Peacham, Henry 3
Peacock, Thomas Love ix, 255
Peel, Bobby 268
penis 160–1
Pennsylvania Dram Shop Act 204
Pepys, Samuel 108, 177, 227
Pérignon, Dom 81, 110
Pernod 109–10
Peter the Great 103, 270
physiology 5–8
Picasso, Pablo 111
Pierce, Franklin 271
Pierre, Frère 81
Piggott, Miss 16
Pilgrim Fathers xii
Pilsen brewery, Bohemia 42
pink gin 107
Pink Lady 122

INDEX

Pinot Noir 64
Pirasununga 51 37
Pitt, William (Pitt the Younger) 231, 265
Platter, Thomas 224
Pliny 21–2
Pliny the Elder 13, 175
Plutarch 242
Poe, Edgar Allan 131
Pollock, John 273
pomace 60
Porson, Richard 245
port 91, 92, 228–9
  passing the 93
porters 44, 46
Priory, The 254
prohibition 118–19, 131, 133, 143, 182, 194, 197–205, 209–11, 217, 221–2, 250
Promises, Malibu 254
proof strength 30–1
Proteas 269
Protestantism 188–9
punch 120
Puritans 189–90
purl 108

R

Rabelais, Francis 224, 240
Raffles, Singapore 142
Ragnaud-Sabourin 36
Raleigh, Sir Walter 247
rape 158
Ratcliffe, Mitch 112
real ales 46, 48
recommended allowances 9–11
Reed, Oliver 10, 178
reformed drinkers 255–8
religion 8, 30, 32, 185–92, 205–8, 214–18, 233, 236
  see also monks/monasteries
Retsina 22
Rhazes, Muhammad 247–8
rhinophyma 248
Richard I, King of England 130
Richard II, King of England 137, 139
Rielsling 64–5
Roberts, Arthur 191
Robinson, Anne 155, 258, 259
Rogers, Will 131
Rohypnol 158
Romberg, Sigmund 233
Roosevelt 194
Roosevelt, Franklin 271
rosacea 248
Royal London School of Medicine 173
Royal Navy 100, 101, 235
Royal Society of Chemistry 121
royal toast 235–6
Royale, Matt 57
rulers 269–73
rum 37, 87–8, 98–101

DRINK | A USER'S GUIDE

Rumpole, Horace 34
Russell, Bertrand 2

S

Sackville, Charles, Earl of Dorset 227
St Bartholomew's School of Medicine 173
St Petersburg Philharmonic orchestra 162
sake 55
Saku brewery 52
Sale of Beer Act 1830 (English) 127
saloons 128–30, 133–4
Salvation Army xiii, 254
sanatoria 249–50
Sapporo 55
Sartre, Jean-Paul 142
Sauvignon Blanc 64
Sayers, Dorothy L. 27
scams 219–22
  see also illicit booze
Scotch 94–6, 97
Sedley, Charles 227
serotonin 244
sex 155–61, 263–6
Sex in the City cocktail 122
Shakespeare, William 8, 28, 93, 160, 224
shari'a 205
Shaw, George Bernard 186, 198

Sheen, Charlie 242, 254, 256
Sheen, Martin 242
Sheridan, Richard Brinsley 232, 245
sherry 91, 92–3
Shilo, Dr 250
Shinauer, Eric 283
Shumann, Robert 256
signs, drinking places 136–40
Sikhism 217
Simpson, N.F. 1
Sinclair, Upton 275
Singapore Sling 122, 142
Skinner, Frank 257–8
Skirrid Mountain Inn, The, Abergavenny 130
Slater, Christian 254
slivovitz 90
Smirnoff 31
Smith, Delia 76
Smithers Alcoholism Rehab Unit 254
Smollett, Tobias x
'sober companions' 246, 254
sobriety tests 169–73
Socrates 126
Spaulding, Steve 68
Speakman, Bill 151–2
Sperling, Spatz 70
spirits 85–113
  see also specific spirits
sportspeople 268–9
Squires, J.C. 3

302

INDEX

Stafford, Jean 276
Stalin, Josef 111, 270, 271
state 192–6
Steiger, Rod 28
Steinbeck, John 142, 274
Stella Artois 46
Stevenson, Robert Louis 101, 132
stills, continuous/pot 86
Stork Club, The, New York 141
stout 26, 44, 46
  alcohol 29–30
  brewing 43
  cocktails 123, 124
  Russian Imperial 50
Stuart, Charles Edward (Bonnie Prince Charlie) 116, 236
Suntory 55
surgical spirits 245
Sutter, Tim 191
Sweat, Noah S. 'Soggy', Jr 287
symposiums 126

T

Taft, William Howard 142
Talmud 186
Tanqueray gin 106
taverns 126, 127, 128, 129, 137, 138
taxation 192, 194–6, 211–14
temperance movement 181–2, 197–204
Tennessee, Army of 234–5
tequila 25, 38, 87–8, 111–13
Terigood, George 32
Thackeray, William Makepeace 140, 142
Theakstons 48
theme pub-restaurants 135, 136
thiamine deficiency 28
Third Reich 250
Thomas, Dylan 143, 240, 266
Thompson, Hunter S. 142
Thucydides 21
thujone 110
Thurber, James 33
tippling houses 129, 133
toasts 232–7
Torrington, Lord 229
Toulouse-Lautrec, Henri de 273
tranquillisers 154
Travis, Walter 277
Trockenbeerenauslese 72
Trotsky, Leon 270
Twain, Mark 26, 94, 235
Two Dogs 124
two-handed loving cups 234
Tynan, Kenneth 104

U

urine tests 172
Uspensky, Boris 102
Utrillo, Maurice 273

DRINK | A USER'S GUIDE

V

vagrants 245
Van Dyke, Dick 268
Van Gogh, Vincent 110, 111, 245, 273
Vatinus 248
Verlaine 110, 224
Vermouth 115
Vernon, Edward 101, 102
Vesuvio, San Francisco 142
Victoria, Queen of England 94–5, 139, 232, 278
Vidal, Gore 273
Vincelli, Dom Bernardo 117
vodka 25, 31, 37, 102–4
vodka sniffing 104
vomiting 12, 246
voting 202

W

Walker, Edwin 83
Walpole, Robert 230–1
Washington, George 43, 92, 138, 190, 200, 212
water x–xi, 6–7, 15
Waterhouse, Keith 259
Wellington, Duke of 196
Wenceslas, King 40
wet/non-temperance/integrated countries 147–50
wheat 41
whisky 94–7, 287
  blends 95, 97
  bluffing connoisseurship 36–7
  bourbon 88, 96–7, 190
  heroics 151
  illicit 210, 211–12
  Irish 95–6, 97
  medicinal properties 25, 26
  production process 87, 88, 96
  Scotch 94–6, 97
  single malt 86, 95, 97
whisky wheel 97
Whitbread's Extra Stout 26
White Horse, New York 143
Whitman, Walt 142
Wienke, Carl 83
Wilde, Oscar 108, 142
William I (of Orange), King of the Netherlands 105, 232
William I (the Conqueror), King of England xii
William III, King of England 230
William IV, King of England 262, 270
Willis, Bruce 121
Wilson, Richard 138
wine 62–84, 210, 225–6
  ageing 67
  alcohol 29, 30
  Arabic 207, 208
  and the British 72–8
  and the church 186–8

304